Behind the Camera: American Women Photographers Who Shaped How We See the World

Maria Ausherman

Foreword by Amy Sancetta

Introduction and Drawings by Fontaine Dunn

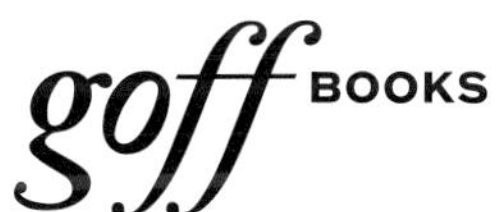

BOOK COVER PHOTO: *Girl with Diploma* (c.1922–1931) by Elise Forrest Harleston

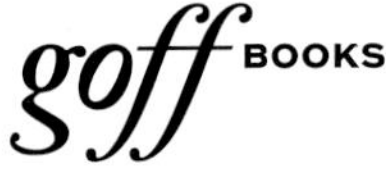

Published by Goff Books, an Imprint of ORO Editions.
Executive publisher: Gordon Goff.

www.goffbooks.com
info@goffbooks.com

USA, EUROPE, ASIA, MIDDLE EAST, SOUTH AMERICA

Author: Maria Ausherman
Foreword: Amy Sancetta
Introduction: Fontaine Dunn
Drawings: Fontaine Dunn
Book Design: Anita Stumbo
Project Coordinator: Alejandro Guzman-Avila
Managing Editor: Jake Anderson

10 9 8 7 6 5 4 3 2 1 First Edition

Library of Congress data available upon request. World Rights: available.

ISBN: 978-1-951541-51-4

Color separations and printing: ORO Group Ltd.
Printed in China.

International distribution: www.goffbooks.com/distribution

ORO Editions makes a continuous effort to minimize the overall carbon footprint of its publications. As part of this goal, ORO Editions, in association with Global ReLeaf, arranges to plant trees to replace those used in the manufacturing of the paper produced for its books. Global ReLeaf is an international campaign run by American Forests, one of the world's oldest nonprofit conservation organizations. Global ReLeaf is American Forests' education and action program that helps individuals, organizations, agencies, and corporations improve the local and global environment by planting and caring for trees.

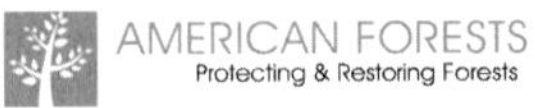

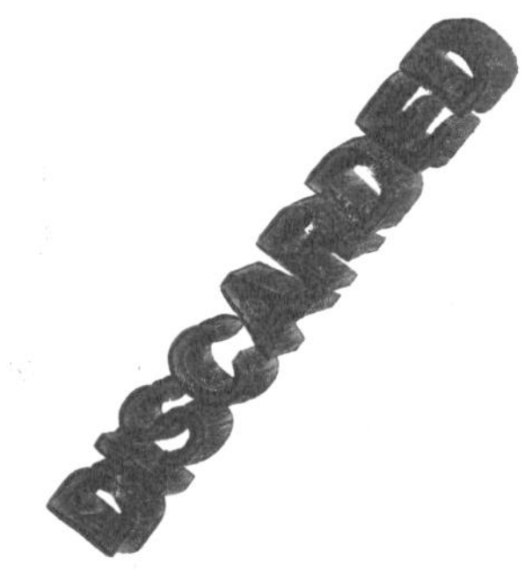

To my cherished daughters Chloe & Lydia
and dear baby granddaughter Emma Jane ...

"Photographs open
doors into the past,
but they also allow a
look into the future."

—SALLY MANN

"A timely, well crafted and sensitive tribute to sixteen women photographers of the late nineteenth century up to the present. The powerful and creative collection of images presented here is further complemented by the individual life stories of each of these photographers and their personal sacrifices to create this slice of history. This is authentic and clearly relevant in these current times and an important read and visual resource of history through the lens of women driven to make a difference"

—KAREN A. HUMMEL, Fine artist, educator

"Maria Ausherman's compilation of 16 pioneering women photographers is a joy to read for anyone interested in our visual history. One life story weaves into the next, with the dominant thread being each woman's willingness to reject social norms and take huge risks in pursuit of her work. This is a beautiful tribute to the famous and some not-so-well known women photographers who came before us."

—ELISE AMENDOLA, Associated Press photojournalist

"*Behind the Camera: American Women Photographers Who Shaped How We See the World* opens doors on history, opening eyes and hearts as it does. Cover to cover, every well written biography in it is an adventure! In a culture that tends to leave out significant women in art's history, here is a rich description of gifted women who brought photography forward both in technical skill and in artistic merit.

It's a very moving journey through to the end of the book: the women portrayed followed their dreams in an astonishing way, defying all the 'norms' of their days in early photography. Young people, young women in particular, will feel genuinely inspired to know of these focused, inspired, and inspiring photographers. Imagine learning of sixteen women, some of whom lived well into the twentieth century, who abandoned all customs of their day to bring this brand-new art form to the world! The book is wonderfully accessible without ever being condescending. The many photographs carry the reader along like a magic spell. It's hard to stop reading, and looking, and feeling the depth of the vision of each of these geniuses. In the early days of adolescence, youngsters need heroes to inspire them and beauty to surround them. This book gives them both!"

—PATRICE MAYNARD, Waldorf teacher, publisher

Table of Contents

Acknowledgments

THE INSPIRATION FOR THIS BOOK rose from my admiration for the stunningly beautiful photographs and eloquent writings of Frances Benjamin Johnston. While conducting research for *The Photographic Legacy of Frances Benjamin Johnston* (2009), I became aware of many other women photographers worthy of more attention and inquiry. They all set the standards for photographers, then and now, and changed the way we see the world.

By studying women photographers, we can view human history, and the history of photography, through the eyes of women. The ability to see what women see is just as diverse and valuable as the male experience. It is my hope that teachers, parents, and budding scholars will find this introductory compilation a welcome addition to their schooling and use it as a springboard for further exploration. Many authors contributed to this brief collection of biographies and their books are listed at the end of each chapter for further reading.

This publication would not have been possible without the assistance of numerous individuals. Fontaine Dunn as artist, fellow teacher, and friend, gave this book her personal touch. Not only did Fontaine edit the stories, but she also wrote the introduction and Helen Levitt story, corresponded with people who helped to obtain copyright permissions and images, and selected some of the photographs for analysis. For her encouragement and resourcefulness, I am grateful. I also received valuable assistance from Hannah Rozenblat who made edits and shared her expertise. Amy Sanchetta, Pulitzer Prize Winner in 1993, provided her fascinating perspective as an Associated Press photojournalist in the foreword.

Special thanks to all those who helped to find photographs and gave permission to reproduce images: Mae Whitlock Gentry, keeper of Elise Forrest Harleston's photographs, Meg Partridge of the Imogen Cunningham Trust, Marvin Hoshino of Film Documents LLC, Tomeka Meon Myers of the Library of Congress Duplication Services, Melissa Lindberg and Jonathan Eaker of Prints and Photographs Division at the Library of Congress, James Kohler of the Cleveland Museum of Art, Maxine Friedman of Historic Richmond Town, Beth Singler and Randy Sullivan of the University of Oregon Library, Monica Park of the Brooklyn Museum, Ann Wolfe of the Nevada Museum of Art, Lauren Lean of the George Eastman Museum, Selena Capraro of the Amon Carter Museum, Marisa Bourgoin, Head of Reference Services at the Archives of American Art at the Smithsonian Institution, Daniel Trujillo of the Artists Rights Society, Jason Tomberlin, Matthew Turi, and Tim Hodgdon of the Louis Round Wilson Special Collections Library of the University of North Carolina at Chapel Hill, Ali Giniger and Rebecca Mecklenborg of the Jack Shainman Gallery, Getty Images, Robert Dunkin and Diana Edkins of Art Resource.

Sincere thanks to Gordon Goff, Federica Ewing, and Alejandro Guzman-Avila of ORO Editions for finding this project worthy of print, appreciating how much the photographs add to the text, and bringing this project the beauty it deserves. I'm also grateful for the graphic design work of Anita Stumbo.

On a more personal note, I remain grateful to Lew Andrews, professor of art history at the University of Hawaii, whose knowledge about photography was unsurpassable. I am grateful to my family—my parents, Charles and Rieneke Ausherman; my daughters, Chloe and Lydia Chapman; my sister, Judy Ausherman; my brothers, Chuck and Steve Ausherman; and my husband, Steven Taylor—for their love and encouragement.

—Maria Ausherman

Foreword

IT'S FUNNY TO THINK that the woman photographers who came up in the 1970s and 1980s, like myself, are sometimes thought of as pioneers of women in photography. We shot without the benefit of autofocus cameras on black and white film. We built darkrooms from 2×4s and black plastic in stadium bathrooms and hotel broom closets. Taking a portable darkroom to the Atlantic coastline for hurricane coverage meant taking down your entire indoor darkroom, squeezing it in your car to transport into the fray, and rebuilding it in a found space at the other end.

And as women in photojournalism, our colleagues were almost 100 percent men. When I covered Philadelphia Flyers NHL games in the early '80s, the only other women in the media area besides me were usually the ones serving the pregame press meals.

For me, Margaret Bourke-White and Dorothea Lange—both who entered the field 50 years before I picked up my first real camera—were huge inspirations. So was my own family.

My first camera was the then-revolutionary Polaroid Swinger, which I received as a gift from my mother when I was a fifth grader. A shy child, I loved the access to people and places that magic little box of plastic gave me.

When I got to high school, I became enthralled with the work of Lange and Bourke-White. I loved the intimate images of everyday people that Lange created. The more you looked at her pictures, the more you saw ... the more you learned. Growing up in suburban Cleveland, looking out the windows of my parents' car, I'd seen the steel mills that were explored by Bourke-White and her camera. I was empowered by the thought of this woman with a camera being able to climb around the hot and dirty mills, making pictures that had not really been widely seen before. I wanted to do that. I wanted to be able to explore the inside of the steel mills and I wanted to make pictures of children working in fields in Alabama. Their experiences and accomplishments, and an encouraging and supportive family, gave me the belief that I could do these things too. And I have.

As a staff photographer for the Associated Press for 30 years, I've explored the insides of working mills, photographed migrant children in sunbaked fields and rundown shanties, captured images of presidents and kings, Olympians and spiritual leaders. I have loved sharing the world I see with others.

The work of these early women photojournalists made me think about seeing—and what seeing the world around you really means.

As Dorothea Lange once said about making pictures, she loved that "a camera teaches you how to see without a camera."

For me, photography is about seeing, sharing that vision, and recording the smallest of things for the next generation. The women chronicled in this book led the way for me, and for so many women photographers to come. I'm inspired by their vision and their courage. I'd like to think that they would have been proud of us.

—Amy Sancetta
Associated Press Photojournalist
Pulitzer Prize Winner 1993

Introduction

EVERY DAY MILLIONS OF PEOPLE around the world use cell phones to document their daily lives. They photograph important moments—a baby's first steps, a birthday party, a family reunion; and special events like first communions, bar mitzvahs, quinceañeras, graduations, and proms. They create visual reminders of holidays, trips, and visits; or record natural phenomena like rainbows, sunsets, eclipses, full moons, and autumn leaves. Then they "post" these "photographs" to social media outlets like Facebook, Snapchat, or Instagram, to name a few.

But this habit of digitally documenting and publicizing one's life is a very recent development. Before that, taking photographs required a camera and a roll of film that had to be developed in a lab. Taking pictures included the cost of the camera, the cost of the film, and the cost of having film developed. And let's say you wanted to send one of those pictures to your six cousins. Then, you would have to pay extra for duplicates.

But worse still, you might get your processed film back only to discover that in ten of the images your thumb was in the way, and seven were "overexposed" (which means there was too much light), so the photo is very pale, and a few were "underexposed" (or too dark), so that you can't see any faces, and in the last picture you cut your uncle's head off at the top! You would not have any way to edit these pictures to make them lighter or darker, or to "crop" out your thumb or to zoom in on your uncle's face. And, too, it would not be so easy to publish these images.

But what if (as was true a hundred years ago), in order to create a photograph, you needed 50–100 pounds of very expensive equipment, including a giant camera and metal or glass plates instead of film? What if you couldn't send those plates out to a lab, but had to develop them yourself with special chemicals in a darkened room? What if the people whose pictures you wanted to capture had to sit for long stretches without moving? And what if traveling around to document historical events or important people was considered "man's work"? These were the conditions for making high-quality photographs from the time the camera was invented in 1839, well into the twentieth century.

Each of the women in this series stepped out of the bounds of physical and social expectations to pursue her personal vision through photography. Some were fortunate to have come from wealthy families who fostered their interests; others had to make their way by supporting themselves, or they found encouragement from other, more established photographers.

All were pioneers in extending the purposes, applications, and scope of making photographs, whether as an art form, a tool for recording, or as a commercial resource. Some were better known for portraiture; others for documenting poverty and hardship, the horrors of war, or the lives of "marginal" people. Various women found joy in photographing the buildings and bustle of city life, including that of recent immigrants and Harlem residents; while some explored the vast terrain and Native American culture of the American Southwest. Several dedicated their lives to the historic preservation of buildings and culture of the South. And, finally, some devoted themselves to nature through their own personal and spiritual connection with the landscape.

Many chose to avoid or leave behind the comforts of married life at a time when marriage provided the primary source of financial security for a woman. All surmounted whatever physical, societal, or financial challenges they encountered in order to pursue their dreams. Their true stories hopefully will inspire you to continue documenting and recording whatever is most important in your life through the ever-evolving and fascinating tool of photography, just as these women did before you.

—Fontaine Dunn

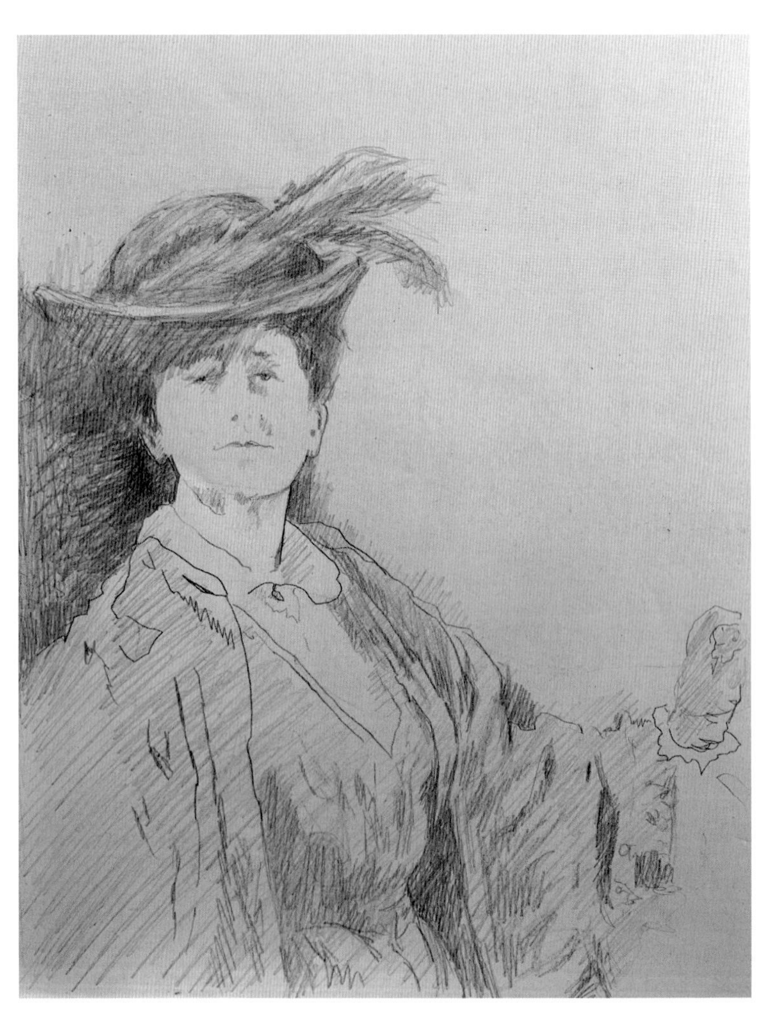

Gertrude Käsebier

1

Gertrude Käsebier

(1852–1934)

Blessed Art Thou Among Women

GERTRUDE KÄSEBIER was born in Des Moines, Iowa, in 1852. During the 1859 Pike's Peak Gold Rush, her father traveled west to make money in the construction business, and would later become the first mayor of the Colorado mining town where he settled. When she was eight, Käsebier's family joined her father. Käsebier made friends with her Native American neighbors, and often she was content to play alone.

Living in a mining town was hard on Gertrude Käsebier's family, though, and after her father's sudden death, the family relocated to Brooklyn when she was twelve where her mother operated a boarding house to support the family.

Käsebier spent a few years living with her maternal grandmother in Bethlehem, Pennsylvania, where she attended the Bethlehem

Female Seminary, later known as Moravian College, the first and one of the best women's schools in the country. She was happy to leave the West so she could attend a good school, especially during a time when education for women was not considered important.

When Käsebier returned to the boarding house in Brooklyn, she met and then married Eduard Käsebier, a successful shellac importer. After having three children, the family moved to New Durham, New Jersey.

Käsebier and her husband did not get along, but they remained married because, at the time, divorce was considered a scandal, so they simply lived apart. In spite of their differences, Eduard Käsebier supported his family financially, and in 1889, at the age of 37, Gertrude Käsebier began to attend the Pratt Institute of Art and Design to study portrait painting and drawing. She quickly became interested in photography, and although studying photography at this school was not an option, she used the school library to improve her knowledge about it. Furthermore, her study at Pratt would become very important to the way she took photographs.

When her husband became ill and could no longer support the family, Käsebier started to develop her own photography business. Working with a chemist, she learned photography techniques beginning in 1893. Three years later, she was employed by a portrait photographer where she learned about the studio business.

Käsebier's first photographs were of her family. She began to photograph before the more portable Kodak camera was available, and always used a large camera with glass negatives. She called her first camera "a clumsy thing with a non-adjustable tripod at least five feet high." Struggling at first, she soon was making photographs that would win contest prizes.

By 1897, Käsebier opened her own portrait studio in New York City, where only the most successful photographers thrived. Over the next decade, she made portraits of the Sioux tribe, no doubt out of nostalgia for the Plains Native Americans she befriended in Colorado. Her portraits show that she cared about indigenous

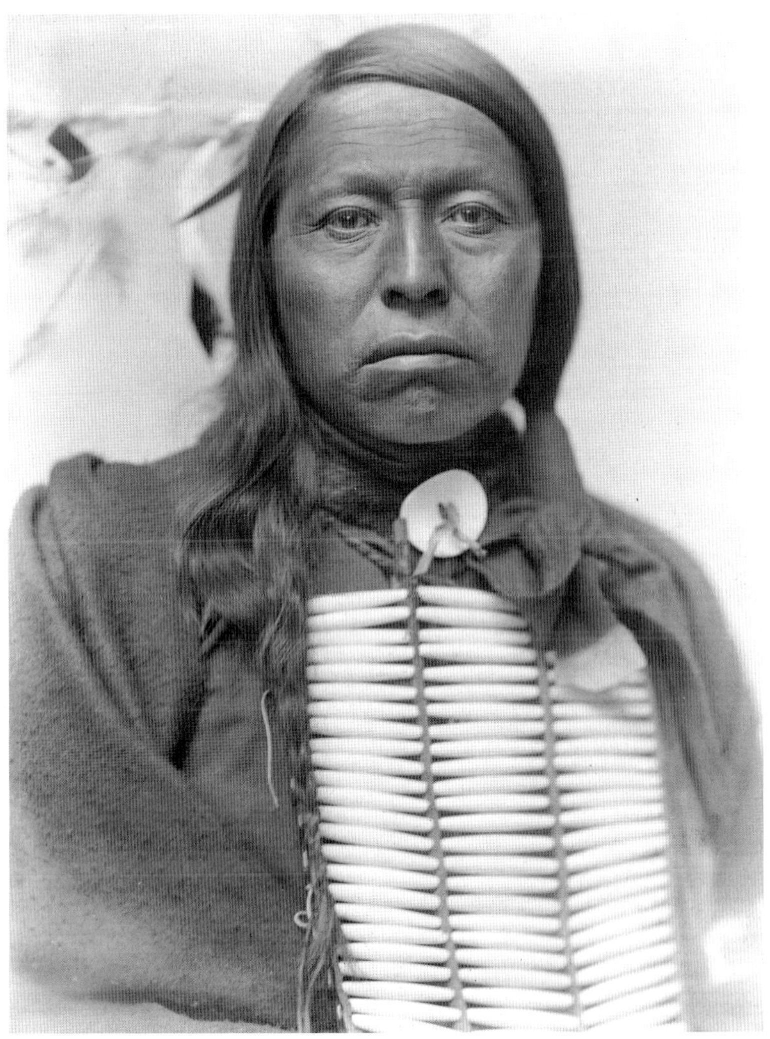

Flying Hawk, 1898

Chief Flying Hawk was an Oglala Lakota warrior, historian, educator, and philosopher. Käsebier focused on his dignified, almost hostile expression to show his fighting spirit. He was a combatant in nearly all of the fights with United States troops during the Great Sioux War of 1876. When this picture was taken, he was new to show business and unable to hide his anger and frustration. Gradually, he would change his outlook and show that he appreciated the monetary benefits of being part of Buffalo Bill's Wild West show by circulating the showgrounds in full regalia and selling his picture postcards for a penny to promote the show.

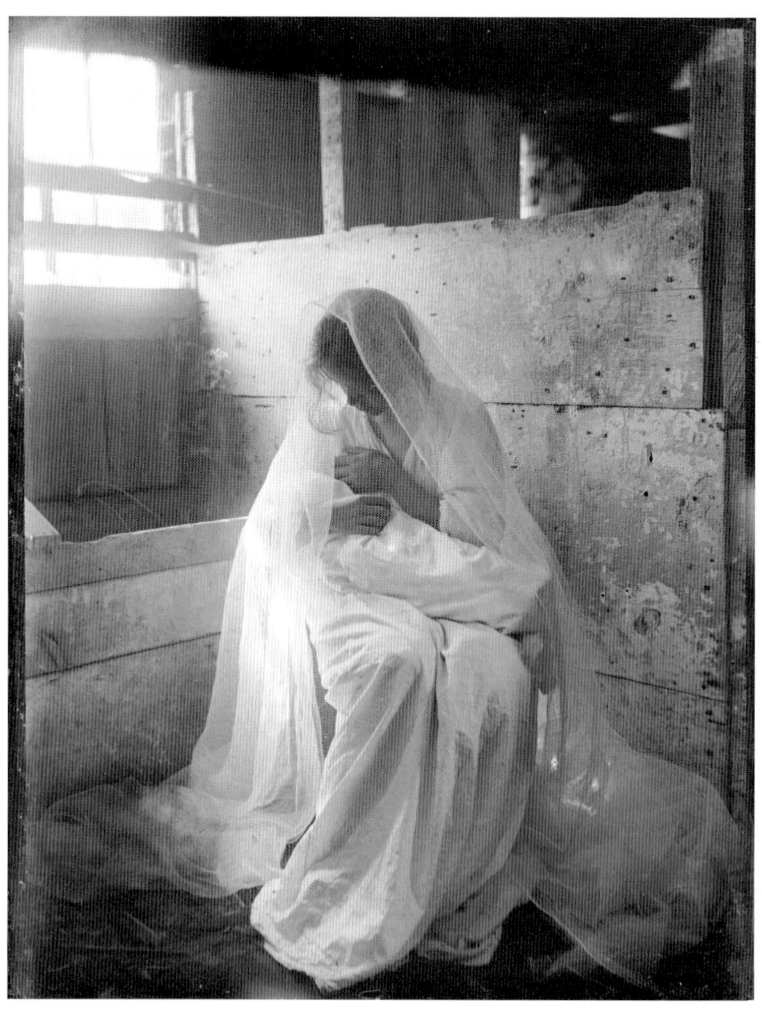

The Manger, 1901

One summer in Newport, Rhode Island, Gertrude Käsebier took this photo in a stable. Her friend posed for the image. There was no baby in her lap—just drapery. The title of the photograph refers to the biblical story of the birth of Christ. By transforming the woman into an archetypal Madonna, Käsebier expresses a reverence for maternity.

Käsebier creates a formal study of shade and tone by obscuring the mother's face in shadow and covering her head with a transparent veil. Likewise, the baby's body is suggested with folds of swaddling cloth. By using a soft focus, she implies her photograph is not a mere transcription of the physical world, but something more universal.

people and considered them prominent members of American society. While at her Fifth Avenue studio, she observed the parade of Buffalo Bill's Wild West show and got permission to photograph members of the troupe who were of the Lakota Sioux people. These photographs, now at the National Museum of American History at the Smithsonian Institution, include nine photographs of Zitkala-Sa, a teacher, writer, and violinist who became a crusader for the rights of Native Americans.

Käsebier also took photographs of many public figures such as author Mark Twain, educator Booker T. Washington, photographer Jacob A. Riis, and photographer Alfred Stieglitz. She later disagreed with Stieglitz, leader of the art photography movement in America, who thought that for photography to be art, it could not be sold. One of her photographs sold for $100, the highest price paid for a photograph at the time.

"The Manger" photograph shows the influence of Stieglitz's "pictorialist" philosophy. At the time, Stieglitz believed that photographs should resemble paintings and therefore not be sharply focused.

Her most famous photograph, entitled "Blessed Art Thou Among Women" and taken in 1900, was a portrait of her friend, Agnes Rand Lee, with her daughter. It became a symbol of the joys of being a mother.

Five of Käsebier's portraits were published in Alfred Stieglitz's *Camera Notes* in 1899. The photographer supported her work and declared she was the "leading artistic portrait photographer of the day." Käsebier would become an influential member of the Photo-Secession, a group that Alfred Stieglitz organized to promote photography as an art.

Eventually, Käsebier would resign from this aesthetic organization, but she continued to participate in exhibitions as a judge and exhibitor. She also continued to publish her photographs in magazines and became one of the most technically expert and prolific photographers in the field.

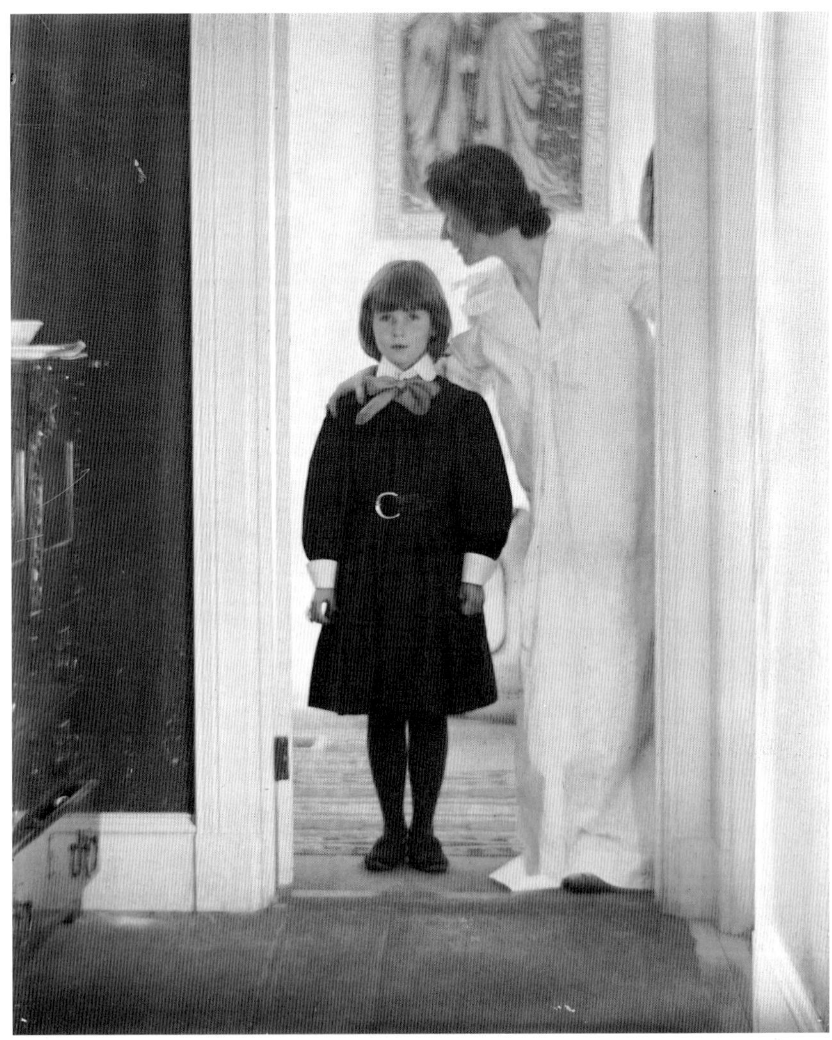

Blessed Art Thou Among Women, 1899

Käsebier's portrait of Agnes Rand Lee, a poet and children's book author, and her daughter, Peggy, at their Boston home reinforces Victorian ideals of motherhood and femininity. While her mother in a white flowing gown gracefully leans over her daughter as if encouraging her to step into the room, the young girl, dressed in dark clothes, stands facing the viewer. The title of the photograph refers to the Bible, and the picture of the Annunciation hangs on the wall behind the two figures. The Annunciation is when the angel Gabriel tells the Virgin Mary that she will become the mother of Jesus.

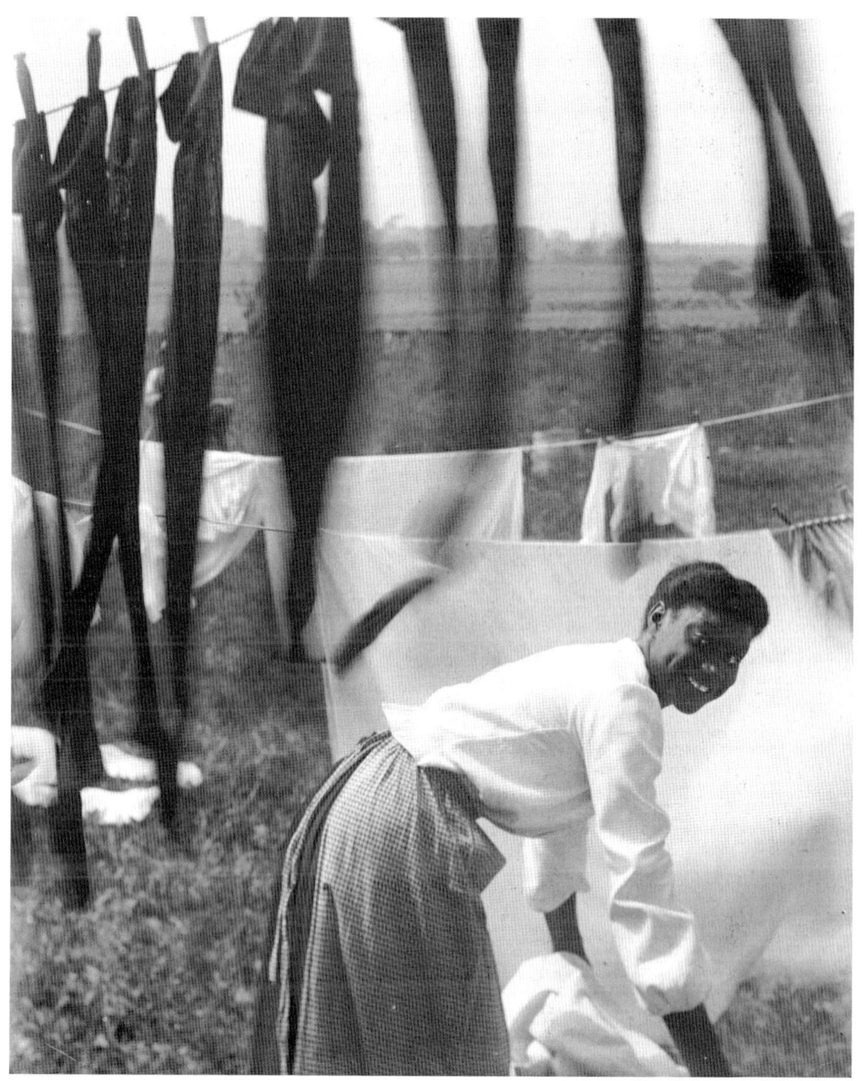

Informal Portrait of a Young Woman Surrounded by Laundry, 1903

Käsebier brings out what she called "the essential temperament that is called soul, humanity" in her informal portrait of a young woman hanging up laundry on a clothesline in Newport, Rhode Island. A line of dark stockings frames the top of the foreground. Underneath, a woman smiles at the viewer as she bends over her pile of laundry. Behind her, sheets wave in the wind. Beyond the clothesline, fields can be seen in the distance.

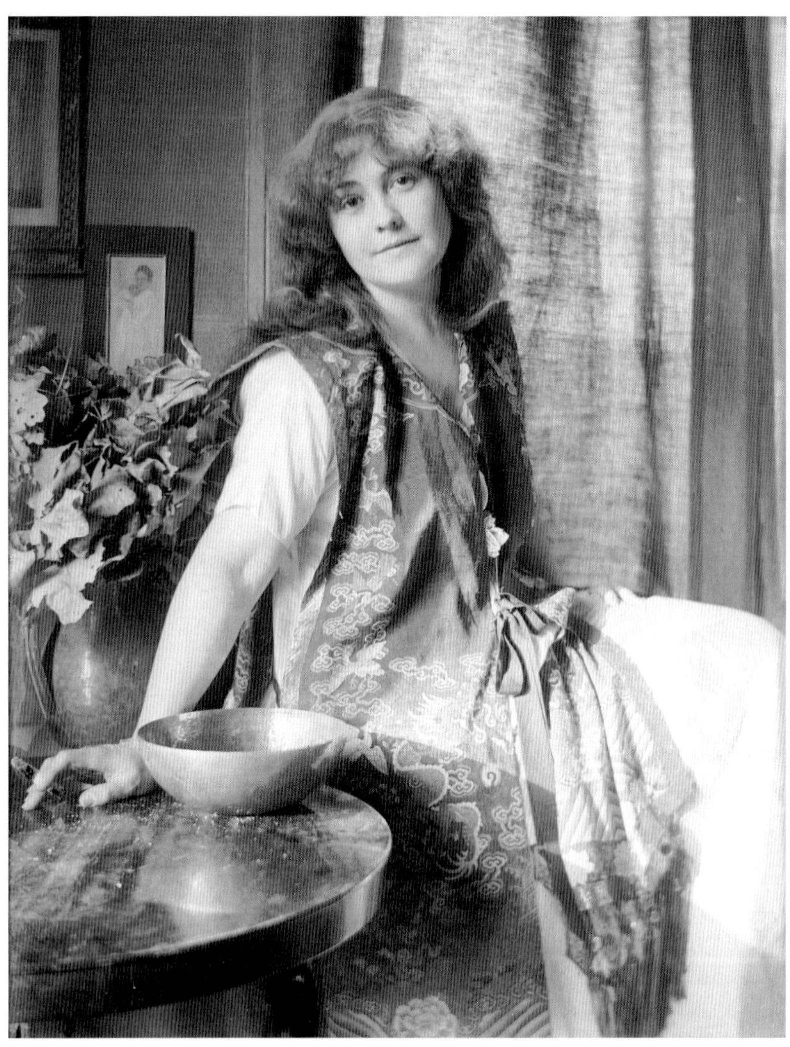

Rose O'Neill, Originator of the Kewpie Doll, 1907

Käsebier brought an artist's sensitivity to portraiture that was uncommon during her time. She encouraged a natural pose for Rose O'Neill, who smiles comfortably at the viewer, surrounded by simple objects of beauty—a bowl, a pitcher containing foliage, and a framed photograph. Active in the women's suffrage movement, Rose O'Neill was an American cartoonist, illustrator, artist, and writer. She earned a fortune by creating Kewpie, a brand of dolls that appeared as baby cupid characters. O'Neill would become the best-known and highest-paid female commercial illustrator in the United States.

She was also one of the photographers featured in Frances Benjamin Johnston's exhibit of female photographers for the 1900 Paris Exposition (World's Fair). The oldest of all the photographers featured in that show, Käsebier was considered to be the most inventive, versatile, and prolific.

Gertrude Käsebier, like Frances Benjamin Johnston, encouraged other women to become photographers. As she explained, "The key to artistic photography is to work out your own thoughts by yourselves. Imitation leads to certain disaster. New ideas are always antagonized. Do not mind that. If a thing is good it will survive." Imogen Cunningham and Laura Gilpin were particularly inspired by Käsebier's art.

Due to failing health, Käsebier closed her studio in 1929, and died five years later. A major collection of her work is located at the University of Delaware and at the Library of Congress.

One of the first American women to elevate photography as an art and have a successful career as a photographer, Käsebier helped shape the way we all photograph today, especially with her timeless images of mothers and children. She was one of the first photographers to focus on the family. Interested in the individual personalities of her subjects rather than in anthropological or symbolic types, Käsebier is also known for her images of Native Americans. Besides inspiring the careers of Imogen Cunningham and Laura Gilpin, Käsebier influenced many photographers today, whether they are aware of her or not.

READING LIST

Delaney, Michelle. *Buffalo Bill's Wild West Warriors: A Photographic History.* Washington, D.C.: Smithsonian, 2007.

Homer, William Innes. *A Pictorial Heritage: The Photographs of Gertrude Käsebier.* Wilmington: Delaware Art Museum, 1979.

Michaels, Barbara L. *Gertrude Käsebier: The Photographer and Her Photographs.* New York: Abrams, 1992.

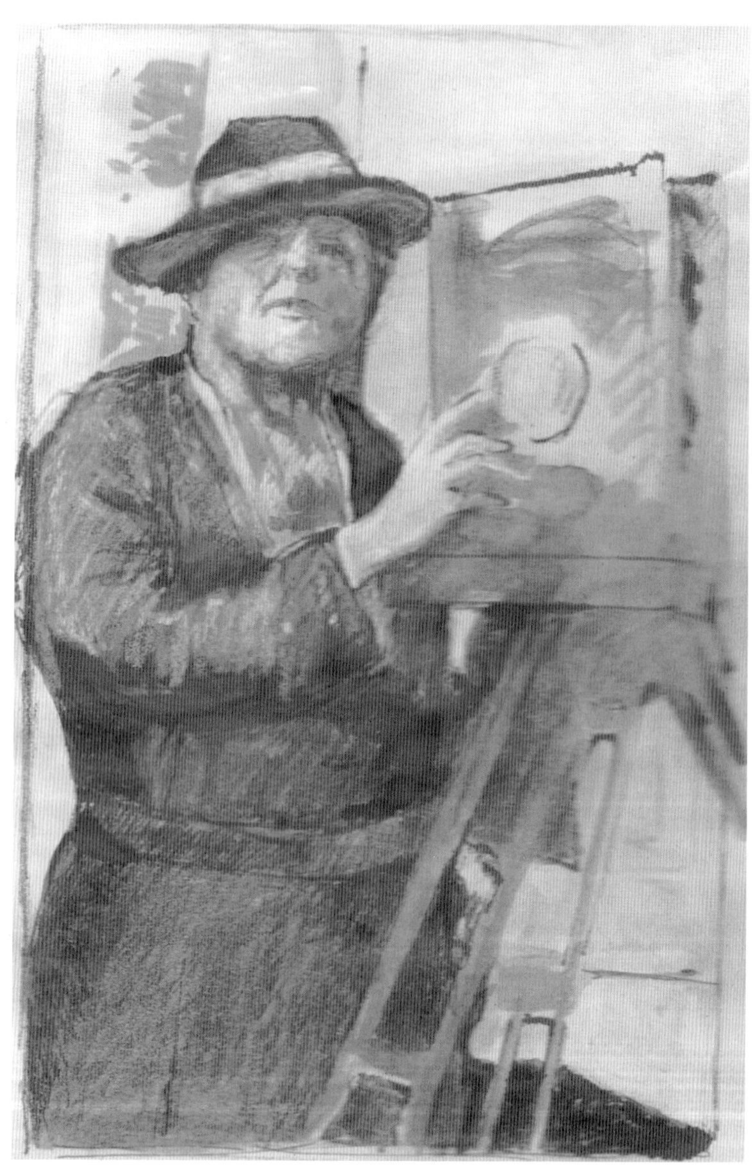

Frances Benjamin Johnston

2

Frances Benjamin Johnston

(1864–1952)

Photographer of Historic Architecture

FRANCES BENJAMIN JOHNSTON was born in West Virginia during the Civil War. She grew up to become one of America's most famous photographers of her day. She is known for her portraits, news photography, garden pictures, and most of all, her documentation of historic buildings.

Johnston was fortunate to have been brought up in Washington, D.C., as part of a wealthy and encouraging family. Her father worked for the Treasury Department and her mother, Johnston's most important role model, was one of the nation's first political reporters and one of the first American women to write on national affairs.

From an early age, Johnston knew she wanted to be a writer, but that was not all. When she showed an interest in art, her parents

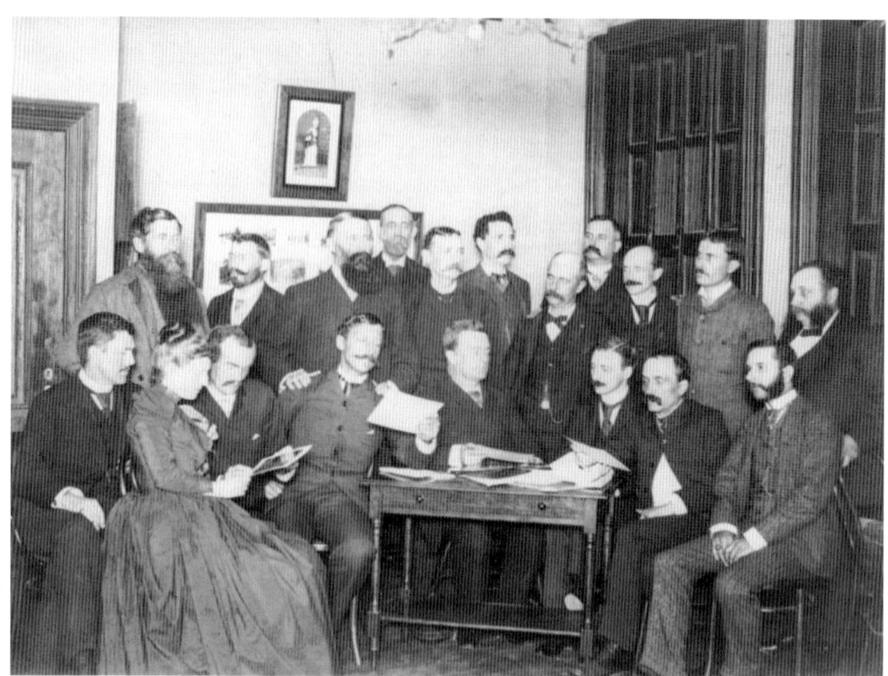

Capital Camera Club, Washington, D.C., 1895

Johnston was not singled out as a female, but was referred to as another Washington photographer who belonged to the Capital Camera Club. Unlike other artists who promoted themselves as struggling artists, Johnston preferred to see herself as a responsible member of a professional community.

gladly sent her to Paris to study drawing and painting. The Académie Julian was one of the few European academies open to women when Johnston studied there. She was proud of her education, and her three years of art studies provided connections that helped her find work.

When Johnston returned to Washington, D.C., she decided to become a magazine illustrator. She could write and draw well. She liked to research and write about history, art, buildings, parks, gardens, and traveling. Most of all, she was fascinated by her own city. Johnston learned about photography from Thomas Smillie, the first

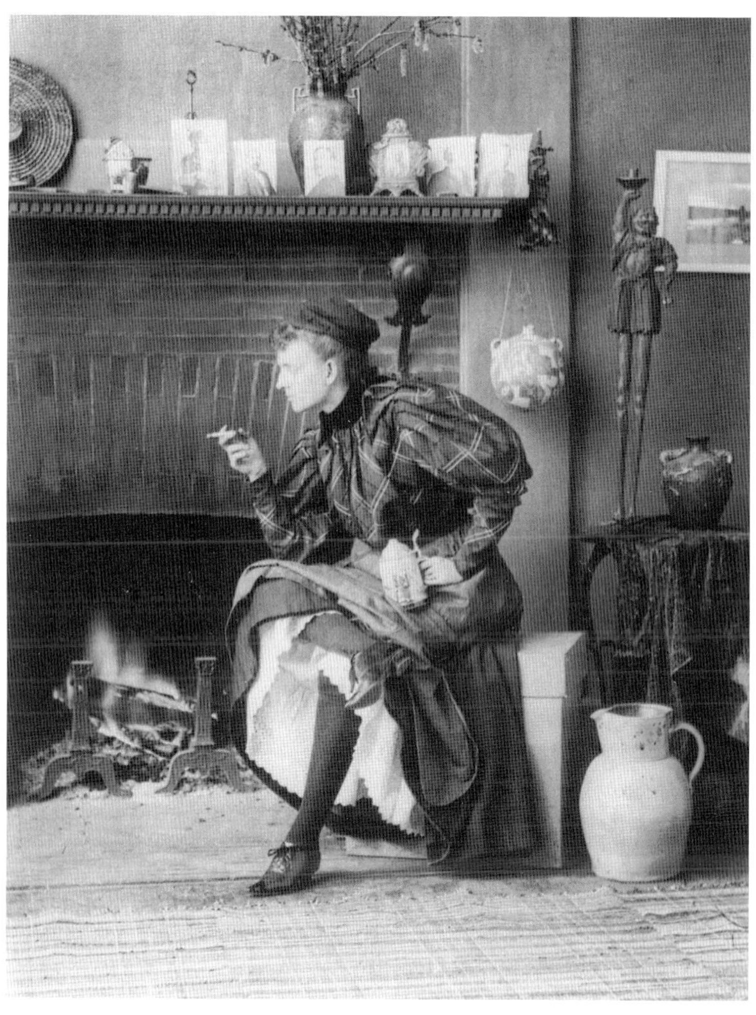

The Rebel, 1896

This portrait, suggesting Johnston's values, has also been adopted as a symbol of feminism, a bold statement of independence in the male-dominated world in which Johnston made a place for herself as a photographer and artist. In her self-portrait, the young woman holds a cigarette in one hand and a beer mug in the other. She sits with her skirt hiked up, showing her petticoats and her legs crossed in a masculine fashion. Committed to breaking conventions, she also wanted to "be one of the boys," to establish herself in her own right. Known for her feistiness and her drive, Johnston's independence and sense of humor sustained her throughout her career.

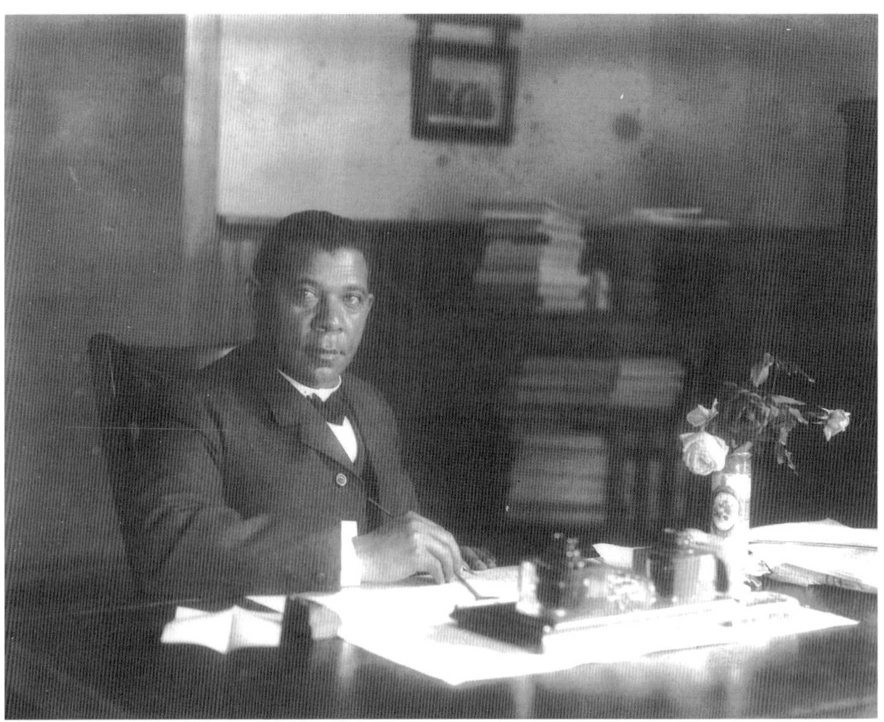

Booker T. Washington, 1906

Johnston's portrait of Booker T. Washington shows him facing the camera, temporarily suspended from his work as he sits behind his desk holding a pen. On his desk are scattered papers and a vase of roses. Light falls predominantly on top of his desk and along one side of his head and hand, catching a very small part of his wooden chair.

As a leading voice during the Gilded Age, Washington advocated for higher education and manual labor to improve the inequality facing African Americans. Johnston's photographs of Tuskegee Institute would be published in *Working with the Hands* (1904), a sequel to Washington's popular autobiography, *Up From Slavery* (1901).

director of the photography department at the Smithsonian Institution, which is a group of museums and research centers run by the government in Washington, D.C. While there, she experimented with different kinds of cameras. Johnston took pictures of all the things she enjoyed.

The inventor of the Kodak camera, George Eastman, was a family friend. He gave Johnston her first roll-film camera in 1888 as soon as it became available. The Kodak camera was a small camera and easy to carry. It used rolls of film that had to be sent to a lab to be developed into prints. Until the advent of digital cameras, this was the main method of taking pictures for the next one hundred years.

For most of her photographs, Johnston used a large, heavy camera that used 8×10-inch glass plate negatives. Long exposures allowed for rich detail in light and shaded areas. Johnston's camera was mounted on three wooden legs, or tripod, allowing the camera to slide and tilt into position.

When Johnston was ready to work on her own, she had a studio constructed behind her family's home on V Street, where people she photographed could be comfortable. Soon she developed a reputation as a portrait photographer. According to the *Washington Times*, Johnston was the "only lady in the business of photography in the city, and in her skillful hands it has become an art that rivals the geniuses of the Old World." Her photographs were compared to famous paintings!

Many important people had their portraits taken by Johnston. Susan B. Anthony (1820–1906) was an American leader who fought for women's rights, especially their right to vote. Booker T. Washington (1856–1915) was an American teacher, author, and leader who improved the lives of the African-American community. Mark Twain (1835–1910) was an American writer known for his books about life along the Mississippi River, including *The Adventures of Tom Sawyer* (1876) and *The Adventures of Huckleberry Finn* (1885). Because of her status in the nation's capital, Johnston also took photographs of five presidents and their families.

Johnston encouraged other women to consider careers in photography. For this purpose, she collected the photographs of 28 female photographers to exhibit at the Paris Exposition of 1900. In another exhibit for the same World's Fair, Johnston brought photographs she had taken of the buildings and students of the Hampton

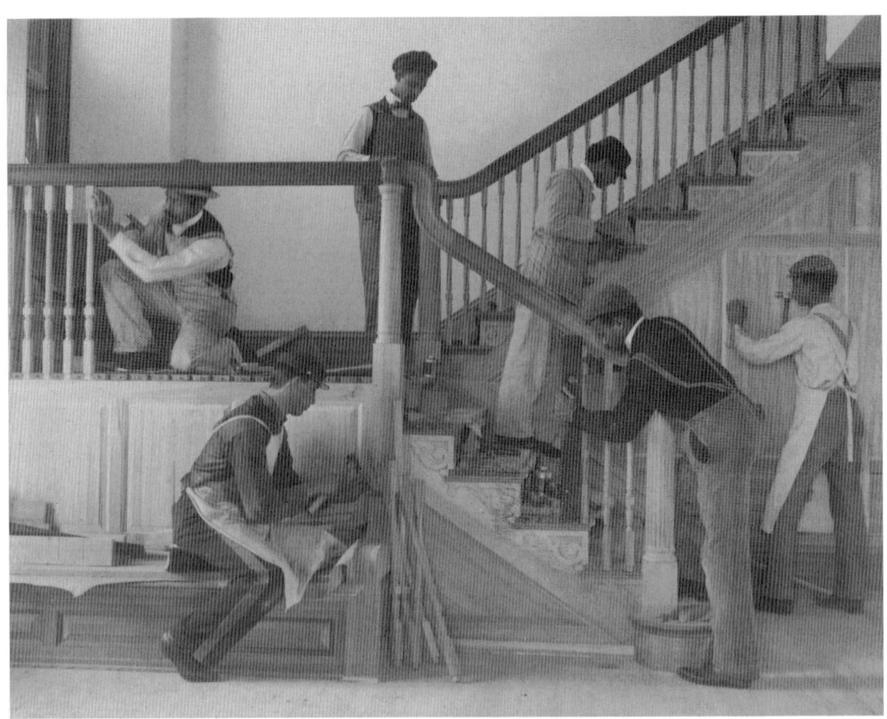

Treasurer's Staircase, Hampton Institute, 1899

This photograph is part of the Hampton Institute series which emphasizes the virtuousness of work. One of Johnston's most frequently reproduced photographs today, and the one for which she is best known, it shows several students at work on the interior stairway of a building under construction, a kind of catalog of carpentry techniques.

The pupils concentrate on various aspects of stairway construction. One man checks to see that the stairs are level. Another person chisels a carving below the balustrade. Someone else hammers a post, while another student inspects the top railing. One hammers paneling below the stairway, and another seems to be inspecting the landing. Working in harmony, their bodies effortlessly follow the horizontal, vertical, and diagonal lines of the stairway.

Institute in Virginia, a school that provided vocational training for ex-slaves and Native American students. Johnston received lots of praise and big awards for these photographs.

During her forties, Johnston moved to New York City where she lived and worked with her partner, Mattie Edwards Hewitt. Johnston was the "boss lady" who taught Hewitt about photography. They operated a studio on Fifth Avenue and took pictures of luxurious estates and gardens for the next eight years. After their partnership ended in 1917, Hewitt continued photographing gardens and mansions.

Johnston would never have a close relationship with another person again, preferring to live independently after she left her most intimate friend in New York.

Johnston saw the historic buildings of the South as fading reminders of the past, disappearing quickly before her eyes. Concerned about their fate, she decided that her job was to hurry "on the road ahead of the march of neglect and progress."

She understood that the story of buildings is the story of the people who made them, and that the history of the country could be written from the study of its architecture. It would be a better history than the ones written from a study of wars, because it would tell about people when they were creating things and not when they were destroying them.

In the summer of 1926, Johnston agreed to go on a tour throughout the Southeast to photograph gardens for *Town & Country* magazine. It was during this trip that she became more interested in the old buildings there. She explained, "It was through my travels [looking for] gardens that I noticed the fine old houses which figured so importantly in colonial history and which are falling to wrack and ruin unhonored and unsung."

During a stop in Fredericksburg, Virginia, Johnston met Helen Devore, who allowed her to photograph her newly restored country estate of Chatham.

After this project, it took Johnston three summers to photograph the historic architecture of the town of Fredericksburg. Her work was exhibited at the local town hall, and Johnston made certain that her photographs received coverage in the national media.

Eventually Johnston's images were exhibited at the Library of Congress, where they attracted the attention of Dr. Leicester Bovine Holland, director of the Library of Congress, as well as administrators from the University of Virginia, and several members of Congress.

Holland and Johnston became friends. They shared a love of gardening, old buildings, and libraries. Holland was very impressed with Johnston's work, and asked her to prepare her photographs for permanent storage and retrieval at the Library of Congress. He said, "I hope you'll let me see more of your material soon!" Holland and Johnston kept in touch for the rest of their lives, and he ended up writing the foreword to her first book.

Johnston donated her work to form the Pictorial Archives of Early American Architecture. It was Johnston's and Holland's hope that the archives at the Library of Congress would become a national foundation for the study of early American architecture and garden design. Her initial contribution of 5,000 negatives was the inspiration for the Historic American Buildings Survey (HABS)—America's largest architectural recording project that continues today.

After the 1929 stock market crash, Johnston was extremely fortunate to be supported throughout the Depression with back-to-back grants from the Carnegie Corporation. Andrew Carnegie (1835–1919) was a wealthy American businessman who made his fortune in the steel industry. He devoted money to libraries, schools, and the arts. Johnston already knew Andrew Carnegie because she had taken a picture of him that he really liked. He gladly supported her photography work in the South. Johnston was lucky to have steady work during the Great Depression, a time when most artists were unemployed.

At the age of 69, Johnston began her photographic survey of nine Southern states, beginning with five years in Virginia. The other states included North Carolina, South Carolina, Georgia, Louisiana, Florida, Maryland, Mississippi, and Alabama.

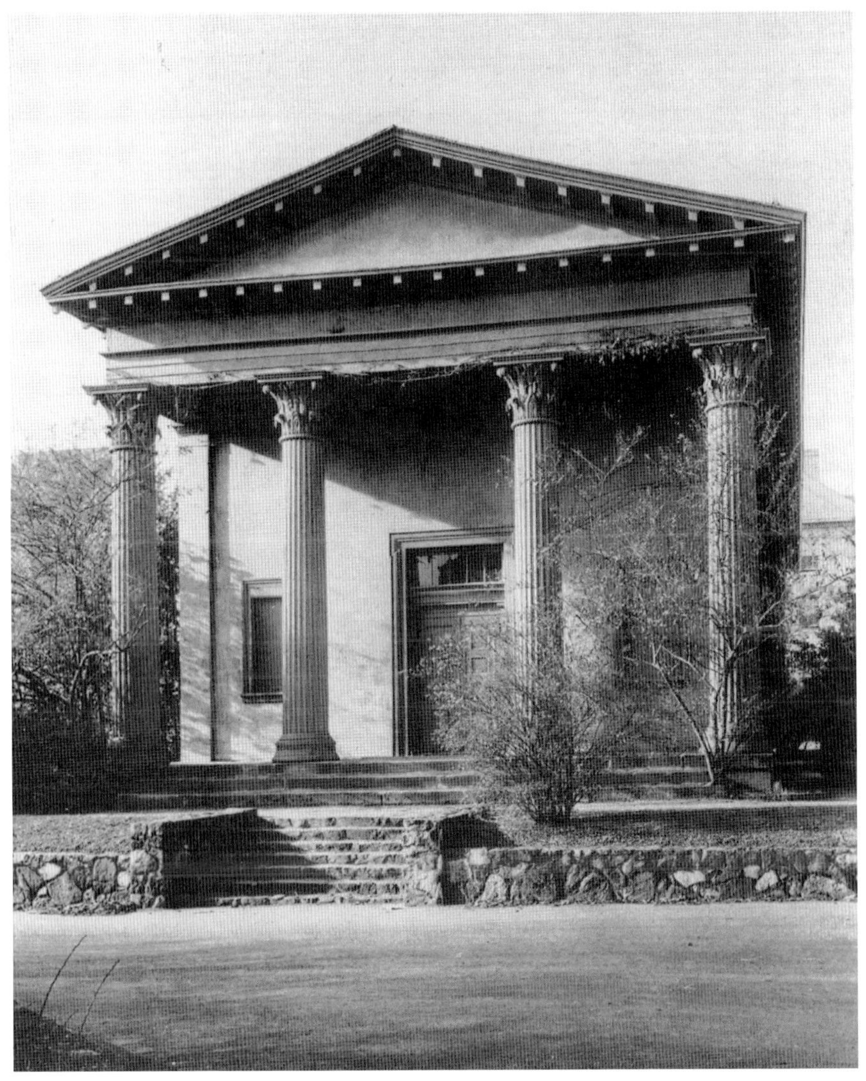

Playmakers Theatre, Chapel Hill, North Carolina, c. 1936

Johnston revered each building she photographed, and the photograph of Playmakers Theatre, located on the University of North Carolina campus where her first book was published, is no exception. The tightly focused portrait of the theater illuminates its individuality and character. The most essential feature of the building, its portico, with fluted columns becomes the primary dramatic interest at close range. Johnston's point of view is level to the facade so that we meet its "gaze" squarely, more like an old friend.

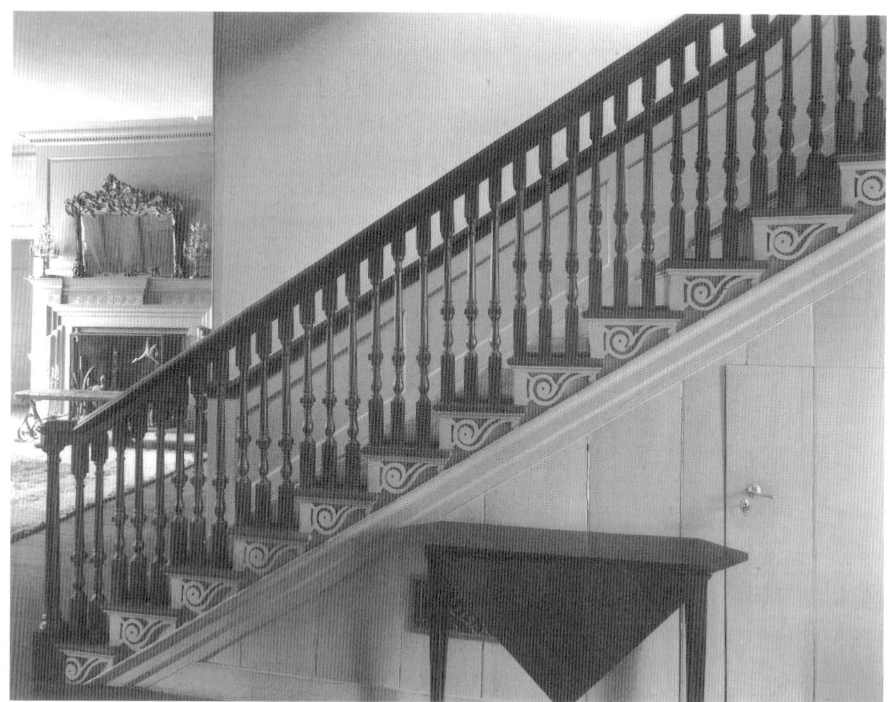

Entrance Hall at Fenwick Hall, Johns Island, SC, c. 1938

Careful attention to the framing of interior views is maintained, allowing for a balanced composition of dark and light elements evenly weighted between the two sides. In Johnston's photograph, a doorway that opens onto a living room mirror and fireplace on one side of a diagonal stairway balances out a dark drop-leaf table in the foreground.

Johnston established a routine. She always began with research of a region and devoted lots of time to studying books on local history and architecture as well as maps. She also contacted local historians, architects, homeowners, and community leaders for information. Johnston enjoyed the help of others, and often, the people who worked with her became lifelong friends. Once in the field, she researched historical records, such as deeds, to verify the dates and owners of old buildings.

Johnston's photographic survey of historic architecture was a success for everyone connected with it. What began as a personal free-lance of a privately-owned estate became a nine-state documentation project sponsored by the Library of Congress, one of the world's largest photographic organizations.

Johnston's work was watched and strongly supported by architects and historians of the National Park Service, the leading government body promoting historic preservation. Johnston's pictures had a direct impact on national preservation legislation and federal work programs. The passage of the American Historic Sites and Buildings Act in 1935 ensured that buildings would be recognized for their artistic merit and historic significance.

Johnston's interest in American architecture inspired her to travel thousands of miles by car through nine states of the South. With money from Andrew Carnegie to photograph historic plantations, churches, and city architecture, the entire project took Johnston twelve years to complete. Considered to be her greatest contribution to the history of architecture, these portraits of buildings are now at the Library of Congress as well as in books.

But Johnston never wanted her photographs to just remain on the walls of museums or inside books. Through her photography she wished for people to appreciate and care for the beautiful buildings she loved so much. She also hoped her photographs would inspire people to remember the history of our country.

You can see many of these buildings for yourself if you travel throughout the southeastern states, and especially if you visit the historic districts that Johnston helped to preserve: Savannah, Georgia; Charleston, South Carolina; St. Augustine, Florida; and New Orleans, Louisiana. Traveling to these historic cities is a fun way to learn more about the history of America.

Near the end of her 60-year career, Johnston bought a house at 1132 Bourbon Street in New Orleans, where she lived for the rest of her life. She died at home at the age of 88 while preparing photographs for another book.

One of the first women to work as an accomplished photographer, Johnston became respected for her portraiture, artistic studies, photojournalism, and garden and architectural photography. She inspired other women to become photographers, and was popular among celebrities of the day. Her most significant contribution to the history and development of photography is her monumental survey of historic architecture in the South.

READING LIST

Ausherman, Maria. *The Photographic Legacy of Frances Benjamin Johnston.* Gainesville: University Press of Florida, 2009.

Berch, Bettina. *The Woman Behind the Lens: The Life and Work of Frances Benjamin Johnston, 1864-1952.* Charlottesville: University Press of Virginia, 2000.

Daniel, Pete and Raymond Smock. *A Talent for Detail: The Photographs of Frances Benjamin Johnston, 1899-1910.* New York: Harmony Books, 1974.

Nichols, Frederick Doveton. *The Early Architecture of Georgia.* Chapel Hill: University of North Carolina Press, 1957.

Stoney, Samuel Gaillard. *Plantations of the Carolina Low Country.* Charleston: Carolina Art Association, 1938.

Waterman, Thomas Tileston. *The Early Architecture of North Carolina.* Chapel Hill: University of North Carolina Press, 1950.

Watters, Sam. *Gardens for a Beautiful America, 1895-1935: Photographs by Frances Benjamin Johnston.* New York: Acanthus Press, 2012.

Alice Austen

(1866–1952)

At Home in Clear Comfort

ALICE AUSTEN was born in Staten Island, New York, in 1866. Abandoned by her father, she grew up with her mother's family in a home known as "Clear Comfort." Built in 1690, this historic landmark offered waterfront views of Brooklyn, the Manhattan skyline, and Jersey City.

As a little girl, Austen was the center of attention. When she was ten years old, her uncle, Oswald Muller, a sea captain, brought home a camera that he let Austen use when he was traveling. Little did he know then that he had changed her life.

Her uncle, Peter Townsend Austen, a chemistry professor at Rutgers University, showed her how to use chemicals to process her photographs and make prints. Uncle Oswald and Uncle Peter built a darkroom upstairs so that Austen could develop her own photographs at home. After her uncles' first demonstrations, Alice "learned by doing." Her family's help and support enabled her to learn photography at a very young age.

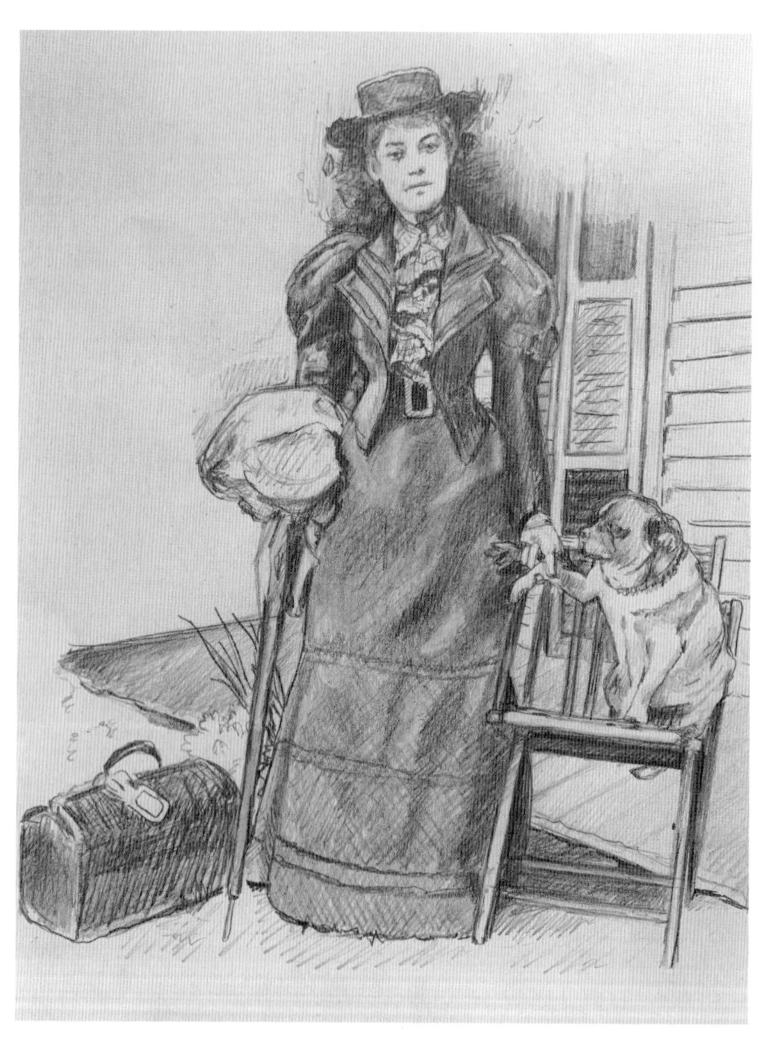

Alice Austen

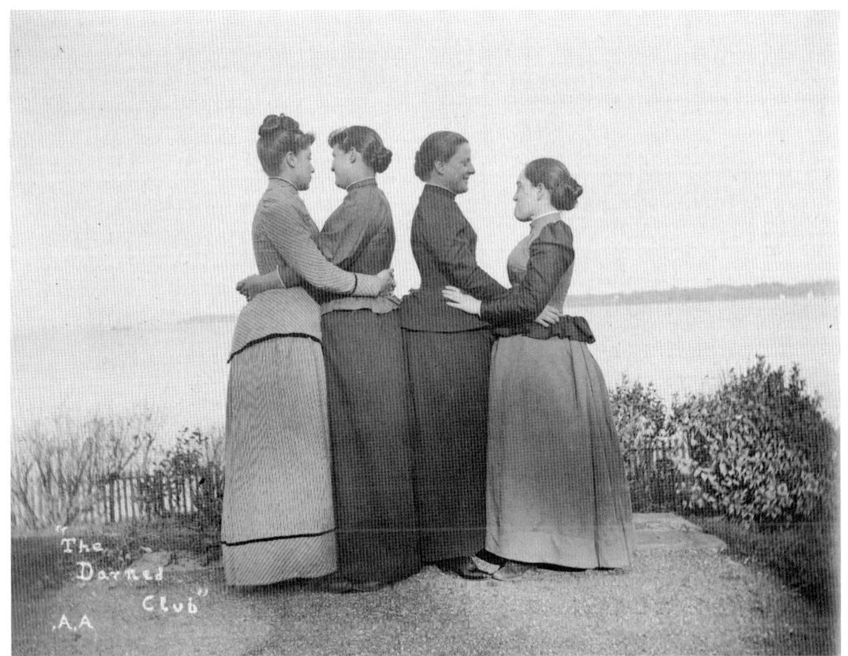

The Darned Club, 1891

This picture of Austen and her three friends standing boldly in profile paired as two couples was taken in the garden of Clear Comfort overlooking the sea. The friends went to school together and spent much time at each other's homes.

The first camera she called her own was given to her by a cousin when she was a teenager. Austen was a professional photographer by the time she was eighteen. Although she did not consider herself an artist, she knew she was a good photographer and she knew what she liked. Her earliest surviving photographs were genteel self-portraits, photographs of her home, her family, and nearby friends.

As a resident who spent much time exploring neighborhoods close to home, Alice was an expert on nineteenth-century life and architecture in Staten Island. She considered photographing all the historic buildings throughout Staten Island, but she decided that using a horse and buggy to travel around the island was too time consuming.

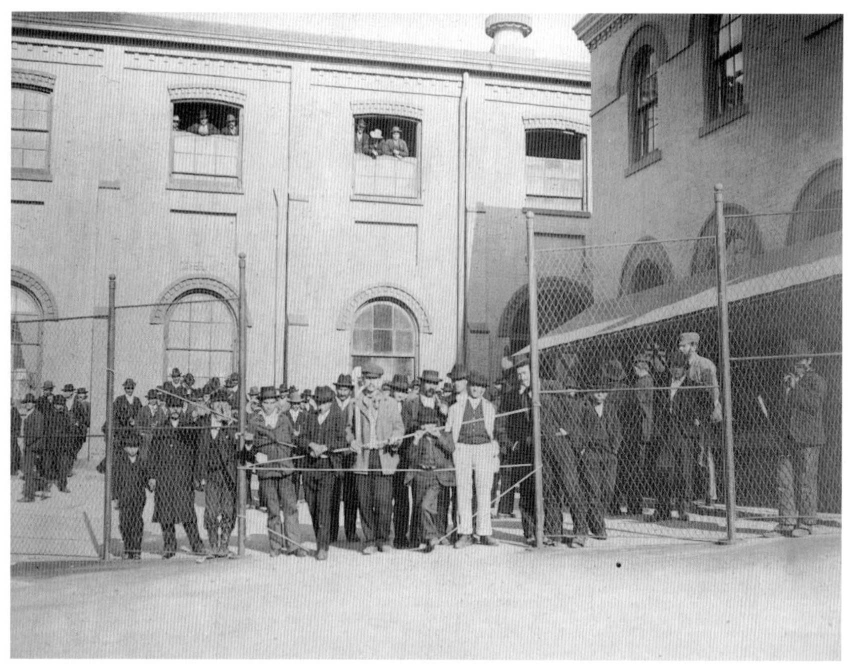

Quarantine, Hoffman Island, 1901

Forlorn immigrants from a ship feared to have a smallpox outbreak are being held for observation behind a fence. Austen documented conditions on Swinburne and Hoffman, two islands off the Staten Island shore for the U.S. Public Health Service. After her one-year commission ended, Austen continued to photograph the quarantine islands for more than a decade. She carefully recorded the buildings, laboratories, and people of the Quarantine Station, a station through which millions of immigrants passed on their way to Ellis Island. If suspected of carrying diseases, the newly arrived immigrants were isolated and treated on these islands, now part of the National Park Service.

Even though she did not complete a survey, Austen recorded events close to where she lived. From her seaside home, she watched the building of the Statue of Liberty as well as the new federal station on Ellis Island. Austen's neighbor, Dr. Alvah H. Doty, the quarantine health officer, commissioned Austen to photograph the Quarantine Station between the fort guarding the harbor and her home.

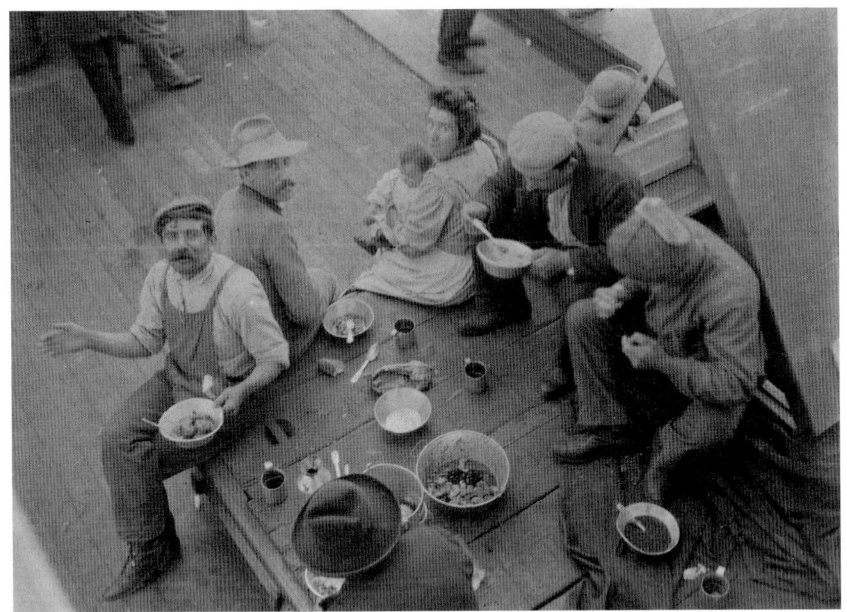

S.S. Finland, Steerage at Supper, 1909

From an elevated viewpoint, Austen shows the deck of a ship. Five men and a woman carrying an infant sit around a wooden platform sharing a meal. Some of the passengers look up at the photographer while others eat. A young boy leans on the edge of an open hatch. The S.S. Finland, a passenger ship built in 1902, usually made trips between New York City and Antwerp, Belgium, but in the year this photograph was taken, the ship made three trips between New York and Naples.

Austen took advantage of the newly opened ferry line across New York Bay to trace the paths of immigrants, past the newly erected Statue of Liberty and across the harbor to lower Manhattan, where they settled and worked. Later, as she traveled with her camera along the streets further uptown, Austen photographed unsentimental portraits of merchants, the first cars, Grace Church, buildings around Washington Square, stores throughout 23rd Street, and Central Park.

Austen took many trips and always brought her camera, along with fifty pounds of equipment. Her photographs mainly document scenes in the northeastern United States, but she also journeyed

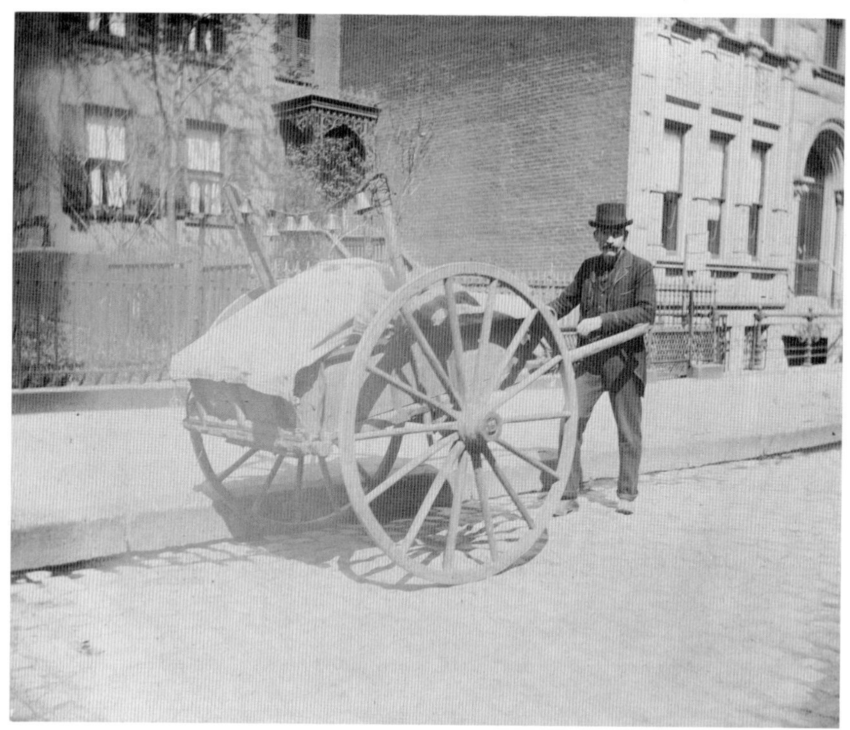

Peddler with Cart, 1896

Alice Austen's photograph of a peddler shows him pushing his large-wheeled wooden cart along the side of a cobblestone street. The mustached man, wearing a suit and top hat, stands in front of a residence with a gated yard. Austen took numerous photographs of merchants in Lower Manhattan to show how many new immigrants settling in New York made a living. These late nineteenth-century photographs mark Austen as one of the earliest female street photographers who captured the changing face of the city at the turn of the century.

north to Quebec, west to Ohio and Illinois, and south to Maryland and Florida. She also made regular excursions to Europe for more than twenty years.

An avid gardener and a prominent member of Staten Island society when it was populated by a wealthy class of landowners, Austen founded the Staten Island Garden Club in 1914. She frequented the country club, where she photographed tennis tournaments, fox

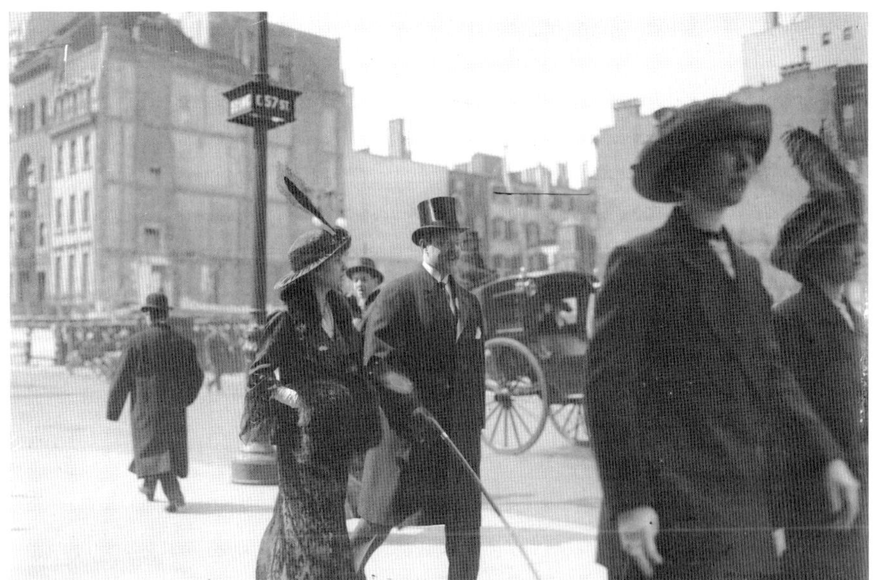

Austen Gray and Wife, 1913

Austen's photograph shows Austen Gray and his wife, Alice Monroe Burnham, enjoying a stroll near East 57th Street on Easter Day. Between the well-dressed couple and two women walking in front of them, a carriage can be seen in the background. Everyone wears a hat and coat, and Mr. Gray carries a cane.

hunting, and the newly popular sport of golf. She was a close friend of people with names like Vanderbilt, Roosevelt, Barrymore, and Cunard, and took photographs of all of them. She and her partner, Gertrude Tate, joined the Colony Club, and every Saturday afternoon they went to the Metropolitan Opera.

In addition to being involved in cultural activities, Austen was civic-minded. For example, she served with the Red Cross by driving an ambulance during World War I. She also was a hostess at a hospital throughout the war years.

Having lived a privileged life, she had a very hard time making ends meet during the Great Depression. In addition to losing all her money at 63, she lost her elegant home.

Publications of her photographs were used to raise enough money for Austen to live the rest of her life in a private nursing home. Around 1950, Austen's photographs were discovered by museum curators and magazine editors. "The publication of her pictures brings Alice Austen, the first important American camerawoman, into the ranks of great American photographers," announced *Life* magazine in 1951. The editors of *Holiday* magazine wrote a year later, "This country's first great woman photographer, a sensitive artist with a camera, drew an affectionate nineteenth-century portrait of her native land—a gentle and long-vanished America."

Austen died in 1952 at the age of 86. Her partner, Gertrude Tate, lived on for ten more years after Austen's death. Today, the Staten Island Historical Society owns most of her extensive photography collection. The Alice Austen House, a seventeenth-century home and National Historic Landmark, now is a house museum devoted to Alice Austen's legacy. As Alice Austen explained, "I am happy that what was once so much pleasure for me turns out now to be a pleasure for other people."

Austen is remembered today for how she extensively recorded the activities of her friends and family, as well as her own life at her home in Staten Island. Personal photographs of Gertrude Tate and other female friends are significant because they show that she questioned gender roles and explored her identity as a Victorian woman. With her camera in hand, Austen also captured street vendors and immigrants in turn-of-the-century New York. In doing so, she helped pioneer documentary photography.

READING LIST

Austen, Alice. *Street Types of New York.* New York: The Albertype Co., 1896.

Khoudari, Amy. *Alice Austen House: A National Historic Landmark: Museum and Garden Guide.* Staten Island: Friends of the Alice Austen House, 1993.

Novotny, Ann. *Alice's World: The Life and Photography of an American Original: Alice Austen, 1866–1952.* Old Greenwich, CT: Chatham Press, 1976.

Zaida Ben-Yusuf

(1869–1933)

The Pleasure of Your Presence is Desired

ZAIDA BEN-YUSUF was born in London in 1869, the eldest daughter of a German mother and Algerian father. After her parents separated, her father remarried. Looking for work, Ben-Yusuf's mother resettled in Boston, where she established her own millinery shop to design and sell women's hats. At the time, hats were considered a very important part of women's fashion.

Following her mother with her three sisters to America in 1895, Ben-Yusuf settled in New York City to become a milliner as well. She needed to earn a living, but she enjoyed taking photographs more. As she explained, "I took up photography at first for amusement, but only for a short time ..."

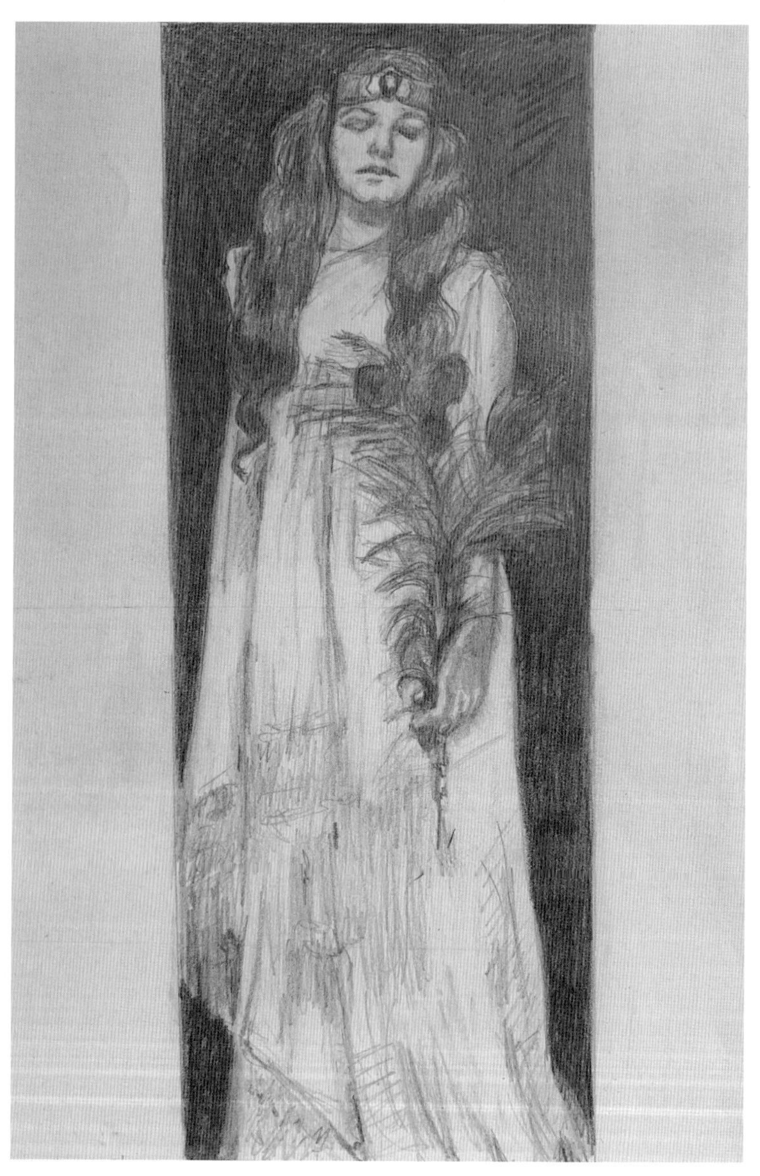

Zaida Ben-Yusuf

One year later, and without formal training, Ben-Yusuf began her photography career. She began to be known as a photographer when she promoted her work in magazines and exhibitions. She also got to know other photographers, who helped promote her career. For example, Alfred Stieglitz, the leader of the art photography movement in America, published her photographs in his journal, *Camera Notes.* In 1898, she held a two-woman show with Frances Benjamin Johnston at the Camera Club of New York.

Ben-Yusuf took portraits of people at her fashionable Fifth Avenue studio, one of the busiest of more than two hundred in New York.

Alone and far from her family, Ben-Yusuf's work allowed her to meet lots of entertaining people. Her portraits included wealthy and famous artists, politicians, actors, and writers, such as Robert Henri, Theodore Roosevelt, Jacob Riis, and Edith Wharton. Robert Henri (1865–1929) was one of the most influential art teachers in the United States in the early twentieth century. Jacob Riis (1849–1914) was a social reformer who wrote and took photographs to help the poor living in New York City. Edith Wharton (1862–1937) was a writer known for many novels, including *The Age of Innocence* and *The House of Mirth.* (Some say that the heroine of Edith Wharton's *The House of Mirth* was modeled on Ben-Yusuf.)

The key to Ben-Yusuf's success in artistic portraiture was how she made each of her sitters look attractive, unique, and full of personality.

Ben-Yusuf considered her photography art. She exhibited her photographs in over fifteen shows and was a member of prestigious photographic societies in England as well as the United States.

Notable photojournalist Frances Benjamin Johnston featured Ben-Yusuf's work in her exhibit of women photographers at the 1900 World's Fair in Paris, known as the Paris Exposition. Ben-Yusuf was also one of the photographers that Frances Benjamin Johnston promoted in one of her 1901 *Ladies Home Journal* articles, entitled, "The Foremost Women Photographers in America."

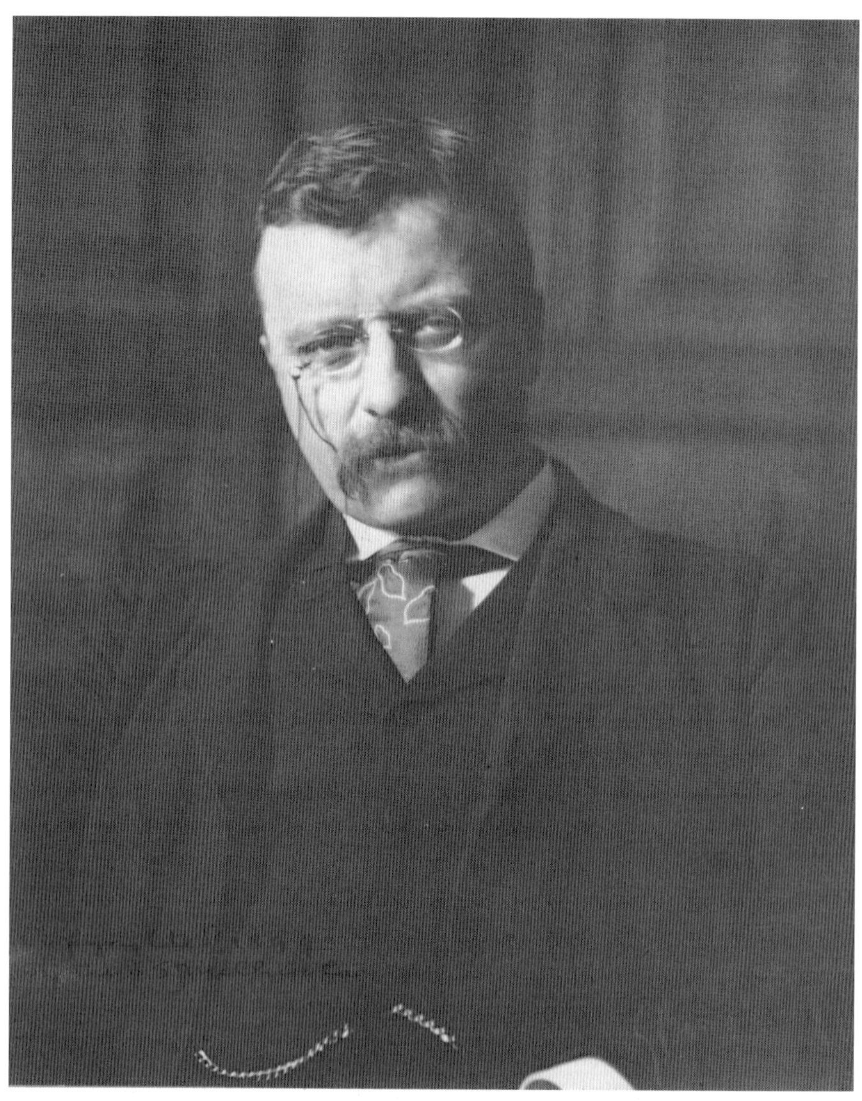

Theodore Roosevelt, 1899

No other American figure was more popular at the turn of the twentieth century than Theodore Roosevelt. A national hero, Roosevelt is known for the break-up of corporate trusts, the building of the Panama Canal, and the conservation of wilderness areas through the formation of the National Park Service. He was the governor of New York when this picture was taken.

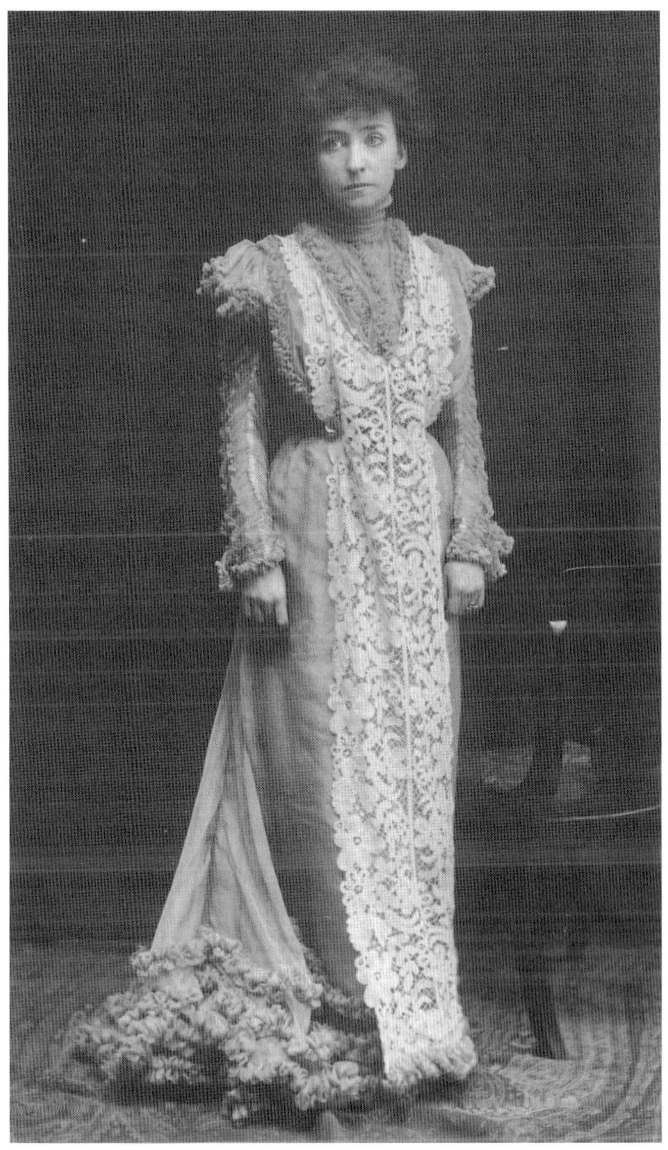

Mrs. Fiske, "Love Finds the Way," 1896

Ben-Yusuf's portrait shows actress Minnie Maddern Fiske (1865–1932) in *Love Finds the Way*, an 1896 play by Marguerite Merington. Fiske was one of the leading American actresses of the late nineteenth and early twentieth century. A prominent animal welfare advocate, she fought against the wearing of egret feathers on hats, fur trapping, and the harsh treatment of cattle on ranges.

In addition to taking portraits of people, Ben-Yusuf brazenly publicized herself, posing before her own camera in elaborate outfits and striking dramatic poses. Appearing confident and assertive, her self-portraits challenged traditional ideas about women's roles. She boasted that she could make a living independently despite the limited number of careers open to women at the time. These images make it clear that she valued women's work and equal rights.

At the time *The Odor of Pomegranates* photograph was taken, Ben-Yusuf's occupation as a commercial photographer was an arduous task. She represents women at the turn of the century who challenged prevailing gender roles. She achieved her goal by living independently, writing, and traveling.

Ben-Yusuf wanted to be as famous as the English photographer Julia Margaret Cameron. She said she wanted to be the "Mrs. Cameron of America!" (Julia Margaret Cameron, 1815–1879, one of the very first pioneering photographers to consider photography as an art, was renowned for her artistic portraits of England's cultural elite.) Likewise, Ben-Yusuf explained, "My best work represents the man of brains, either in business or professional life, and the thoroughly modern, clever woman, and these are the ones I enjoy photographing when I am in the mood for work ..."

Most of all, she admired women whose lives were even more unconventional than her own. For instance, one magazine published her portrait of Nancy Huston Banks, who served as a reporter on the war in South Africa. Other portraits include those of Agnes C. Laut, author of *Vikings of the Pacific*, and explorer May French Sheldon, who led an expedition to Kilimanjaro.

But Ben-Yusuf's career only lasted a little more than a decade. Operating a New York City studio became too much of an economic challenge. After making many portraits, she left her studio at the end of the First World War and spent the next twenty years traveling around the world and writing.

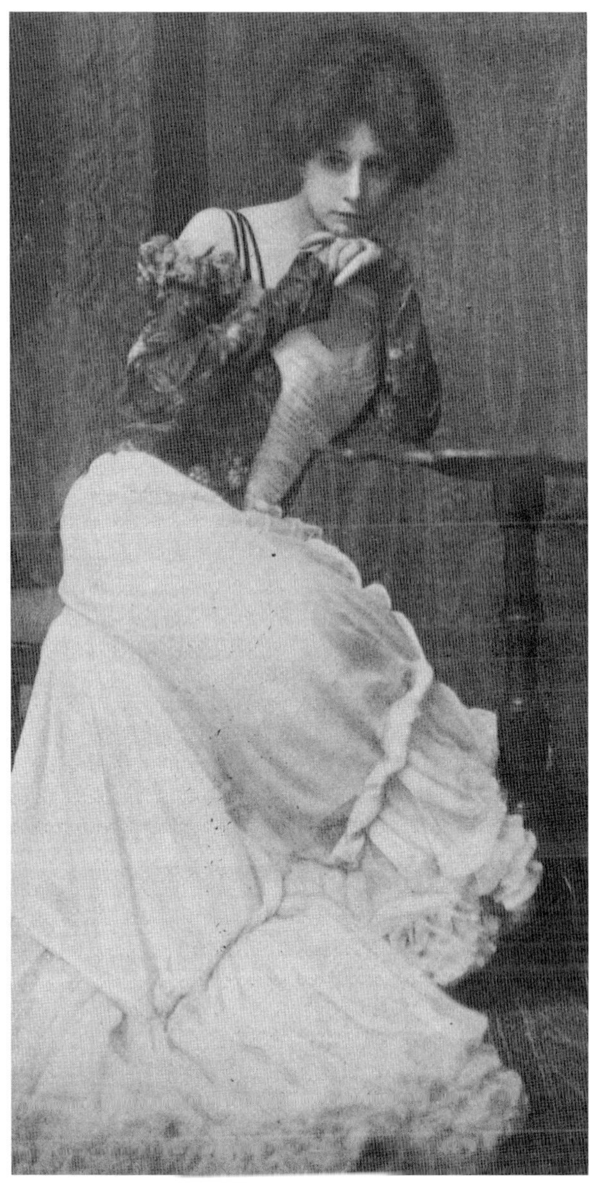

Self Portrait, 1901

In this portrait of herself, Ben-Yusuf clad in crinoline gazes pensively at the viewer. Her portrait accompanies her article published in *Metropolitan Magazine* entitled, "The New Photography—What it Has Done and is Doing for Modern Portraiture."

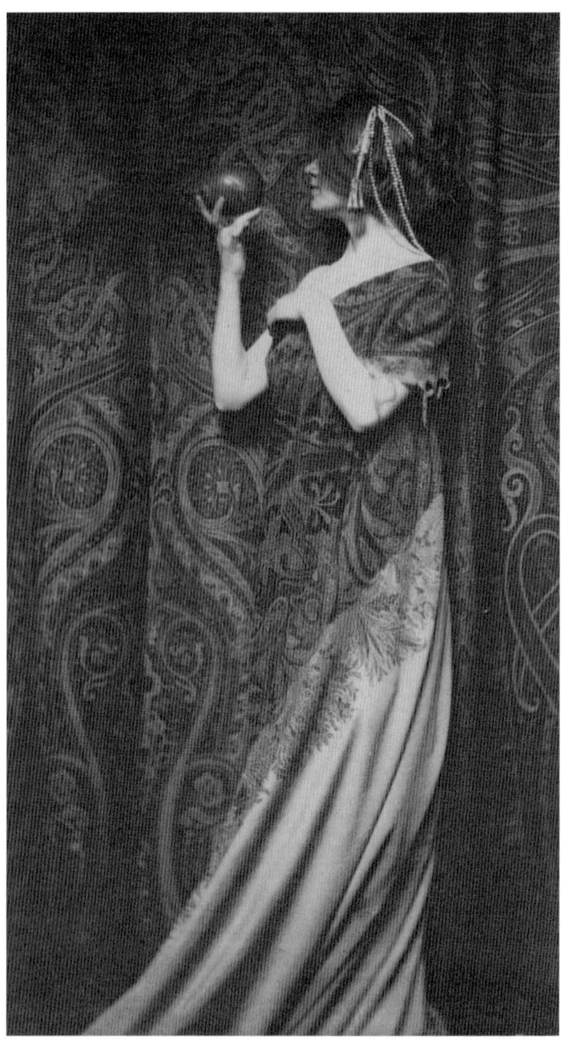

The Odor of Pomegranates, 1901

In Greek mythology, Persephone eats the pomegranate that Hades gives her, so that she must follow him to the underworld, where she lives only part of the year. After winter is over, she can return to her home on earth until winter begins again. Perhaps the pomegranate in this portrait, so often exhibited and published at the beginning of the twentieth century, can be viewed as a symbol of resurrection. The model's dress blends with the folded drapery backdrop, showing the influence of Art Nouveau, a movement that had swept through Vienna and Paris, which was characterized by elongated forms and floral motifs.

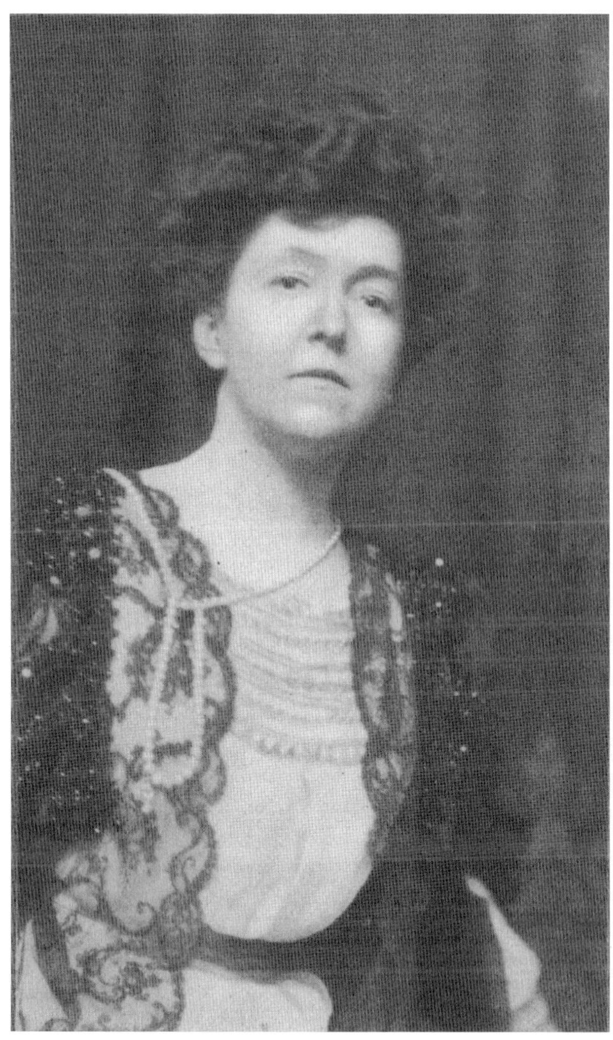

Miss Elsie de Wolfe, 1901

Elsie de Wolfe (1865–1950) was an American actress, author, and one of the first women interior decorators. She replaced heavy Victorian-style rooms with lighter, more intimate, and uncluttered spaces popular in late eighteenth-century France. In her autobiography, she called herself a "rebel in an ugly world." Ben-Yusuf's portrait of Elsie de Wolfe was taken while she was still acting in the play *The Shades of Night.* Eventually, de Wolfe left the theater to become a successful full-time decorator. At the peak of her career, she designed interiors for many prestigious people on the East and West Coasts.

When she returned in 1922, she took up needlework. She also began working for the New York-based Reed Fashion Service and lectured on fashion topics in department stores. Always conscious of fashion, Ben-Yusuf started a women's clothing business.

She died in Brooklyn in 1933 at the age of 63. The Library of Congress Prints and Photographs Division contains thirteen of Ben-Yusuf's original photographs. (Most of her work does not belong in a single institution.)

One of the most active photographers in New York City in the early twentieth century, Zaida Ben-Yusuf focused on making artistic portraits of people, especially celebrities of her day. She was attracted to ambitious figures who achieved great success, and she worked hard in her studio to show how they were special. Besides photographing individuals of accomplishment, Ben-Yusuf frequently posed before her own camera dressed in elaborate outfits, one of the first to use herself as subject matter. Although her portraiture career was brief, she contributed greatly to making photography a fine art.

READING LIST

Goodyear, Frank H., III. *Zaida Ben-Yusuf: New York Portrait Photographer.* Washington, D.C.: National Portrait Gallery, 2008.

Poulson, Elizabeth. *Zaida.* History of Photography Series, no. 18. Tempe: School of Art, Arizona State University, 1985.

5

Anne Brigman

(1869–1950)

Child of the Tropics

ANNE BRIGMAN was born in 1869 into a close-knit family descended from the islands' earliest Christian missionaries in Hawaii. The oldest of eight children, she grew up in Nu'uanu Pali, a lush mountainous region above Honolulu on the island of Oahu.

Although she never met her grandfather, Reverend Lorrin Andrews, Brigman knew of his distinguished reputation as a Christian minister. Not only did her mother's father establish a seminary to train young missionaries, but he also prepared a Hawaiian dictionary, translated the Bible into the Hawaiian language, and founded the first Hawaiian newspaper. Brigman was proud of her grandfather for what he had accomplished, and admired the way he kept local traditions alive.

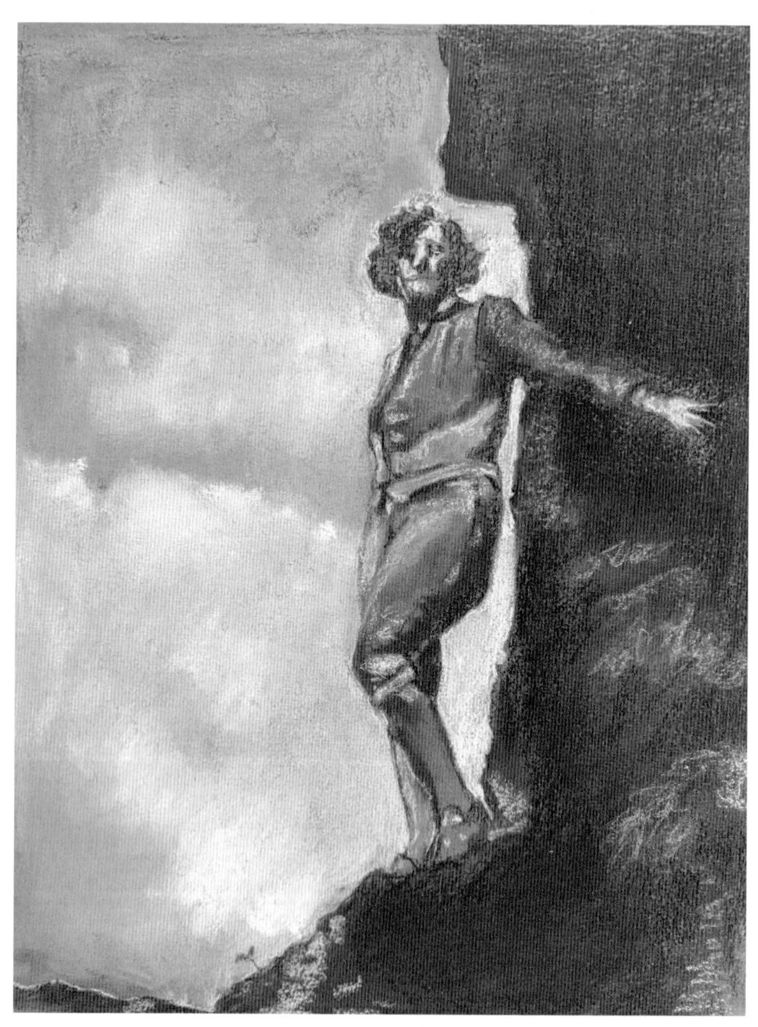

Anne Brigman

Brigman received a classical education as well as instruction in religion and modern science at Punahou School in Honolulu, which was founded in 1841 for missionary children. She was not particularly devout, and resented how the Hawaiian children "ran shoeless and wild" while she had to sit for hours during Sunday prayers.

Members of her family were strict and pious Christians, but Brigman preferred Hawaiian mythology and legends, and stories about the ancient Greek gods and goddesses. She believed male and female spirits were to be found everywhere–in rocks, the water, and trees as well as the sky.

She could speak the Hawaiian language, knew much about the local plants, and called herself a child of the tropics, where "mountain peaks and blue sea, trees and clouds, flowers and fruits and birds were as near and as complementary as one's right hand is to the left."

Life was full of adventure for Brigman and her spunky group of young companions. They "were into everything for miles around ... vivid young savages, primed to the brim with living." Being high in the valley above Honolulu was magical–full of colors and delicious smells.

"Mango trees, tall and ample in their glossy foliage, hung in season with huge jewel-like clusters of yellow, pendulous fruit, red-cheeked at the stem-end ... the golden globes of the guava and the heavy abundance of the banana and the papaya ..." (From unpublished foreword for *Songs of a Pagan* by Anne Brigman, 1939.)

When she was sixteen years old, Brigman's family moved to California. Nine years later in 1894, she married Martin Brigman, a sea captain from Denmark who was twenty years older. With a thirst for adventure, she accompanied him on some of his voyages. During one of their trips, Anne Brigman may have returned to Hawaii for a visit.

The couple eventually settled near Oakland in a bungalow where Brigman taught herself photography. By 1903, her parents had separated and her mother and sister moved in with Brigman and her

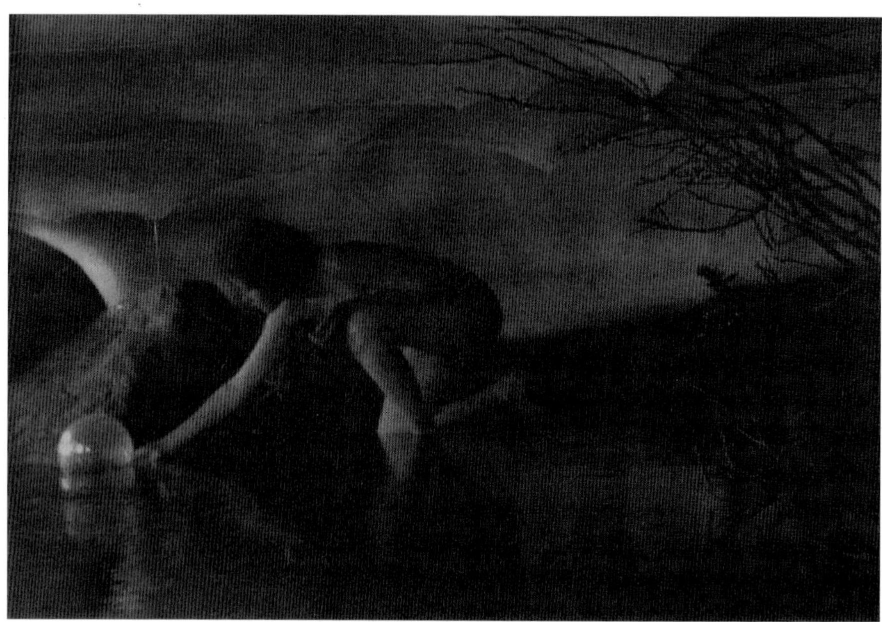

The Bubble, 1906

Rejecting the feminine as maternal, this picture shows a young nymph within an ice cave stretching her right arm to reach a translucent sphere floating in the water. Brigman often uses the image of the fragile orb. The crystal globe beside the figure of a woman transforms her material body into a spirit of nature.

husband. Brigman made portraits using herself and her sisters as models, and soon after displayed her pictures with other members of the California Camera Club at the 1902 San Francisco Second Photographic Salon.

Brigman's earliest photographs show women in traditional roles, such as sentimental mothers surrounded by children and flowers. Often, the women look more like decorative objects than real people.

Brigman's first excursion to the Sierra mountains in 1905 reminded her of her time outdoors. It also marked the beginning of her maturation as an artist devoted to direct encounters with

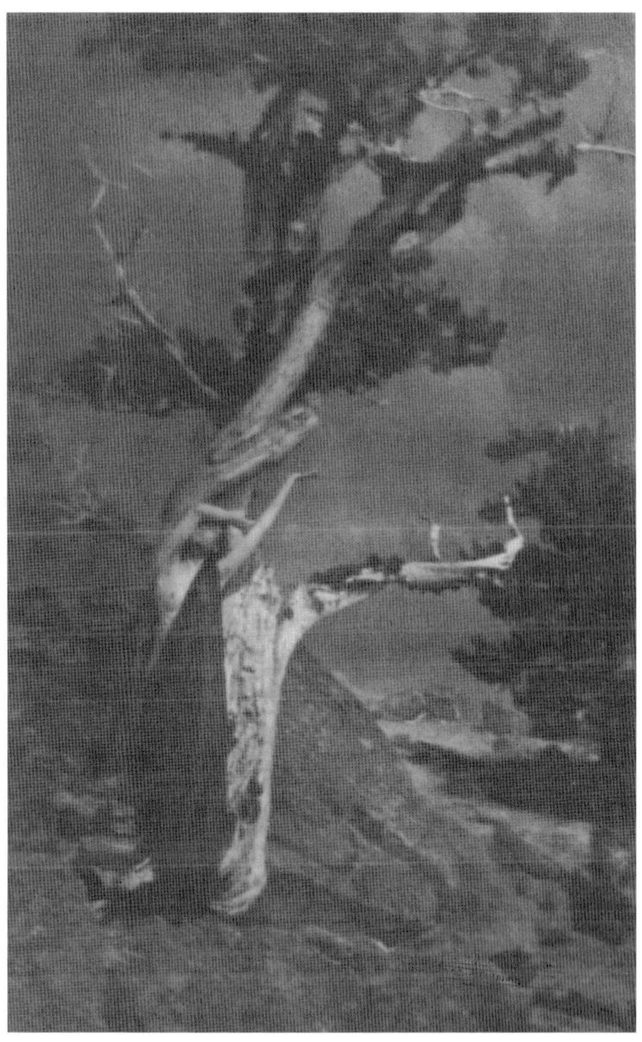

The Dying Cedar, 1906

Taken in the wilds of California, this image is a poetic commentary on how women are connected to nature as living beings. Often in Brigman's photographs, the women are active participants in nature—strong, engaged, and interconnected with their surroundings. The woman in this picture, a nymph dressed in a loose-fitting gown, stands in front of the gnarled tree trunk with her eyes closed. Her energetic arms resemble the limbs of the tree behind her. The picture can also be seen as a feminist statement of yearning for some sort of freedom in the way the woman's arms stretch toward the sky.

nature. Her most famous photographs, which give human expression to the natural environment, were taken in California during the first two decades of the twentieth century.

"The Bubble" shows a young nude woman on bended knee at the edge of a still mountain pool. As a nymph, she stretches her right arm to reach a large translucent sphere floating in the water. The fragile orb seems to hold some kind of mysterious power.

In "Soul of the Blasted Pine," the nude female stands inside the crevice of a tree that appears to have been struck by lightning. The woman grips the trunk with one hand and stretches the other towards the sky recreating the way the tree once stood and struggling to break away.

Seeking freedom from social constraints, Brigman was the first photographer to make self-portraits in the wilderness. For her, the female body was a source of creative energy that was liberated in nature, "far from the carp of busybody tongues." Freedom meant leaving the civilized world long enough to enter a dialogue with the surrounding landscape. As she explained, "Where I go is wild—hard to reach ... because there are things in life to be expressed in these places." Brigman's favorite destination became the wilderness of the high Sierras among the ancient pine, cedar, and juniper trees.

Wearing knickerbockers and a vest instead of a more traditional corset and long dress, she walked on barely explored terrain without trails or maps that hikers have today. Sometimes she remained on location for days at a time to produce photographs that displayed her deeply held beliefs about the interconnectedness between humans and the natural environment. Her desire to explore, enjoy, and protect the wilderness was similar to the outlook of the Sierra Club founded a decade earlier by preservationist John Muir (1838–1914).

Brigman often brought along books such as those by the American poet Walt Whitman (1819–1892) for inspiration. Whitman wrote about the beauty and freedom of the human body and how it is a part of nature. In his poem, "Song of Myself," he wrote, "I will go to

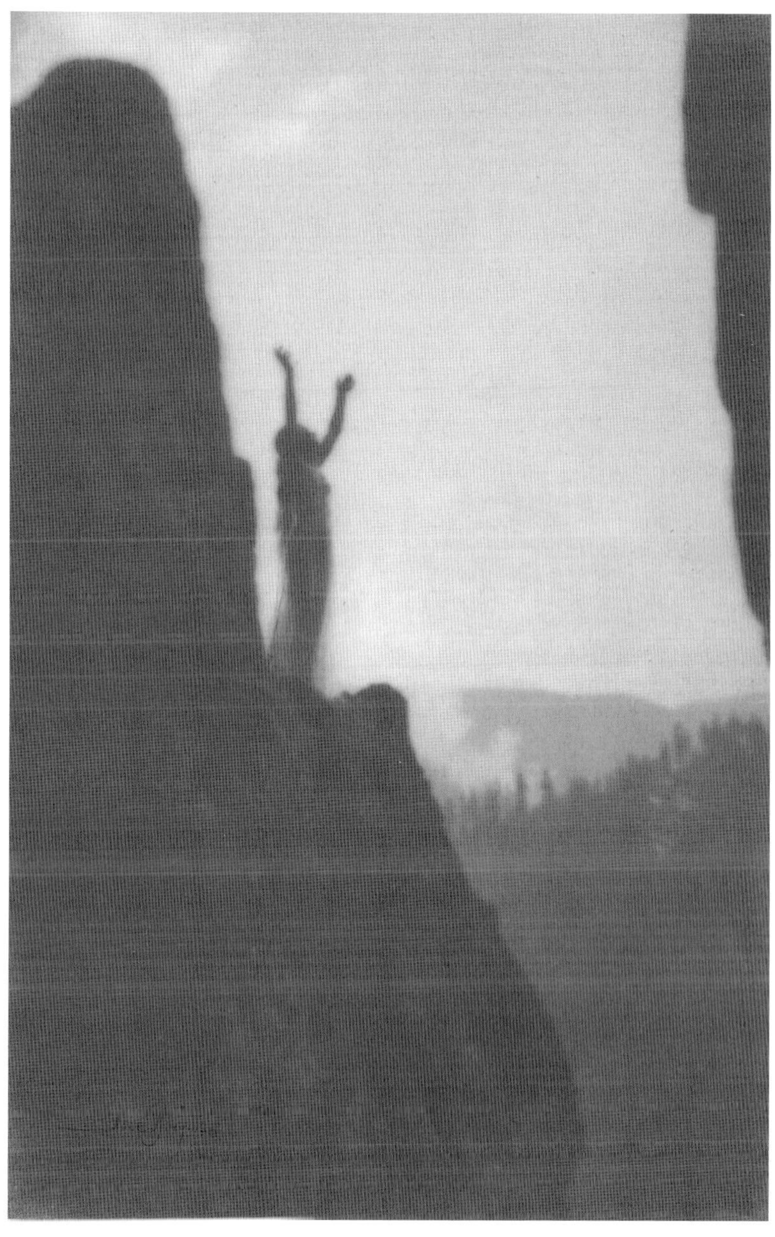

***Incantation*, 1905**

On the side of a distant mountain, a nymph stands on a rocky cliff and stretches her arms up to the sky in awe of the beauty of nature. Perhaps she is appealing to the gods, casting a magic spell, or chanting words of praise in honor of life itself.

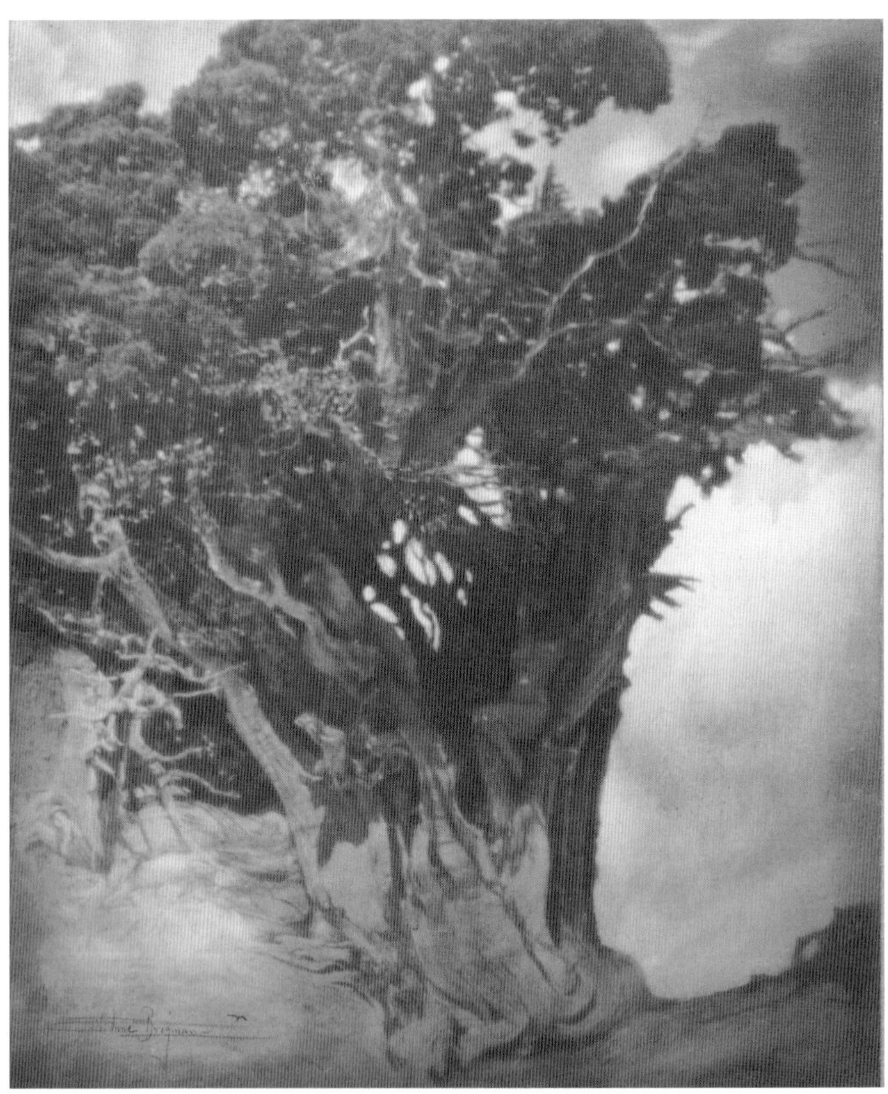

The Hamadryads, 1913

In Greek mythology, a hamadryad is a nymph whose life begins and ends with a specific tree. Here, two females represent wood nymphs basking among the flowing forms of a massive, old tree in the Sierra Nevada mountains.

the bank by the wood and become undisguised and naked." Quoting from Walt Whitman's "Song of the Open Road," Brigman said she has "a hunger for the clean, high, silent places, up near the sun and the stars." Her photographs remind us that our nation's natural resources are irreplaceable and deserve to be treasured.

During her excursions, Brigman developed relationships with specific trees and rock formations and returned many times to visit and see how her old "friends" were doing. She considered them sacred sites, full of life and power.

Although she often journeyed with others, Brigman was not afraid of being alone in the mountains. Nor did it bother her that the journeys she made were difficult, with dusty stagecoach rides, pack mules, and heavy camera gear. It was more important for her to be free. She said, "Fear is the great chain which binds women and prevents their development, and fear is the one apparently big thing which has no foundation in life."

Brigman used images of trees to express freedom from social constraints. For example, "The Dying Cedar" shows a woman reaching from a gnarled tree to the sky. This image is a reference to a Roman myth about Daphne, a beautiful young nymph being pursued by Apollo, the sun god. She tries to evade his advances, and just before he can catch her, she pleads with the other gods to save her. The gods respond by transforming her into a tree.

Hiking in the mountains made Brigman a stronger and more independent person and changed her forever. She described her experience: "You remember too, the long steep trails that lead zigzag, mile after mile, away from trees and brooks, up into the heat of rocks blessed by the sun, where your lungs ache and your heart hurts from the struggle—and then you find it—the Vision!—the glory of the things beyond. The memory and the wonder of it goes with you to the lowlands, into the daily life, and you are glad you had the courage."

At the height of her career, Brigman operated a teaching studio, gave lectures, and staged artistic salons where photographers, writers, and painters could share ideas. Although she hosted small gatherings in her studio, it was her private space where she could develop her voice and work alone. Brigman edited photographs in her darkroom and manipulated the negatives. With her etching tool she could scrape away anything she thought was useless.

Brigman began making more regular trips to the mountains after the 1906 San Francisco earthquake. Even though the earthquake lasted less than a minute, it ignited several fires around the city. These fires destroyed nearly 500 city blocks, killing 3,000 people and leaving half of the city's 400,000 residents without homes.

Recognizing the beauty of Brigman's photography, Alfred Stieglitz, the famous photographer who promoted photography as art, invited her in 1910 to the East Coast to become one of two California members of his art photography group known as the Photo-Secession. But she did not like spending time in New York City and soon retreated to the fresh air of Maine, where she took part in Clarence White's first summer school of art photography. Although Brigman had only stayed in New York City for a short while, Alfred Stieglitz made sure that three issues of his publication, *Camera Work*, featured her photographs. He also exhibited her pictures at his New York City gallery. As a result, Brigman came back to California with even more self-confidence and ambition about her art. She also separated from her husband at this time.

Alfred Stieglitz was inspired by Brigman's images of the expressive female body when he took pictures of Georgia O'Keeffe, and O'Keeffe, in turn, admired Brigman's photographs as well. She liked the way Brigman depicted natural objects, and felt they were kindred spirits. Like Brigman, O'Keeffe defended the intentions of her art. Both were not trying to be sexy for the admiration of men. For O'Keeffe, a flower is just a flower, and for Brigman, a tree or rock is simply what it is and not symbols of sexuality. Both female artists simply wanted to exist harmoniously in nature and to express their unique visions unencumbered by societal or sexist expectations of the time.

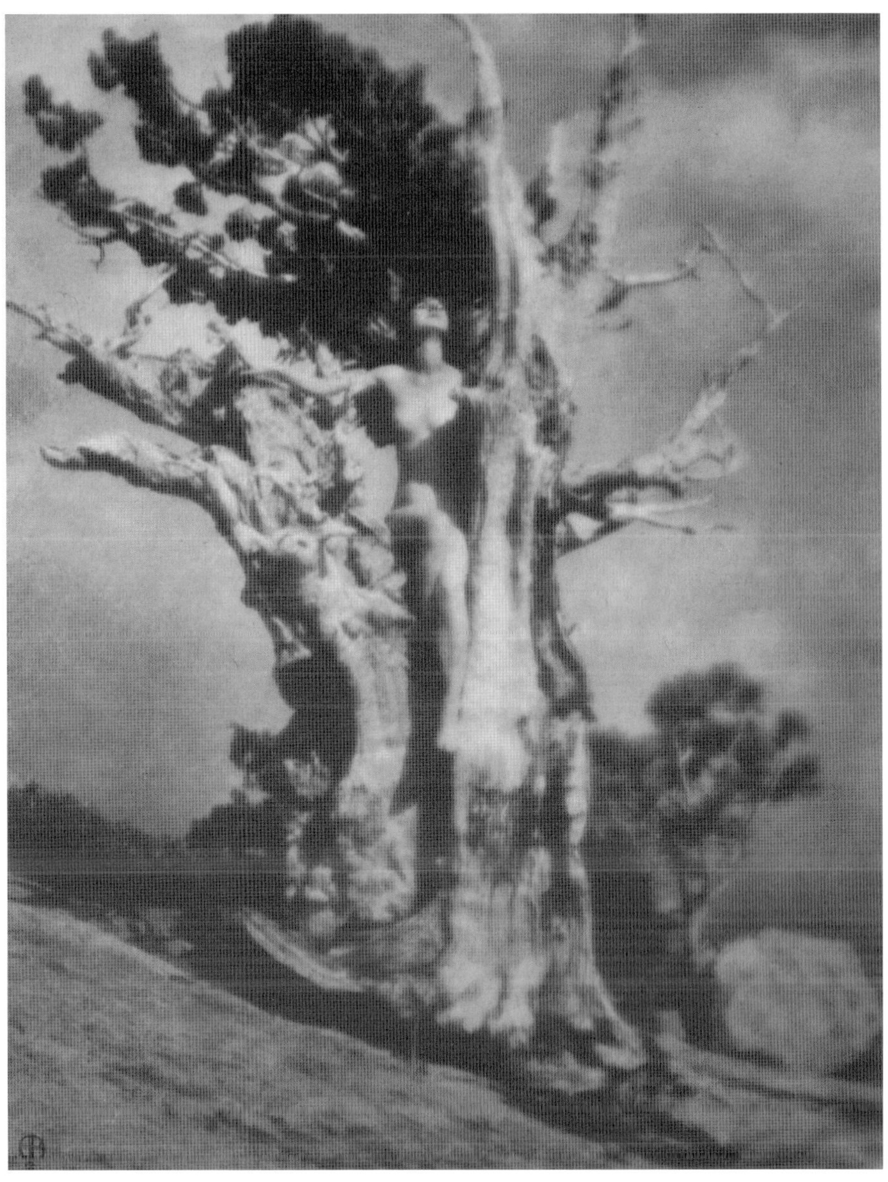

***Invictus*, 1924**

Invictus is the Latin word for "unconquered." In Brigman's photograph, a nymph appears to rise from a juniper tree as if part of the same life force. Juniper trees are known to be so hardy they can even grow on the sides of rocky cliffs. Like the juniper tree, the woman's resolute position reminds us that there is strength in the face of adversity.

In 1929, Brigman moved to Long Beach in southern California to live near her sisters and elderly mother. There, she was deprived of the grandeur of the mountains, but she renewed her deep connection to the sea, photographing sand patterns along the shore. She also took pictures of the ocean, emphasizing the movement of waves. She ended her photography career one year later due to her failing vision, but continued to write.

Brigman published *Songs of a Pagan*, a book of her poems and photographs. A year later, she died at the age of 80. At the time of her death, she had completed a second collection of poetry and photographs entitled *Wild Flute Songs*, and had made drawings for a book, *Child of Hawaii*.

Anne Brigman will always be celebrated for her poetic landscape photographs that express her rapport with the mystery and grandeur of nature. Ahead of her time for depicting the female nude in the wilderness when women were still confined to corsets, Brigman would inspire fashion photographer, Louise Dahl-Wolfe. Brigman's legacy also continues through the work of contemporary artists, including Ana Mendieta, Laura Aguilar, and Judy Chicago. Their works also stage their bodies amid the landscape to show the interconnectedness of humans and nature as well as to illuminate the personal feminist struggle.

READING LIST

Brigman, Anne. *Songs of a Pagan*. Caldwell, ID: Caxton Printers, 1949.

Ehrens, Susan and Anne Brigman. *A Poetic Vision: The Photographs of Anne Brigman*. Santa Barbara Museum of Art, 1995.

Heyman, Theresa Thau. *Anne Brigman: Pictorial Photographer, Pagan, Member of the Photo-Secession*. Oakland, CA: The Oakland Museum, 1974.

Pyne, Kathleen. *Anne Brigman: The Photographer of Enchantment*. New Haven: Yale University Press, 2020.

Wolfe, Ann W., Susan Ehrens, et. al. *Anne Brigman: A Visionary in Modern Photography*. New York: Rizzoli, 2018.

6

Jessie Tarbox Beals

(1870–1942)

The Greenwich Village Scene

JESSIE TARBOX BEALS was born in 1870 in Ontario, Canada. Her parents owned a Victorian mansion surrounded by landscaped grounds in one of the best residential sections of the city. Due to her father's financial misfortunes, creditors took the mansion, and the family moved to a smaller, more modest home. Jessie's father became an alcoholic and eventually left.

A precocious child, Beals did well in school, and when she was fourteen years old, she was admitted to a prestigious school, the Collegiate Institute of Ontario. Two years later, when faced with making a living, Jessie asked the Board of Education for a nonprofessional examination to allow her to apply for certification as a teacher.

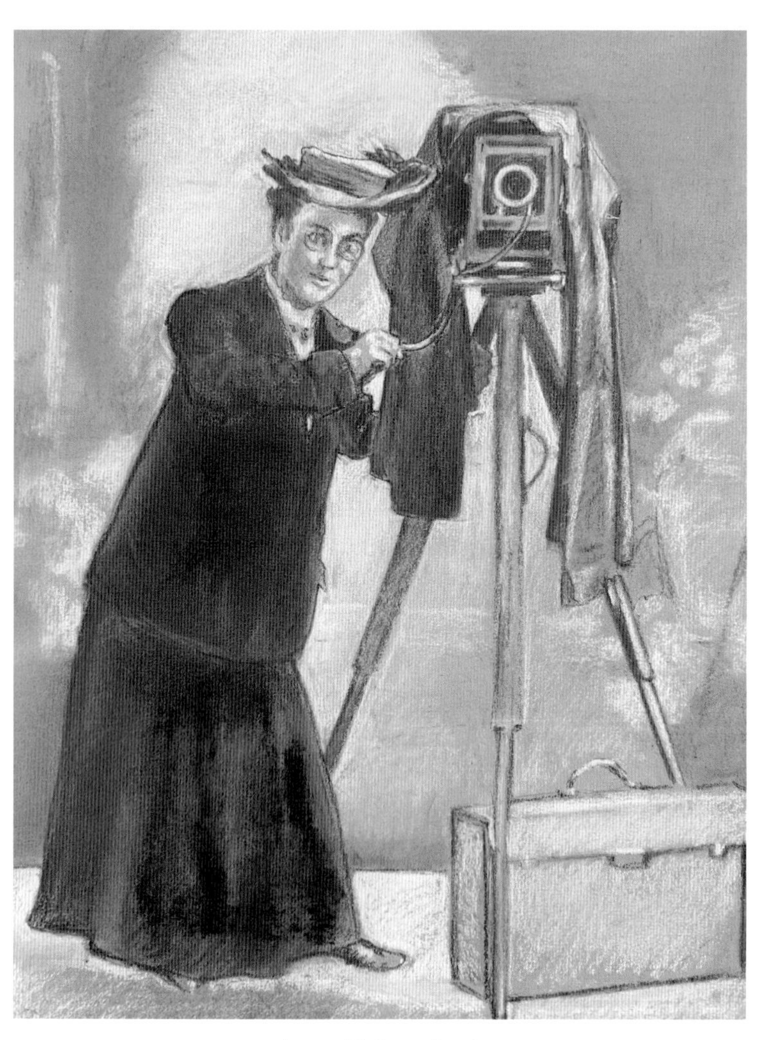

Jessie Tarbox Beals

She was seventeen years old when she took her first job teaching seven students of various ages in a one-room schoolhouse. It was located in a remote area, five miles from the small town of Williamsburg, Massachusetts, where her brother resided. Soon her mother moved there to live with Jessie.

In 1888, Beals won a simple, small camera by selling magazine subscriptions. She immediately used the camera to take pictures of her students and their surroundings. "I learned to love to use it. I soon found that it was a wonderfully satisfying way of recording impressions. Of course, at first they were not so subtly accurate as I would have liked, but at least they aroused the train of association and reminiscence that I connected with each scene."

Soon Beals bought a higher quality Kodak camera and, as a side hobby, set up a photography studio in the front of her house. It would be the first one in Williamsburg. Beals earned more money part-time making portraits of students who attended local colleges than with her teaching job.

After admitting that teaching was boring and not financially rewarding, Beals realized her true calling. An enthusiastic reader on the subject of photography, she constantly experimented with different photographic processes and took pictures of everything she could find around her home, including birds feeding their young. During a visit to the 1893 World's Columbian Exposition in Chicago, she met and was inspired by two famous female photographers, Frances Benjamin Johnston and Gertrude Käsebier. Upon returning home, she decided to photograph new places.

In 1897, she married Alfred Tennyson Beals, a botanist and expert on mosses and lichen, who worked as a machinist in a factory. She stopped teaching after her marriage, and became a full-time photographer.

Beals taught her husband photography and he became her assistant. He worked in the darkroom and she was the photographer and business manager. That same year, one of her photographs was published in a newspaper for the first time.

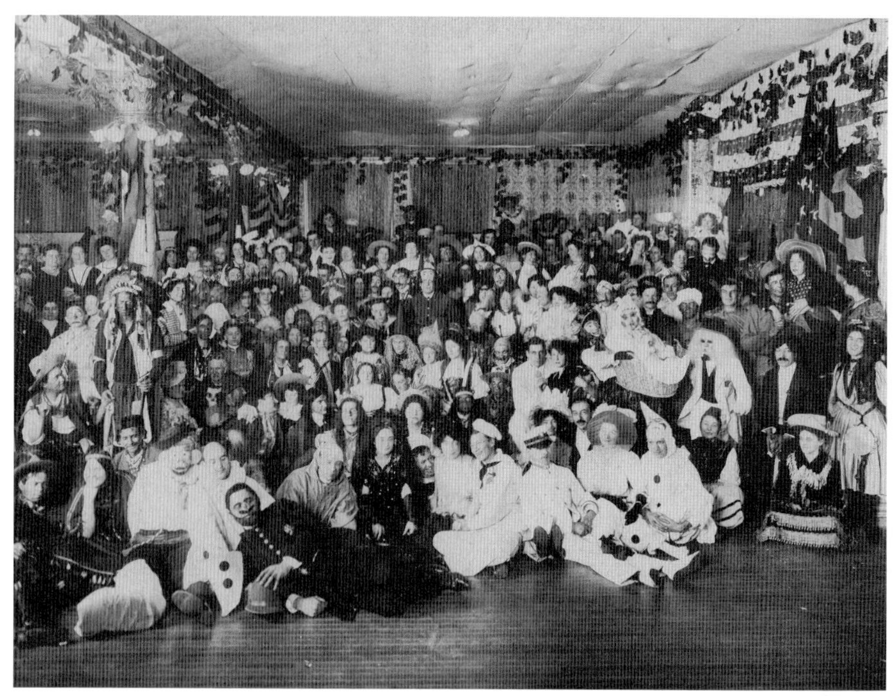

Kit Kat Club, New York City, 1920

This photograph epitomizes the gay, carefree days of the 1920s. Beals, as a freelance photographer, took this group shot of Jazz Age hipsters for Walter Kuhn, an American artist. Kuhn is best known for the major role he played as organizer of the Armory Show of 1913, America's first large-scale introduction to modern art. During the 1920s when this photograph was taken, Walter Kuhn worked as a designer and director for revues and circus acts. Some of his most memorable portraits are of circus and vaudeville entertainers.

Two years later, Beals was hired as a staff photographer for two Buffalo, New York, newspapers, the *Buffalo Inquirer* and *The Courier* where she covered events of daily life. Her editor received numerous letters of praise for the artistic merit of her photographs. It was during this time that she received national recognition for her portrait of Sir Thomas Lipton, inventor of the teabag. He was the first international celebrity she photographed.

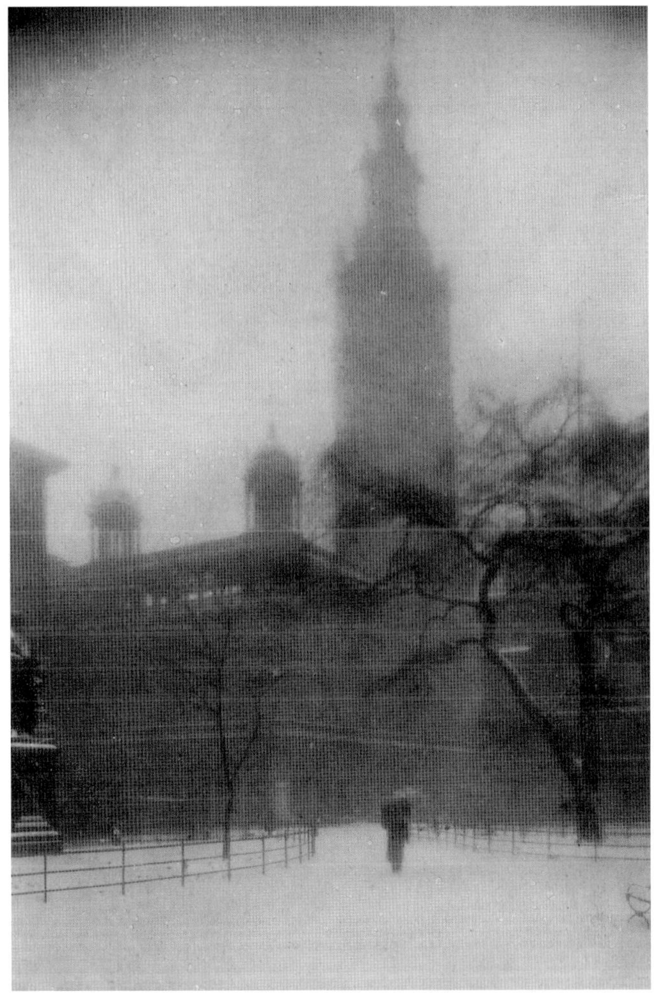

Diana in the Snow, 1915

Beals shows a woman walking near the Madison Square Garden building on a snowy day. "Diana" refers to the Goddess of the Hunt, depicted as an iconic sculpture that stood for three decades on top of the building. Commissioned by architect Stanford White and made by his close friend Augustus Saint-Gaudens, the nude form was quite shocking for New Yorkers during the Gilded Age when it was scandalous for a lady even to expose her ankles in public. Diana was taken down in 1935 just before the building was sadly demolished. Beals no doubt appreciated the beauty of the statue, seen in soft focus at the very top of the distant building.

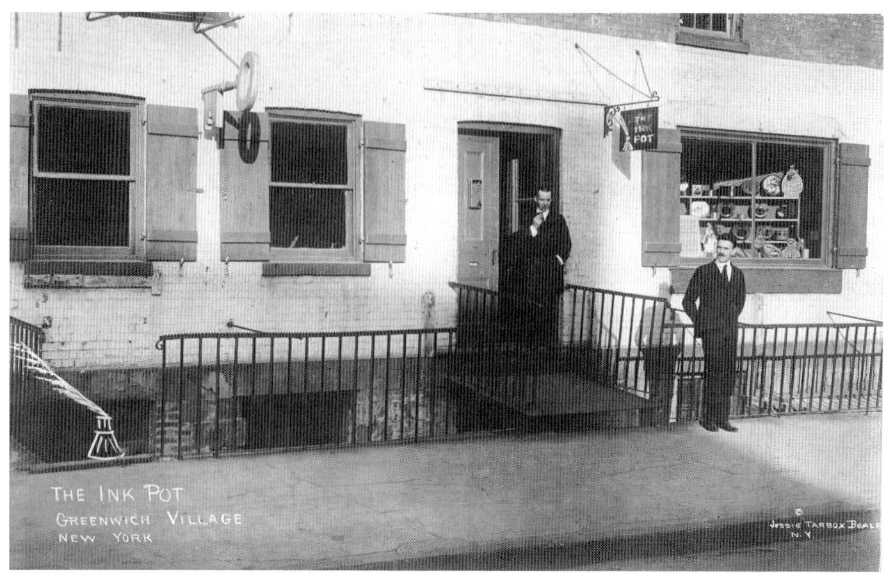

The Ink Pot, Greenwich Village, New York, 1917

Two men, Peter Newton and Forest Mann, stand in front of a shop called The Ink Pot, located on Sheridan Square. At the time, *The Ink Pot* was a small monthly magazine that began publishing stories from its headquarters. The editor, Peter Newton, ensured that the neighborhood publication covered the colorful lives of various Greenwich Village residents. Forest Mann was part of the editorial staff of *The Quill*, a similar magazine with an office on West 4th Street. This building and its neighbors have long been replaced by a much taller apartment building.

Soon Beals became a fully accredited press photographer for three other publications as well as all the newspapers in Buffalo. As the only woman with full press credentials, she became essential for the publicity of the 1904 St. Louis Purchase Exhibition. There, she took photographs of President Theodore Roosevelt and his family, and future president, William Howard Taft.

At the time, she said, "Many a mile have I walked in a day taking sixteen to thirty photos of every description. Those who have grown weary tramping around the Fair carrying a little 4×5-inch camera will understand the difference of doing the same thing with

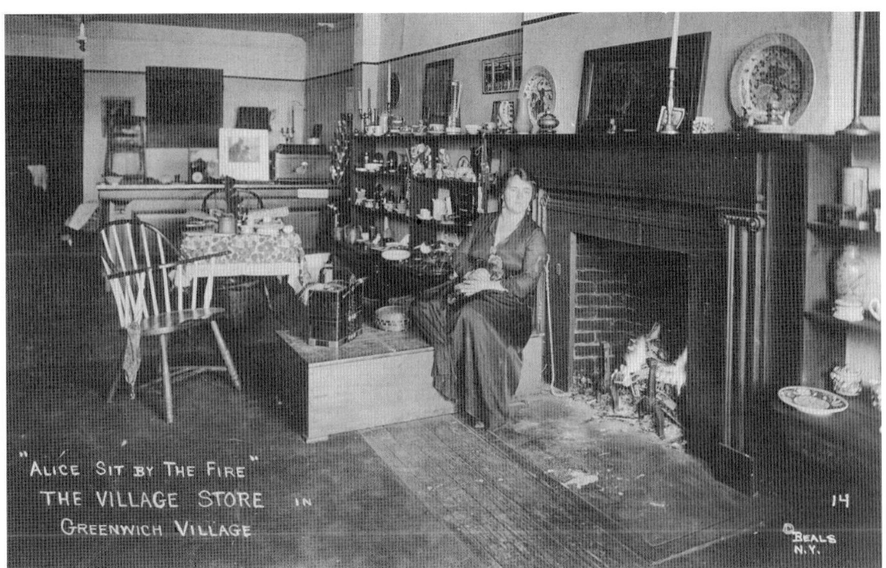

Alice Sit By The Fire, The Village Store, Greenwich Village, 1917

Shop manager Alice Palmer sits comfortably next to the fireplace, surrounded by shelves holding items from her small but cozy one-room store. The items for sale include fine china, teacups, bowls, decorative plates, and candlesticks. An empty chair next to the chest where Ms. Palmer rests makes it clear that this is more than a store. It is a place where customers can stay awhile – relax, chat, and perhaps have tea as well.

a heavy 8×10-inch camera and a tripod to match, the 12 holders with glass plates alone weighing about 30 pounds ... [It] was an experience calculated to wear out the strongest, but full of interest and the joy of success."

Beals knew what it takes to be a newspaper photographer. "If one is the possessor of health and strength, a good news instinct ... and the ability to hustle, which is the most necessary qualification, one can be a news photographer."

After so many successes, Beals and her husband moved to New York City. Sadly, they grew apart and divorced twelve years later.

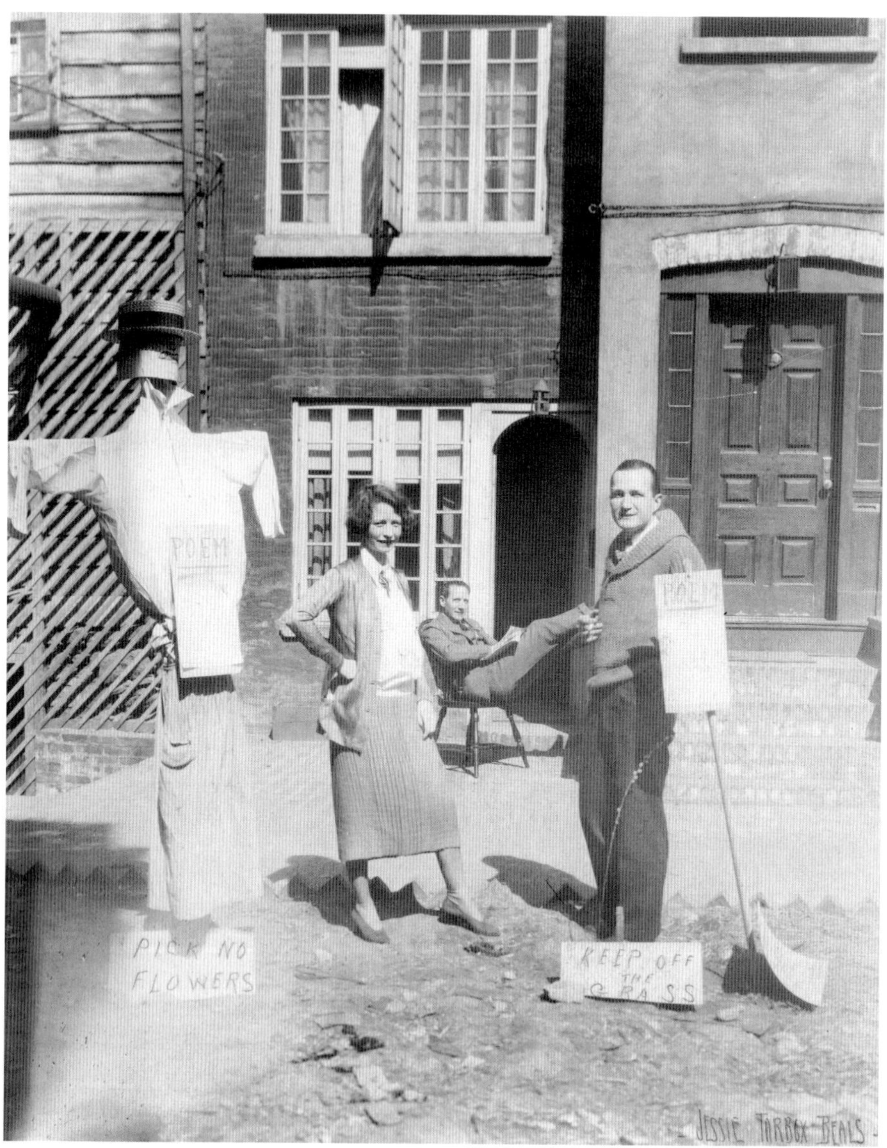

Edna St. Vincent Millay and Edmund Wilson, 1923

Beals took this picture of famous poet and playwright Edna St. Vincent Millay with her friend, critic Edmund Wilson, at Millay's home in Greenwich Village, New York City. Millay's husband, Eugen Boissevain, sits behind them. The year this photograph was taken, Millay received the Pulitzer Prize for poetry and was the third woman to win the award.

Jessie Tarbox Beals continued to take on a variety of photography assignments, while raising her young daughter.

In 1920, Beals and her daughter moved to Greenwich Village, where she opened a studio, art gallery, and tea room. Greenwich Village was the center of New York City's bohemian culture in the early and mid-twentieth century. Beals sold prints and postcards of her work while taking portraits of the neighborhood writers and artists. Some of her best-known photographs depict Bohemian Greenwich Village and notables such as playwright Eugene O'Neill, authors Sinclair Lewis and Theodore Dreiser, dancer and choreographer Isadora Duncan, and poet Edna St. Vincent Millay. Beals's quick wit and often brilliant conversation made her a popular companion. Inspired by these writers and artists, Beals began to write poetry, continued to take pictures, and dreamed of her success as an artist.

During the 1920s, Beals continued her freelance news photography and portraiture, as well as the photography of gardens and homes of the wealthy. Twenty-nine of her photographs were printed in the original 1915 edition of Louise Shelton's *Beautiful Gardens in America*. Frances Benjamin Johnston was another major contributor to this classic book.

Beals explained, "One cannot rush upon the gardens, snap them as they are at the moment, hoping merely for a pretty picture. One must school oneself to arrive early and stay through hours of lengthening shadows. A garden is a bashful and wistful thing, hesitant, disinclined to reveal itself in haste, and the only possible portraits of it that are good will be those that are a distillation of its many moods."

However, during the Great Depression, which was especially hard on artists, Beals experienced hard times. She died in poverty at Bellevue Hospital at the age of 71.

The Museum of the City of New York and the New York Historical Society hold extensive collections of Beals's works. The archives

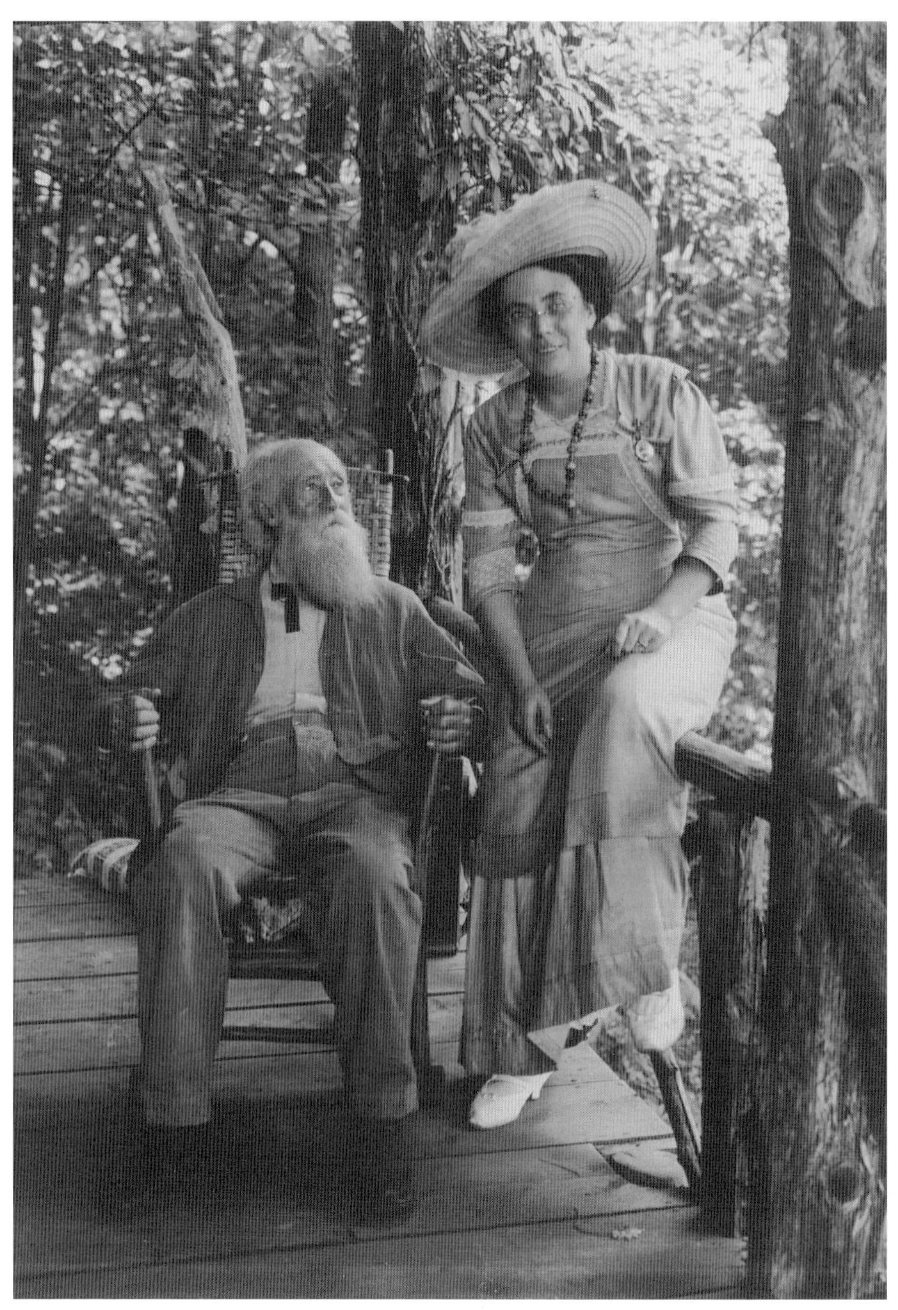

Jessie Tarbox Beals with John Burroughs, 1908

This photograph shows Beals with conservationist John Burroughs sitting on the porch of his summer cabin, Slabsides, in West Park, New York.

of Jessie Tarbox Beals are now housed at the Schlesinger Library at Radcliffe College in Massachusetts.

One of the first female photojournalists, Jessie Tarbox Beals accepted all kinds of assignments. She made illustrations for calendars, postcards, and books, as well as portraits of wealthy clients, Greenwich Village residents, and documentary photographs of children in New York slums. A storyteller with a camera, Beals was one of the first to create photo essays, or series of photos with captions to document newsworthy subjects. She paved the way for Dorothea Lange and Margaret Bourke-White and countless news photographers today.

READING LIST

Alland, Alexander, Sr. *Jessie Tarbox Beals: First Woman News Photographer.* New York: Camera Graphics Press, 1978.

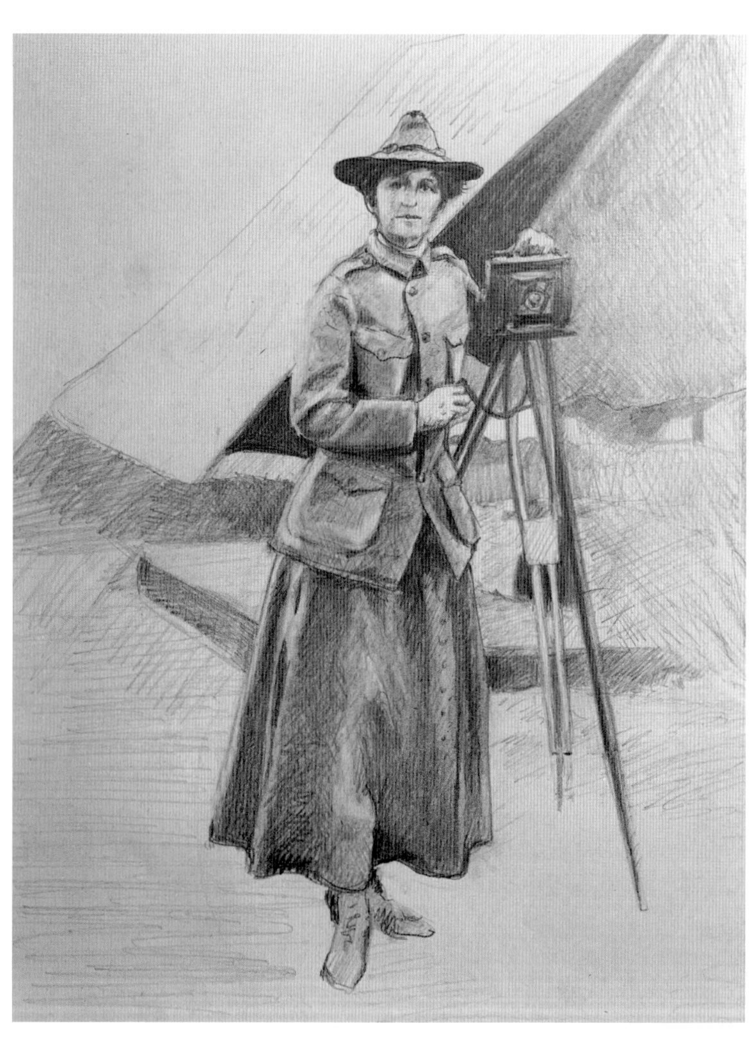

Bayard Wootten

Bayard Wootten
(1875–1959)
Carolina on Her Mind

BAYARD WOOTTEN was born in 1875 in the small eastern riverfront town of New Bern. She is known today as the most important photographer from North Carolina.

The port and trading center of New Bern, located where two rivers meet, has many wonderful old homes, stores, and churches built in the early 1700s—years before our nation even began. Wootten's grandparents' pre-Civil War home where she was born still stands today. It is no wonder that Wootten loved to photograph beautiful historic buildings!

The oldest child in her family, Wootten was the first to leave her home. She went to college in Greensboro knowing she wanted to become an artist and a teacher. She wrote to the president of the school that her family was very poor, adding, "I am determined to

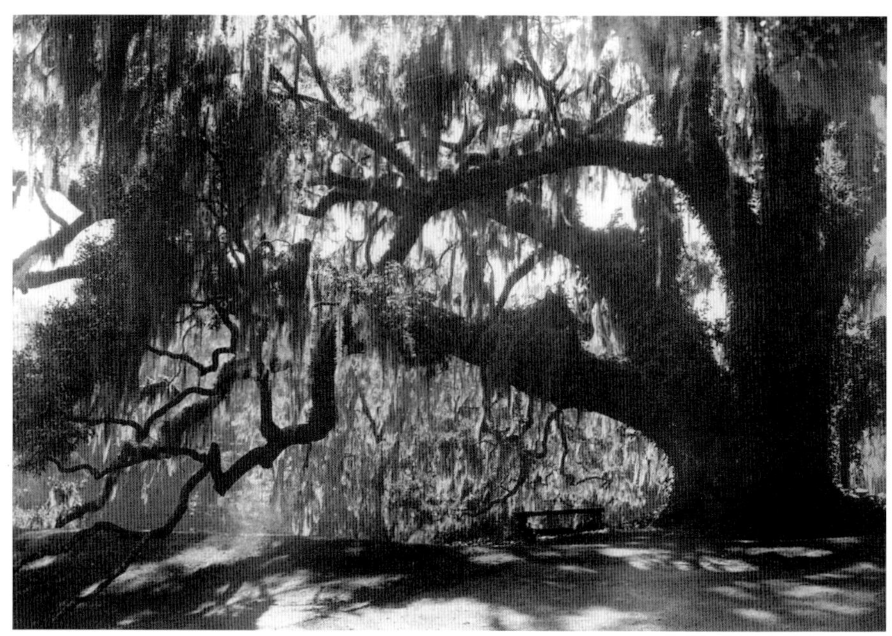

Oak at Middleton Place, Charleston, South Carolina, 1930s

The largest live oak at Middleton Place, Charleston, South Carolina, is 67 feet tall and has a thick trunk about ten feet in diameter. Bayard Wootten focuses on the massive canopy, with a number of branches several feet in diameter, that extends outward to form a broad low crown. The limbs, covered in Spanish moss, throw shadows on the ground.

make my own living, and if I cannot do it by teaching, I shall have to do it by sewing, and therefore I am very anxious for an education."

After her art instruction, she taught art at the Georgia School for the Deaf for four years. At the school she met her future husband, Charles Wootten, who worked at odd jobs and sometimes practiced law. The couple had a difficult marriage and after having two children, divorced.

Upon returning to the family home in New Bern, this time with two young sons, Wootten worked with her mother hand painting designs on fans, dresses, calendars, invitations, and parasols. Around this time, Caleb Bradham, the inventor of Pepsi-Cola who

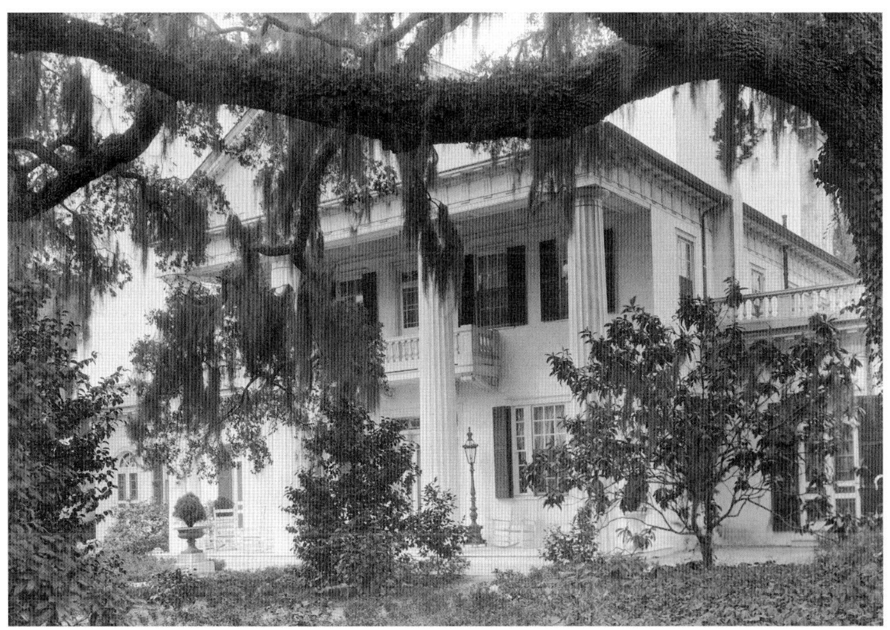

Orton Plantation, Winnabow, North Carolina, 1930s

The Orton Plantation, a well-known example of seventeenth-century antebellum architecture, is located in Brunswick County, North Carolina, about fifteen miles down river from Wilmington. In Wootten's image, a branch in the foreground covered with Spanish moss partially obscures the view of the front facade. The landscape of this rice plantation adds historic context and helps to frame the photograph.

lived next to Wootten's home and saw that she was a very talented artist, asked her to create the first design for the Pepsi-Cola label.

Wootten taught herself how to use a camera since it was a faster process than painting, and soon she opened a photography studio next to her home. She looked for instruction in photography wherever she could find it, especially salesmen from Eastman Kodak and the other photographic companies that spent time in New Bern. Then she went to Asheville to study photography under Ignatius Brock, who became her mentor and a lifelong friend.

Specializing in making postcards early in her career was good for business. Postcards were not the mass-produced glossy images

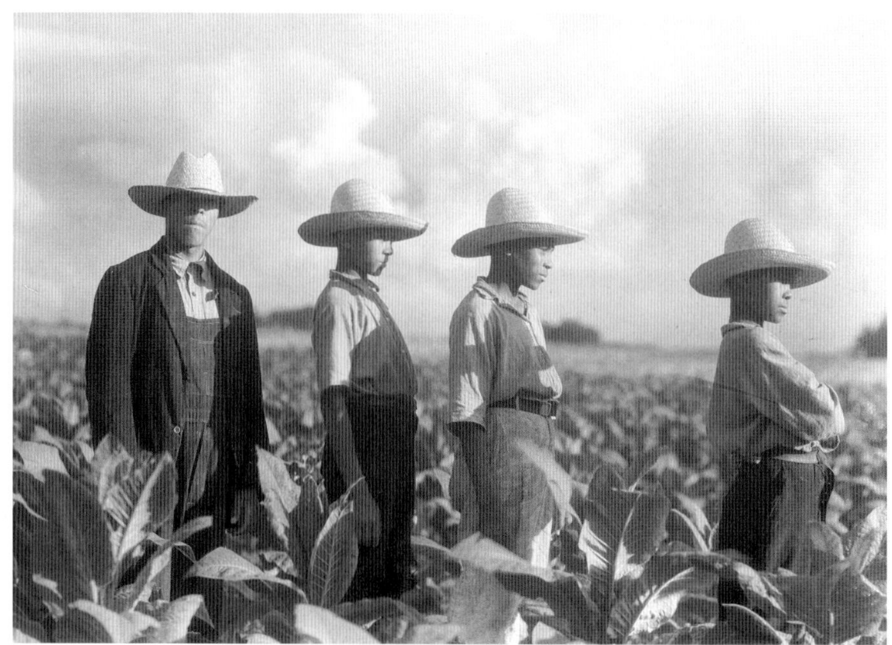

A tobacco farmer and his three sons, North Carolina, 1930s

In the middle of a tobacco field rising up to the waist, a tobacco farmer looks at the viewer. Next to him are his three sons, standing in profile, lined up in a row. The composition of Wootten's photograph emphasizes the togetherness of this family. All wear broad-rimmed straw hats for protection against the sun. The third son farthest to the right folds his arms as he waits. They all look ready for work. Tobacco growers put North Carolina on the map as early as the mid-seventeenth century. Tobacco is still one of the most important industries in the state.

of today. It was common for people of all income levels to send picture postcards of themselves to family and friends for just a penny postage. At that time, most people did not have telephones (even "landlines"), so this was an important way to communicate.

But photography in New Bern dwindled during the summer months when some residents moved to escape the heat and farmers were busy with their tobacco and cotton crops. So, Wootten moved her shop to Camp Glenn, a National Guard summer training camp in nearby Morehead City. At first, the commander of the camp discouraged her by saying she was just a camp follower. Nonetheless, she persisted. He soon realized that the postcards were good for the soldiers' morale because they loved sending them to their families. What motivated her was her need to take financial care of her children, plus her drive to be considered an equal. After that, he appointed her "Chief of Publicity," the first woman in the North Carolina National Guard. She proudly wore her uniform every day for twelve of the sixteen years she worked at the camp.

In addition, Wootten took the first aerial photograph made by a woman. Flying from a plane that had been made by the Wright brothers, she took the aerial photograph by pointing the camera down between her feet to look over New Bern with views of the rivers. The local New Bern newspaper marked the event with front-page coverage. "Mrs. Wootten is probably the only lady in New Bern who has been up in an aeroplane, and she is very proud of this fact. As the big machine soared over the race track far into the clouds, the spectators craned their necks and followed its flight with their eyes until it had alighted and Mrs. Wootten had alighted amidst the cheers from many throats."

Unlike the experience of Frances Benjamin Johnston, Gertrude Käsebier, and Zaida Ben-Yusuf, Wootten's attempt to base a photography studio in New York City lasted only a few months in 1917. After the setback, she soon admitted that North Carolina was her home, and that the South would suit her best.

Wootten moved to Chapel Hill, home of the University of North Carolina, where she opened a photography studio with her half brother, George Moulton. Their partnership would last for decades. Working in a university town was good for business. Most of the students went to her for their yearbook portraits. People associated with the theater, including author Thomas Wolfe, had their portraits taken at her studio, too, since Bayard was the official photographer for the Playmakers Repertory Theatre.

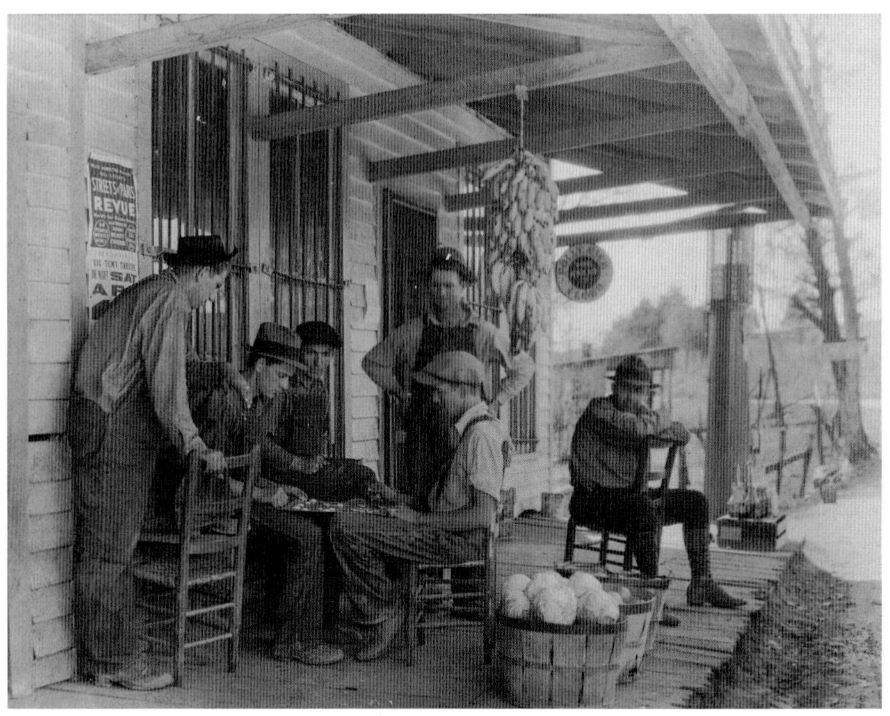

Bain's Store, near Sevierville, Tennessee, 1930s

Wootten pictures the activities taking place on a wooden porch of a small country store. Two men play checkers as three others watch intently. Another person sits on a chair backwards, looking on from a distance. Baskets of fresh produce adorn the edge of the porch and a bundle of bananas hangs from one of the rafters.

Wootten also worked on murals made from her photographs. These appeared in homes and public buildings throughout the Carolinas. One of these in a courthouse showed the Wright Brothers Memorial at Kitty Hawk, where the first airplane was flown.

In Chapel Hill, Wootten exhibited her work. Publishers who came across her work through these exhibitions became interested in images for book illustrations. At the peak of her career, she provided photographs of buildings and gardens for several books. Those featuring her photographs published by the University of North Carolina Press include *The Story of North Carolina*, *Back-*

woods America, and *Cabins in the Laurel.* Her favorite book containing her photographs was *Charleston: Azaleas and Old Bricks*, published by Houghton Mifflin. She considered it the fruition of her long career and especially was pleased that the format was much larger than any of the previously published books. This book was followed by *New Castle, Delaware, 1651–1939.*

Wootten also provided photographs for *Old Homes and Gardens of North Carolina*, and a second book on North Carolina's historic buildings, *The Early Architecture of North Carolina*, with photographs by Wootten and Frances Benjamin Johnston.

In some cases, Wootten took pictures of some of the same historic buildings as Johnston, for example, the Orton Plantation in Winnabow, North Carolina. Wootten's picture, however, shows greater emphasis on landscape and vegetation. They also both photographed the Brothers House in Winston-Salem, North Carolina. Their photographs look almost identical except for the different shadowing, which is evidence that the photos were taken at different times of the day.

Both photographers also gave lectures with slide projectors to show their pictures of historic buildings and gardens at women's groups and garden clubs in the Carolinas. This financial and moral support helped sustain their careers. Both exhibited their work in some of the same places, and so they knew some of the same people and shared some of the same friends.

Not surprisingly, the two women were casual friends with similar career interests because they had much in common. But Wootten identified herself as a North Carolina photographer while Johnston was a better-known "out-of-towner" visiting North Carolina as part of her nine-state survey of historic architecture.

Wootten also knew about the work of a contemporary photographer, Doris Ulmann of New York City. Both were talented women who took photographs of people living in the southern Appalachian region around the time of the Great Depression. Both emphasized the dignity of manual labor in quiet rural settings. Rather

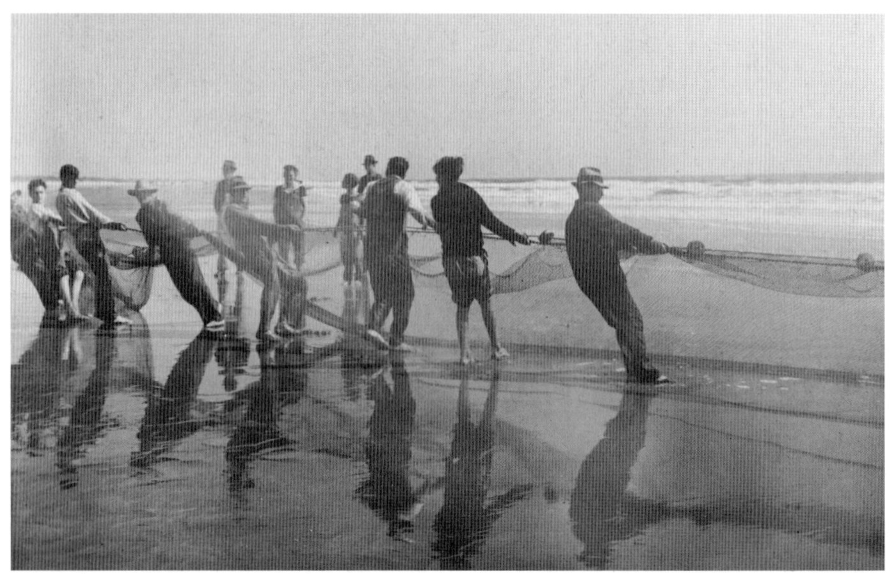

Reflections from the East, Ocean Drive, South Carolina, 1930s

than focusing on the despair of the national crisis, their photographs celebrate stoic and optimistic human character.

Two years after Ulmann's death in 1934, a local college exhibition of Appalachian photographs taken by both Wootten and Ulmann opened to the public. The April 23, 1936, issue of the Berea Citizen newspaper noted that "both photographers caught the life of the mountains and related it with accuracy and understanding." There were ordinary scenes of the "fireside, poses of leisure, men and women going to market, whetting and grinding implements, carving, weaving, carding wool, splitting boards with a froe, making pottery ... as well as country stores, interiors and exteriors of log cabins, faces rich with character, and faces that have aged with charm ..."

Wootten easily approached people and was proud of the way she could put them at ease, whether they were former slaves or tobacco workers. "She could go to the mountains and those people are mighty skittish about people they don't know, but they would invite her to spend the night and have supper. She just had a way

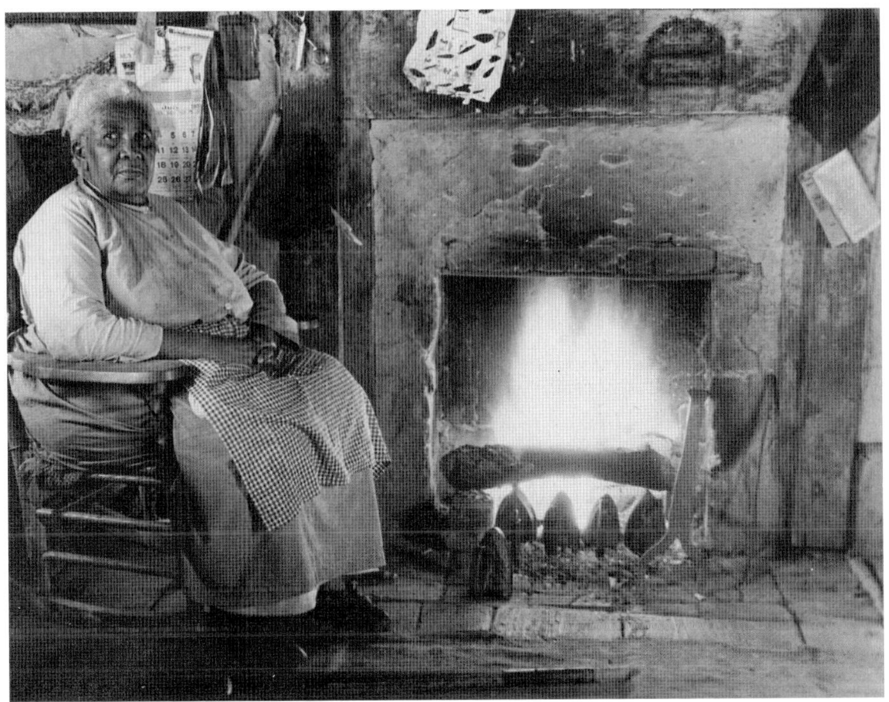

Irons in the Fire, c. 1933

To prepare for ironing clothes, a woman wearing an apron sits in her rocking chair next to a fireplace where a fire is heating four of her five irons. Wootten's portrait makes it apparent that ironing without electricity was quite an undertaking. This testament of working-class respectability shows sacrifices were endured.

of talking to people," admitted one of Wootten's studio assistants. She saw herself as a Southerner most of all, and identified strongly with others who were financially responsible for their families.

Through her photography, Wootten had a successful career, became a great artist, and was able to support her two sons as a single parent. She admitted that there was nothing more satisfying to her than the business of photography, even though the financial returns were not always that satisfying. The people she met, the places she visited, and her adventures as a photographer meant more to her than money.

Toward the end of her life, Wootten started to go blind and deaf. When she retired, she depended on relatives for financial aid and returned to her home in New Bern, where she lived for the remainder of her life.

Wootten died in New Bern in 1959. Late in her life, she said, "I have always been chasing something. But one of the surprises that life has held for me is that I am happier as an old woman than I ever was as a young one. Perhaps the reason for this is that I realized now it does not matter whether we arrive. The joy is in the going."

One of the South's leading photographers of the early twentieth century, Bayard Wootten was an adventurous trailblazer. She designed the first Pepsi-Cola logo, became the first woman member of the North Carolina National Guard, and the first female aerial photographer in America. Her life and work paved the way for photographers today, including Sally Mann who described Wootten as having a "susceptibility to myth and obsession with place, family, death and the past." Her successful career, despite economic challenges and discrimination, helped advance women's rights. Her photographs are now part of the North Carolina Collection at the University of North Carolina main library.

READING LIST

Cotton, Jerry W. *Light and Air: The Photography of Bayard Wootten.* Chapel Hill: The University of North Carolina Press, 1998.

Wootten, Bayard, illus. *Backwoods America.* Text by Charles Morrow Wilson. Chapel Hill: University of North Carolina Press, 1934.

Wootten, Bayard, illus. *Cabins in the Laurel.* Text by Muriel Earley Sheppard. Chapel Hill: University of North Carolina Press, 1935.

Wootten, Bayard, illus. *Old Homes and Gardens.* Text by Archibald Henderson. Chapel Hill: University of North Carolina Press and the Garden Club of North Carolina, 1939.

8

Doris Ulmann

(1882–1934)

Life in the Rural South

DORIS ULMANN was born into a very wealthy family on the Upper East Side of New York City in 1882. As a young child, she developed a stomach ulcer and underwent three separate bouts of surgery, but she never fully recovered. Ulmann trained for three years as a kindergarten teacher at the Ethical Culture School, a socially liberal organization that championed individuals regardless of ethnic background or economic condition, but she did not really need to work full-time. She first took up photography as a hobby and used a simple box camera to document her family and their activities.

Ulmann married Charles Jaeger, a doctor and photographer, and in 1914 began to study psychology and law at Columbia University. While there, she became one of Clarence White's most devoted photography students. Photographer Laura Gilpin was a classmate. (Margaret Bourke-White and Dorothea Lange also became Clarence White's students.)

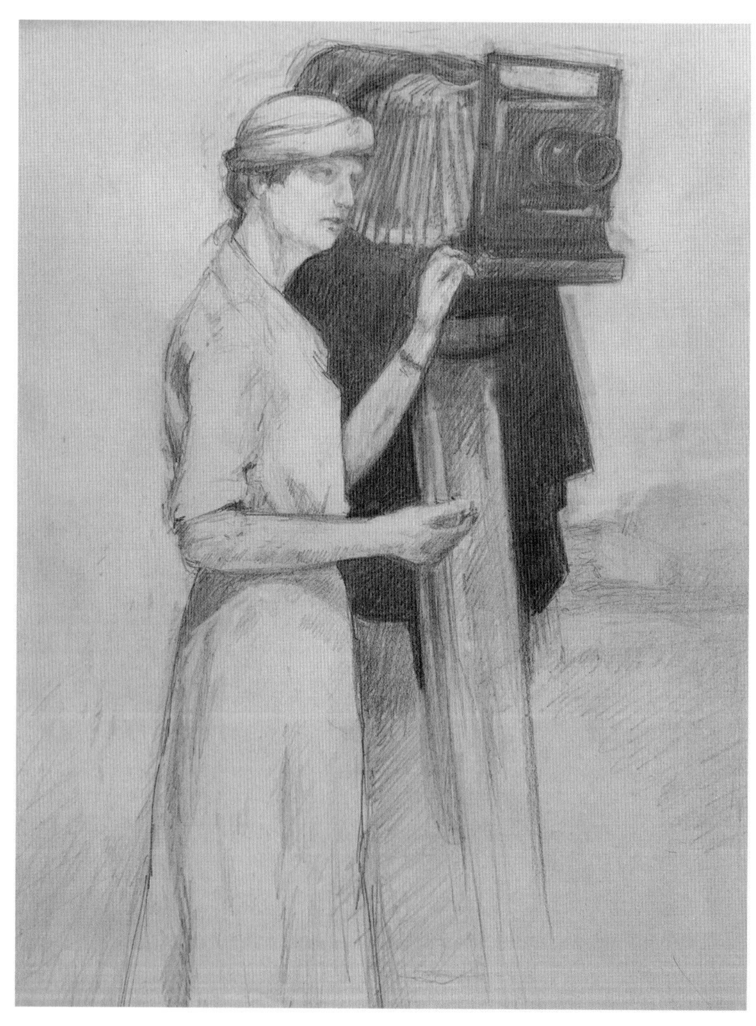

Doris Ulmann

Four years later, Ulmann adopted photography as her profession. Her economic and social standing, as well as her appreciation for literature and the arts allowed her to meet celebrities from all over. In her studio at her Park Avenue home, she was the Annie Leibovitz of her time, taking photographs of prestigious doctors, lawyers, artists, explorers, and important writers of the day, such as Robert Frost, Thornton Wilder, Edna St. Vincent Millay, and Paul Green. These portraits were carried by *Vanity Fair* magazine and Sunday newspapers. Thomas Wolfe used his 1927 portrait on the dust jacket of his first novel, *Look Homeward, Angel.*

When making a portrait, Ulmann asked her sitter to do certain things for one photograph and then other things for other photographs. She explained, "... I try to know the individuality or real character of my sitter and, by understanding him, succeed in making him think of the things that are of vital interest to him. My best pictures are always taken when I succeed in establishing a bond of sympathy with my sitter ..."

When she got tired of living among successful, wealthy people in New York City, she decided she wanted to explore different ways of life in the South.

She wanted to record things that she felt people in New York City were missing, a quality measured not by wealth but by character. Her focus on pre-industrial America included the pride of a southern African American man holding his violin, the dignity of a couple at the doorway of their home, the diligence and concentration of a woman weaving at her loom.

Ulmann's method of taking portraits would be the same for everybody she photographed—whether they were rich and famous, or poor people living in the Appalachian mountains whose families of English and Scots Irish ancestry had settled there in the eighteenth century. She also photographed people living on the coast of South Carolina who were the descendants of African slaves. She explained her reason for taking pictures. Ulmann was inspired by the revived

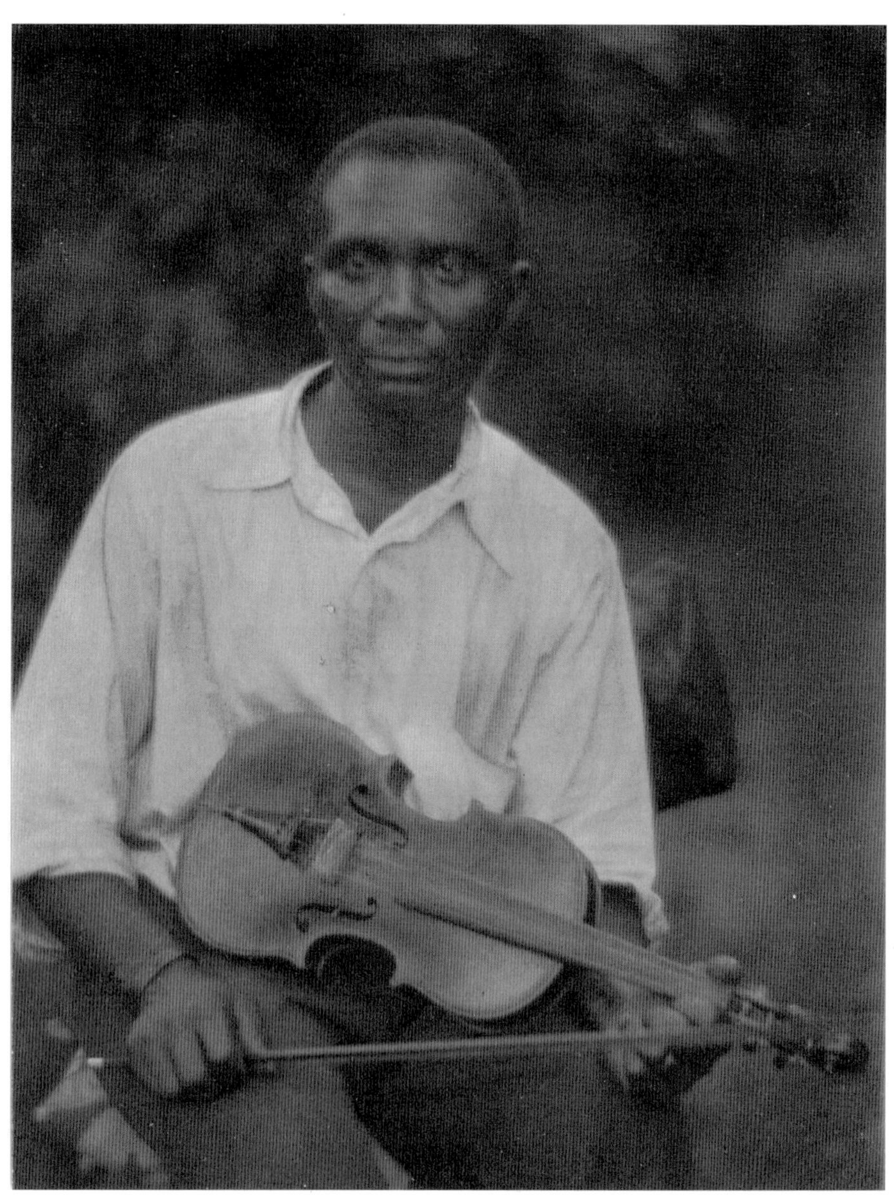

Man with Violin, 1930

Also known as a fiddle player, a seated musician with his violin poses for his portrait. Ulmann took this picture while accompanied by John Jacob Niles, composer and collector of American folk ballads.

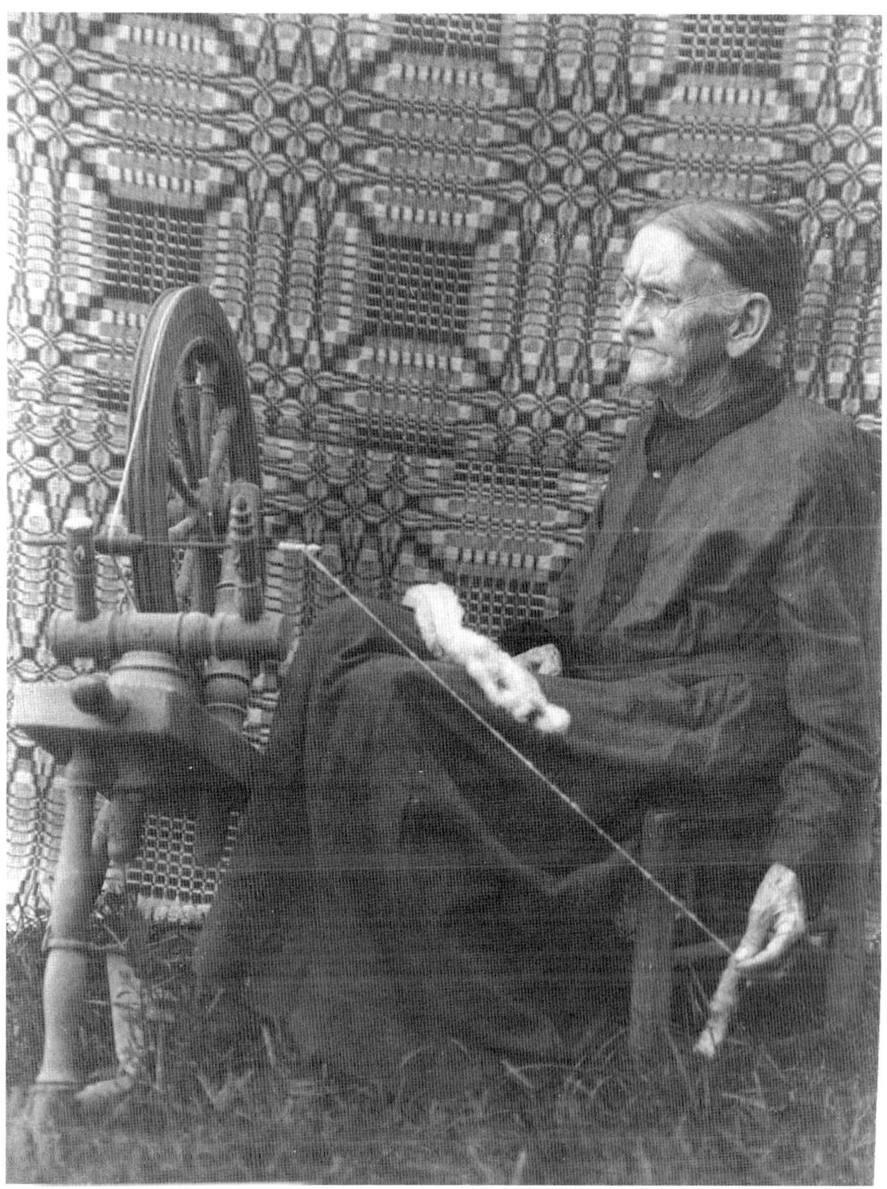

Aunt Lou Kitchen, Spinner and Weaver, Shootin' Creek, N.C., 1933

Doris Ulmann photographed an elderly woman spinning in front of a nicely woven cloth that is displayed on the wall behind her. The patterned cloth, the end result of her labors, helps to construct a strong geometric composition.

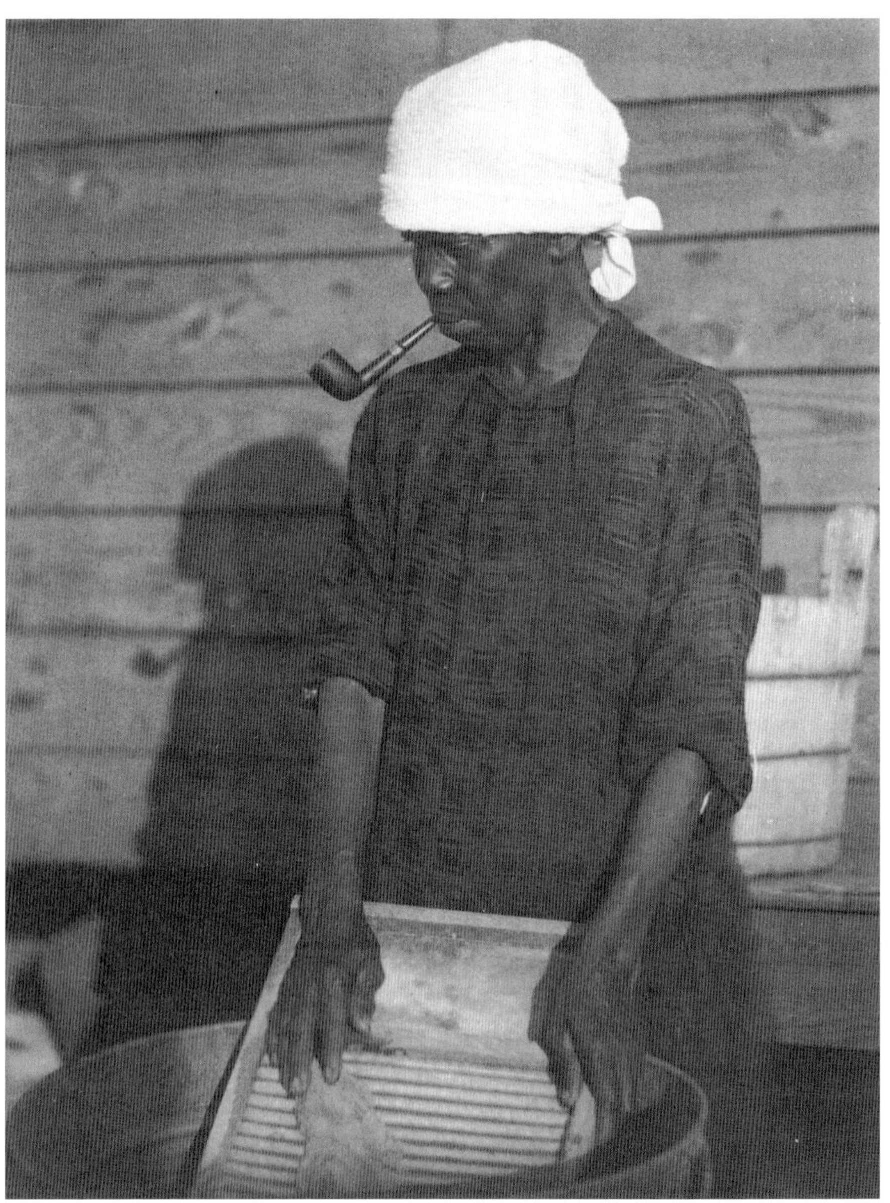

Katie Jones, 1930

A woman wearing a darkly patterned dress and white turban smokes a pipe as she washes with a scrub board. Her shadow projects onto the unpainted clapboard wall behind her. A wooden pail on the table can be partially seen.

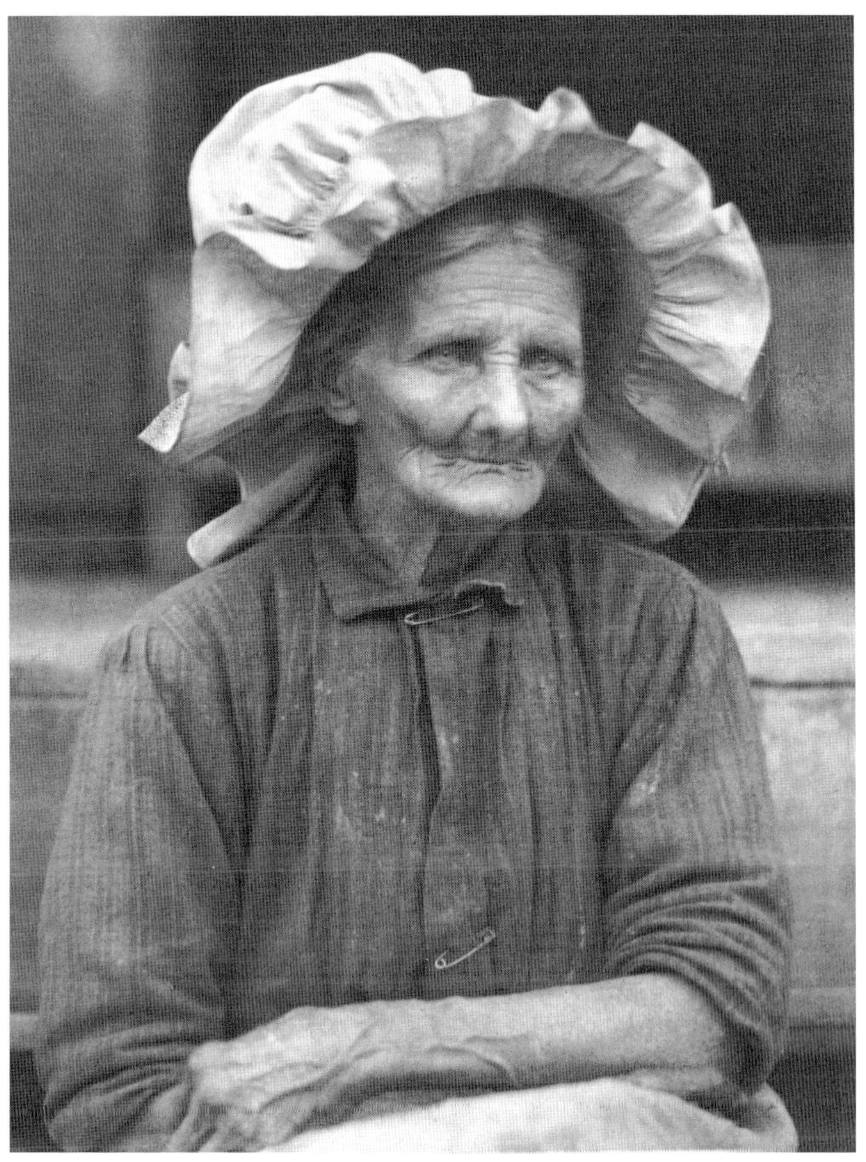

Woman in a Sun Bonnet, 1930

Ulmann brought to her task a profound respect for her sitters, as exhibited in this portrait of an elderly woman whose face has been lined and hardened by a life of poverty and relentless hard work. Although she lacks teeth and her shirt is held together with giant safety pins, she presents a stoic and dignified self-containment which Ulmann documents with sensitivity and compassion.

interest in rural customs and the making of handicrafts, such as basket weaving. Her ethnographic photography became a way of preserving America's heritage in the countryside before industry replaced their way of life.[1]

"I am glad to have people interested in my pictures as examples of the art of photography, but my great wish is that these human records shall serve some social purpose."

In 1925, Ulmann divorced her husband and set out with John Jacob Niles, a musician and native of Kentucky who wanted to conduct research on musical traditions. Together they traveled to Virginia, Kentucky, and North and South Carolina. As her field assistant, Niles helped Ulmann with the transport of her heavy equipment which included a view camera, a tripod, and glass plates. He sometimes carried Ulmann either on his back or in his arms when the terrain was rough, muddy, or steep.

Ulmann used a soft focus and natural light for a dreamy look in her portraits of people. She admired how her subjects valued simplicity and closeness to the soil more than progress, money, and fame. Ulmann's photographs helped change the way we see people in rural communities, showing them not as picturesque peasants, but as dignified and talented individuals with purpose in the modern world.

She explained why her southern portraits meant so much to her. "A face that has the marks of having lived intensely, that expresses some phase of life, some dominant quality or intellectual power, constitutes for me an interesting face. For this reason, the face of an older person, perhaps not beautiful in the strictest sense, is usually more appealing than the face of a younger person who has scarcely been touched by life."

All in all, she took photographs for several books. After she met South Carolina novelist Julia Peterkin, who had won the Pulitzer Prize for a novel the same year she met Ulmann, she collaborated

1. Ethnography is the study of individual cultures and ethnic groups.

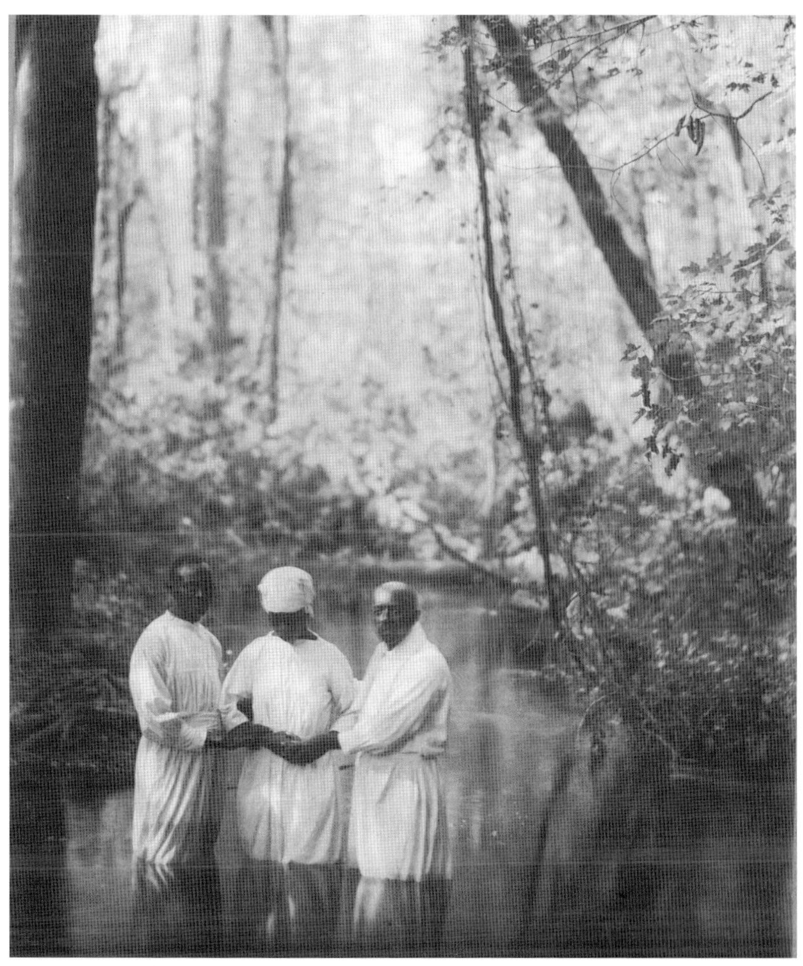

Baptism, South Carolina, c. 1929–1931

Immersion in a river that runs through a forest serves as a metaphor of rebirth and renewal in Doris Ulmann's photograph entitled "Baptism." This scene of a river baptism was featured in Julia Peterkin's *Roll, Jordan, Roll* (1933). Bathed in natural light, the softly focused photograph depicts a southern African American Christian ritual. A group of three people, all dressed in traditional white gowns, stand knee-deep in the still water. The woman in the middle lowers her turbaned head and clasps her hands, ready to publicly confess her newfound faith through immersion. The two men flanking her hold her arms and look toward the viewer. The beautifully balanced composition is enhanced by a sense of stillness and reverence.

with her for the book, *Roll, Jordan, Roll.* It documents the vanishing Gullah culture of the descendants of West African slaves who settled on the tiny sea islands of South Carolina and Georgia. Inspired by their simplicity, Ulmann was most interested in their humility, inner strength, spirituality, and sense of community, as can be seen in her focus on rituals.

One of her most memorable photographs is "Baptism." It shows an African American woman standing in knee-high water flanked by two men. The photograph captures the uniqueness of the southern landscape and its religious practices.

Ulmann was able to locate people to photograph in the Appalachian mountains through her work with the Russell Sage Foundation in New York. This organization was designed to support research methods that could lead to improved social policies. Allen Eaton, an employee in the foundation, saw Ulmann's prints at a Knoxville, Tennessee, exhibit. Two years later, while working on a book of native crafts, he asked her to provide illustrations. He wanted certain handicrafts documented, and provided Ulmann with an itinerary of places to go and people to see. This project, resulting in Ulmann's largest body of work, culminated in the publication of *Handicrafts of the Southern Highlands*, with 58 photographs taken by Ulmann.

The last two years of her life, Ulmann took photographs for Allen Eaton's landmark book, *Handicrafts of the Southern Highlands.* Often in frail health due to her ulcers, she spent much of her last summer working in the southern Appalachians assisted by a nurse. Despite her deteriorating condition, Doris made her last photographs at the home of a rural family near Asheville, North Carolina, in 1934. She returned to New York, died within a month, and would not live to see the publication of Eaton's book. Tragically, she was only 52.

Ulmann's photographs are archived at the University of Oregon. Days before her death, she endowed the John C. Campbell Folk School in Brasstown, North Carolina, and established the Doris Ulmann Foundation at Berea College in Kentucky. Through her photography and endowments to two Appalachian schools, Ulmann linked her legacy with crafts in Appalachia.

One of the first photographers to portray people in the rural South, Ulmann promoted their unique regional cultures. Acting on her humanist beliefs, she helped change the way we view ordinary people outside the American mainstream, whether they be craftsmen, musicians, or members of religious communities. All are seen as people with dignity and purpose.

Photographers influenced by Doris Ulmann as a documentarian and portraitist include Kael Alford, who documents native tribes affected by rising sea levels in South Louisiana, and Scott Dalton, who deals with issues on the border with Mexico.

READING LIST

Clift, William and Robert Coles. *The Darkness and the Light: Photographs by Doris Ulmann. Millerton,* New York: Aperture, 1974.

Gillespie, Sarah Kate. *Vernacular Modernism: The Photography of Doris Ulmann.* Athens, Georgia: Georgia Museum of Art, University of Georgia, 2018.

Featherstone, David. *Doris Ulmann: American Portraits.* Albuquerque: University of New Mexico Press, 1985.

Jacobs, Philip Walker. *The Life and Photography of Doris Ulmann.* Lexington, Kentucky: The University Press of Kentucky, 2001.

Rosenblum, Naomi. *Documenting a Myth: The South As Seen By Three Photographers: Chansonetta Stanley Emmons, Doris Ulmann, Bayard Wootten,* 1910–1940. Portland, Oregon: Reed College, 1998.

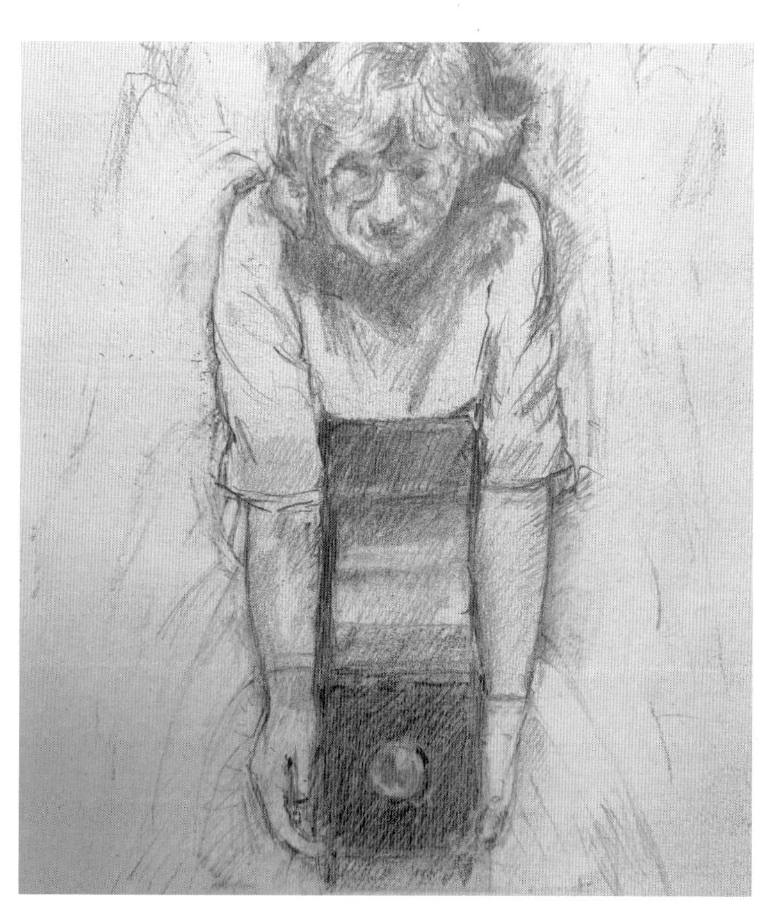

Imogen Cunningham

9

Imogen Cunningham

(1883–1976)

Flowers Up Close

IMOGEN CUNNINGHAM was born in 1883 in Portland, Oregon. Her father had three children from his first marriage, and when his wife died, he soon remarried. Cunningham, the first of seven children born to his new wife, was his favorite of all. Named for the princess in *Cymbeline*, Shakespeare's play about early Britain, she began taking photographs at the age of 18 when she bought her first camera.

The family struggled financially but Cunningham's father always found the money to pay for her art lessons during the summer. He was a very well-educated man, although self-taught, and wanted the best for her. After Cunningham began taking photos, he even built her a darkroom in their woodshed despite his disapproval of photography as a career choice.

Cunningham was inspired by the work of photographer Gertrude Käsebier while a chemistry student at the University of Washington. She said she saw some Käsebier photographs in a magazine and told herself, "I want to be just as good as she is."

After graduating in 1907, Cunningham became a studio assistant for Edward S. Curtis, the well-known photographer of Native American tribes, who captured the authentic ways of life of over 800 tribes and whose work was published in twenty volumes. At his Seattle studio, she gained knowledge about the portrait business.

In 1909, Cunningham was awarded a grant to study photochemistry for a year in Germany. The branch of chemistry concerned then with the chemical effects of light, photochemistry is the basis of photosynthesis, vision, and the formation of vitamin D. While in Germany, she saw the International Photography Exposition of 1909, which contained photographs from all of Europe and the United States. After seeing the exhibition, she stated that she had seen "the best of American photography placed side by side with the foremost work of the European artists, and in technical skill, good taste and real pictorial values, the American work stood first."

Three years later, Cunningham opened her own portrait studio in Seattle, Washington. Although she is now mainly known for her images of plants, Cunningham enjoyed taking pictures of people, too. She explained, "I photograph anything that light falls on ... but people began to interest me very early. I don't know why. Perhaps ... because in people there are no duplicates. You must say that. If you see a sunrise, it happens another day, too. But people are always different. They are different every second."

Cunningham's first photographs imitated paintings of softly focused, sentimental subject matter resembling the Pictorialist work advocated by photographer Alfred Stieglitz. Her artist friends posed in the woods dressed in loose robes. Years later, Cunningham changed her style. Now she made sure her photographs became more sharply focused, and some of them were even abstract.

In 1915, Cunningham married Roi Partridge, a printmaker and

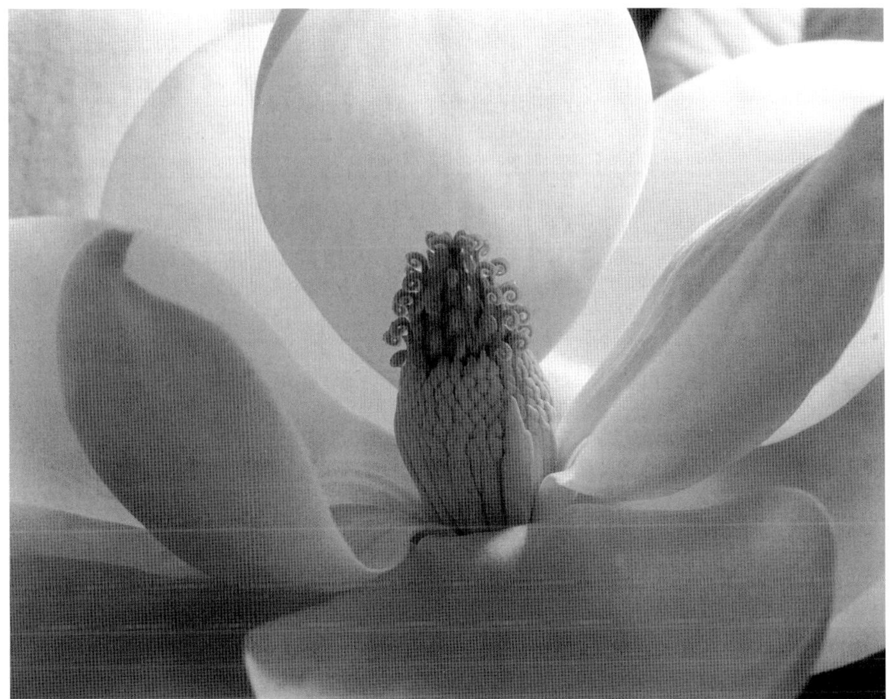

Magnolia Blossom, 1925

This close-up view allows us to examine the natural beauty of a newly opened magnolia blossom. The elegant, perfect flower fills the entire frame. The pistils and stamens are sharply focused and clearly detailed. Through Cunningham's masterful lighting and composition, the petals have become translucent. This was an important image for Cunningham, a two-year-long in-depth study of the magnolia blossom, one that has endured so resonantly within her oeuvre.

teacher, and the couple would have three children. Cunningham loved being a mother. She said, "I feel no woman has really lived without the experience of motherhood ..." She also wrote that she had "one hand in the dishpan and one in the darkroom." Her days of early motherhood were filled with taking and developing photographs, tending a flower garden, cooking meals, and taking care of her family.

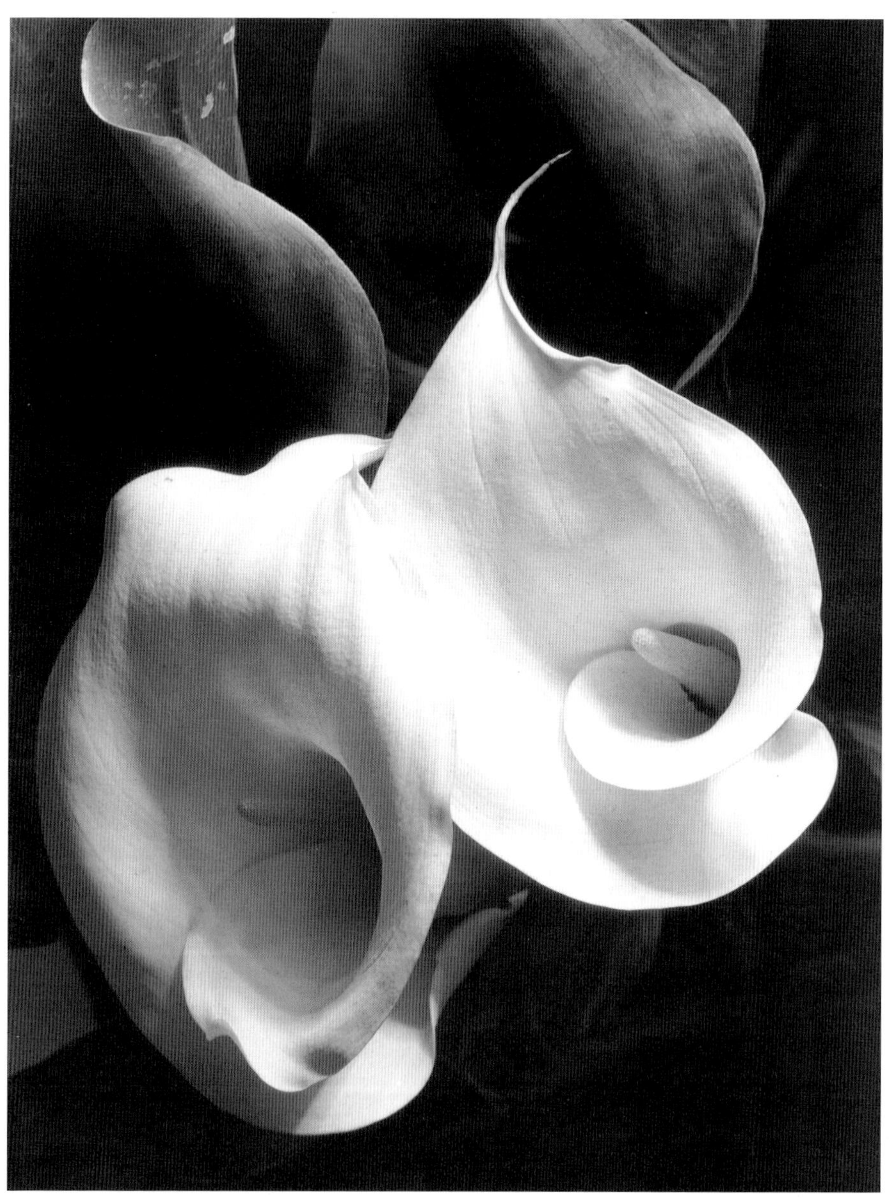

Two Callas, 1920s

This breathtaking image of two calla lilies becomes almost abstract at close range so that the white flowers become two balanced spirals. The detail is so incredible that one can imagine the silky texture of the delicate bloom and the roughness of the stems. The dark corners of the photograph serve as a frame leading the eye to the central focus.

Both Cunningham and her husband were highly professional people, and their house was their shared workplace. The matting and printing room was in the attic, where both etchings and photos were cut and mounted. The etching room and the darkroom were in the basement.

Cunningham photographed her three sons, and while they napped in the afternoon, she also took close-ups of her flowers. She was very interested in the decorative quality of plant forms. She knew a lot about plants, and she took pictures of them at close range illuminated by natural light. Her photograph of magnolia blossoms became her best known. Another one of her most notable works is "Two Callas."

Cunningham explained why she was drawn to photographing flowers. "The reason I really turned to plants was because I couldn't get out of my own backyard when my children were small. That was when I started photographing what I had in my garden ..."

Friends thought Cunningham could have become an excellent botanist because she was so interested in plants. When she photographed them, she talked about the general placement of the leaves and the relationship of the petals of a flower. She spoke about the line, the way the flower was placed, and the lights and darks.

Cunningham founded the California Horticultural Society and her interest in the Horticultural Society sustained her for many years. The little garden in the front of her house as well as the plants on her front porch were important to her. Every plant was personal to Cunningham and she cared about how they looked each season of the year. Usually, she gave cuttings to her friends. During family camping trips into the California Sierras, Cunningham continued to express her appreciation for nature by taking unsentimental pictures of aging juniper trees and closely focused images of wildflowers, craggy rock walls, fields of grasses, tree roots, trunks, branches, and leaf studies. What interested her most were textures of natural forms.

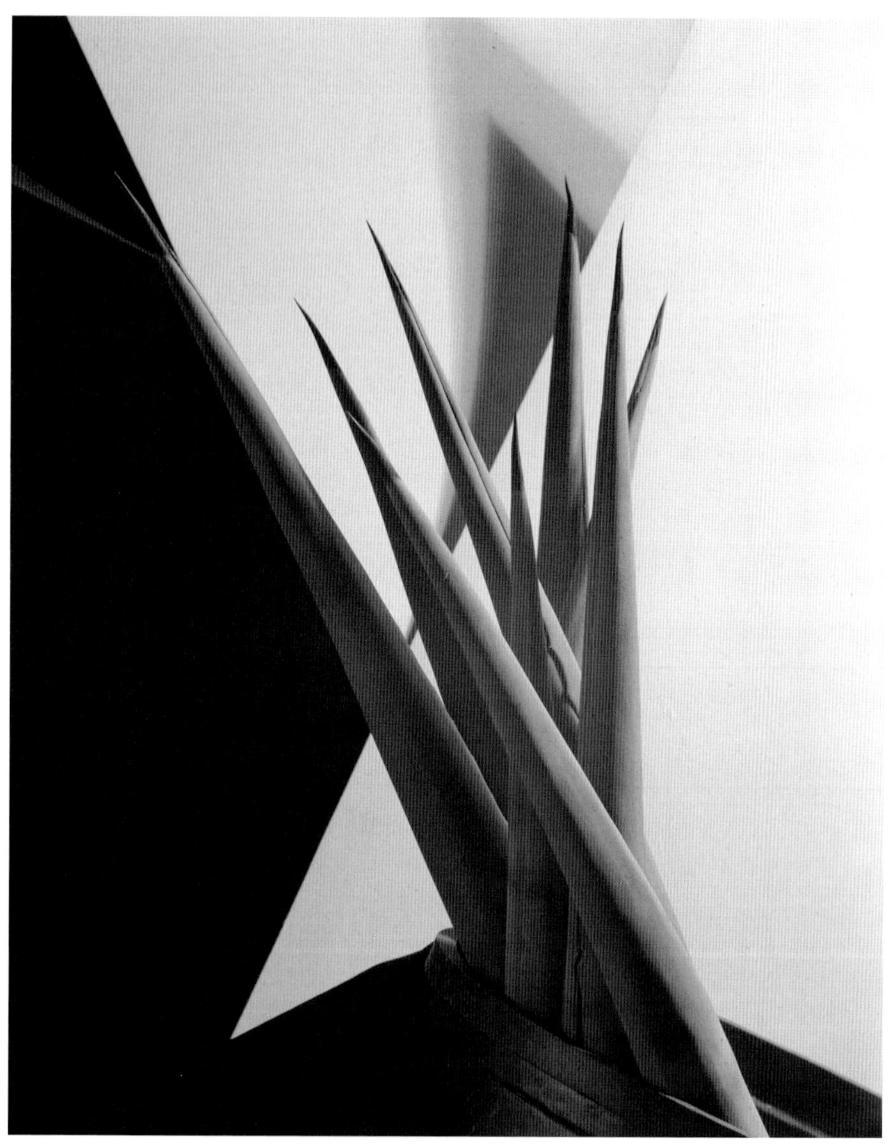

Agave Design I, 1920s

Though Cunningham's photographs of plants often were used for documentation, her images, as seen here, also helped photography attain recognition as an art that could be used to explore pure expression and experimentation of abstract form and design.

In addition, Cunningham took photographs of many important people. She created a stunning portrait when she met the dancer Martha Graham and was inspired by the intensity of her modern choreography.[1]

In the 1930s, Cunningham worked for the magazine *Vanity Fair.* Leaving her family to visit the editor and take pictures in New York caused a major disagreement with her husband, and soon afterwards the couple divorced. Cunningham would never remarry but continued to contribute photographs of famous people for two more years. Later she would also take pictures of artists like Frida Kahlo, poets such as Theodore Roethke, and curators such as Beaumont Newhall, many of whom were her friends, including Laura Gilpin.

Cunningham became an influential member of the prestigious photographic society known as Group f.64. Named for the f.64 camera setting that has a very small lens opening, the group of San Francisco photographers was interested in sharing their ideas about sharply focused and finely detailed images within a greater depth of field. Cunningham enjoyed their company and took photographs of her colleagues, including Ansel Adams and Edward Weston.[2]

Cunningham was invited by photographer Ansel Adams to become a teacher at the California School of Fine Arts in 1945.

In the 1950s and 1960s, she photographed poets of the Beat Generation, a literary movement started in the 1950s by a group of authors who rejected consumerism and conventional society. Cunningham also photographed flower children in the Haight-Ashbury

1. An American modern dancer and choreographer, Martha Graham's modern dance style is still taught all over the world.

2. Photographer Ansel Adams helped form this group of West Coast photographers to advocate for sharply focused pictures, a direct contrast to Alfred Stieglitz's East Coast "fuzzy" aesthetic principles. Depth of field is the distance between the nearest and farthest objects in a scene that is sharply focused.

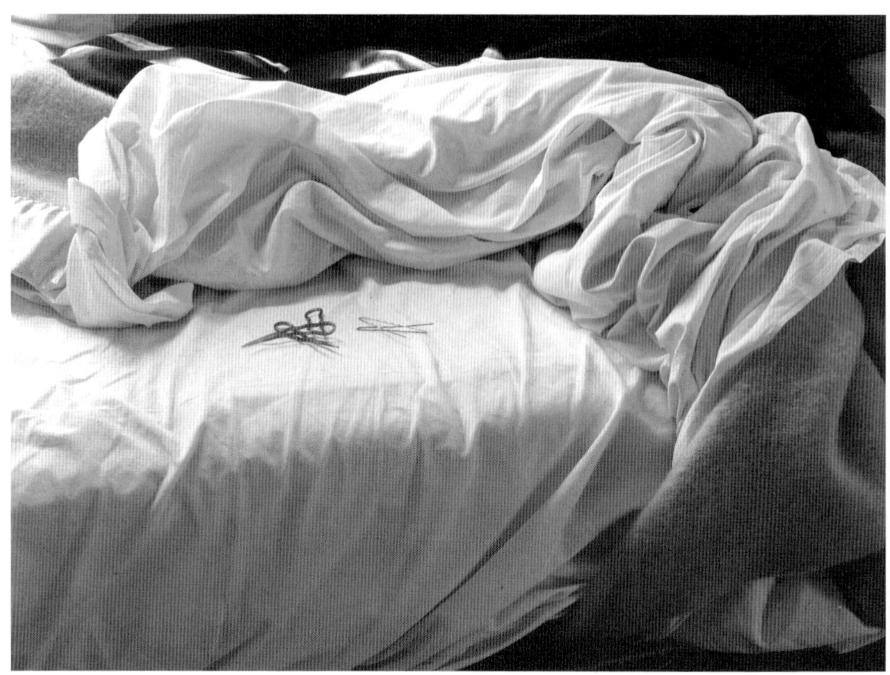

The Unmade Bed, 1957

Cunningham brings to this photograph the same love of sensuous form she exhibits in her close-up images of flowers or peppers. The swirl of rumpled sheets provides a rich range of blacks, grays, and whites that are the hallmark of an expert photographer. The organic, almost landscape-like shapes formed by the sheets lie in extreme contrast to the hard metal hairpins. But there is more: Cunningham has created an air of mystery, suggesting that a woman has slept here and perhaps only recently awoken. Or could another person be sleeping in the dark upper portion of the picture? If so, could the woman have left abruptly, leaving her hairpins behind?

district of San Francisco, the birthplace of countercultural hippies who opposed the Vietnam War and supported world peace. In 1974, *Life* magazine declared her "the best-known woman photographer in America," and *Newsweek* called her "The Queen: the blithe spirit of American photography." Two years before her death, she set up the Imogen Cunningham Trust to preserve her negatives and

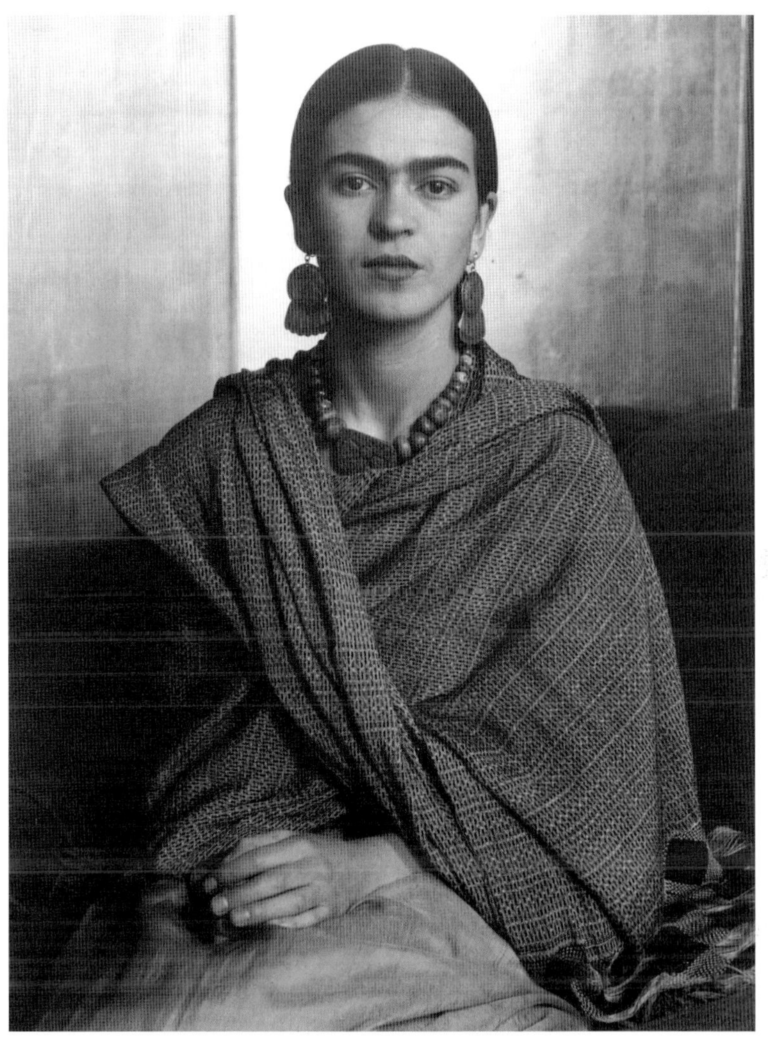

Frida Kahlo, 1931

Cunningham belonged to an international set of painters, writers, photographers, and philosophers, so it is not surprising that she would create a portrait of the Mexican artist Frida Kahlo.

Kahlo was very proud of her heritage and delighted in wearing the traditional clothing of her upbringing, rather than trying to appear more sophisticated or cosmopolitan. Again, Cunningham brings her eye for sensuous detail to the patterns of folds and drapes in the woven fabric, contrasting with the rougher texture of the rattan basket. At the same time, she captures Kahlo's steely resolve to be taken seriously.

publish her prints. She died in San Francisco in 1976 at the age of 93, just a year before her photography book of people over 90 was published.

Cunningham popularized photography in its early years and helped others see it as an art. Well-read and knowledgeable about art, Cunningham is known for her career as a teacher, and her many friendships with other artists. Her photographs ranged from scientific experimentation, nudes, botanical specimens, and portraits to still lifes and street photography. She excelled in different genres and took photographs every day of her life. Horticulturalists and other scientists still use her pictures of plants in their work. Her Pictorialist work influenced artists such as Francesca Woodman. Her photographs also have also inspired the work of Judy Dater, Abigail Ekue and Vivienne Maricevic.

READING LIST

Cunningham, Imogen. *After Ninety.* Seattle: University of Washington Press, 1977.

Dater, Judy. *Imogen Cunningham: A Portrait.* Boston: New York Graphic Society, 1979.

Lorenz, Richard. *Imogen Cunningham Flora.* New York: Bulfinch Press, 1996.

Rosenblum, Naomi. *A History of Women Photographers.* New York: Abbeville, 2014.

10

Elise Forrest Harleston

(1891–1970)

Charleston, The City by the Sea

ELISE FORREST HARLESTON was born in Charleston, South Carolina in 1891. She attended Avery Normal Institute, a private school established by the Amerian Missionary Association, graduating in 1908. She then taught at a rural school. In 1913, She met Edwin Harleston in Charleston and was attracted to him right away. They spent time together often since his brother was married to her sister. During their courtship, Edwin Harleston gave her a Brownie camera. Before Edwin Harleston left to study painting at the School of the Museum of Fine Arts in Boston, he asked Elise Forrest Harleston to enroll in a photography class so that after his return, they could be married and open a portrait studio.

In 1919, Elise Forrest Harleston attended the Emile Brunel School of Photography in New York City. (Emile Brunel was a German

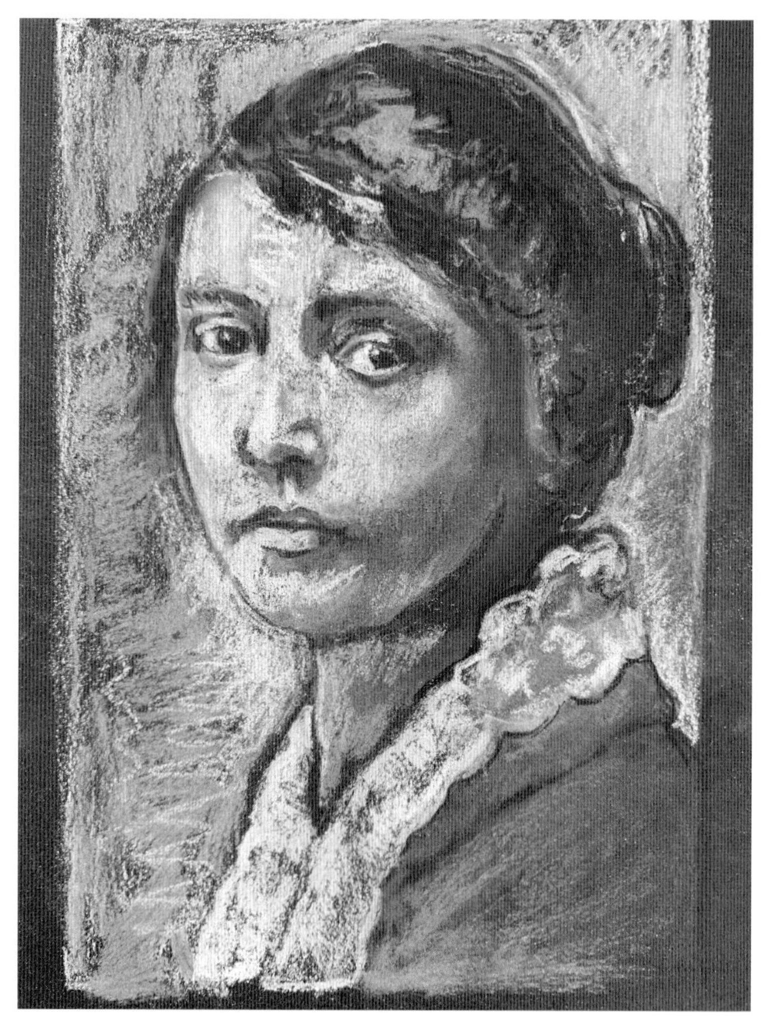

Elise Forrest Harleston

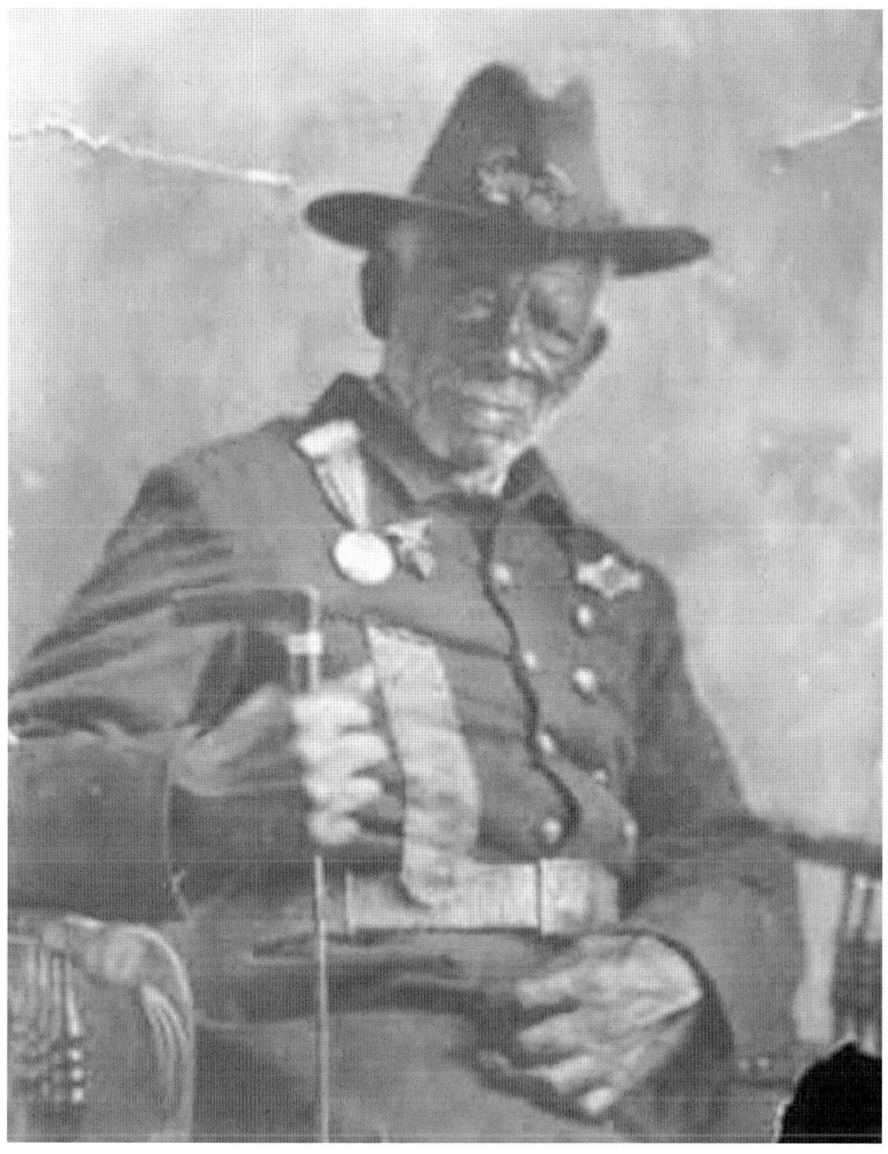

Grand Army Veteran, c. 1922–1931

Smart Chisholm, a member of the 128th Regiment of the U.S. Colored Infantry during the Civil War, posed for Elise's camera in his Grand Army of the Republic uniform. Edwin Harleston later painted a portrait of the G.A.R. veteran based on Elise's photograph.

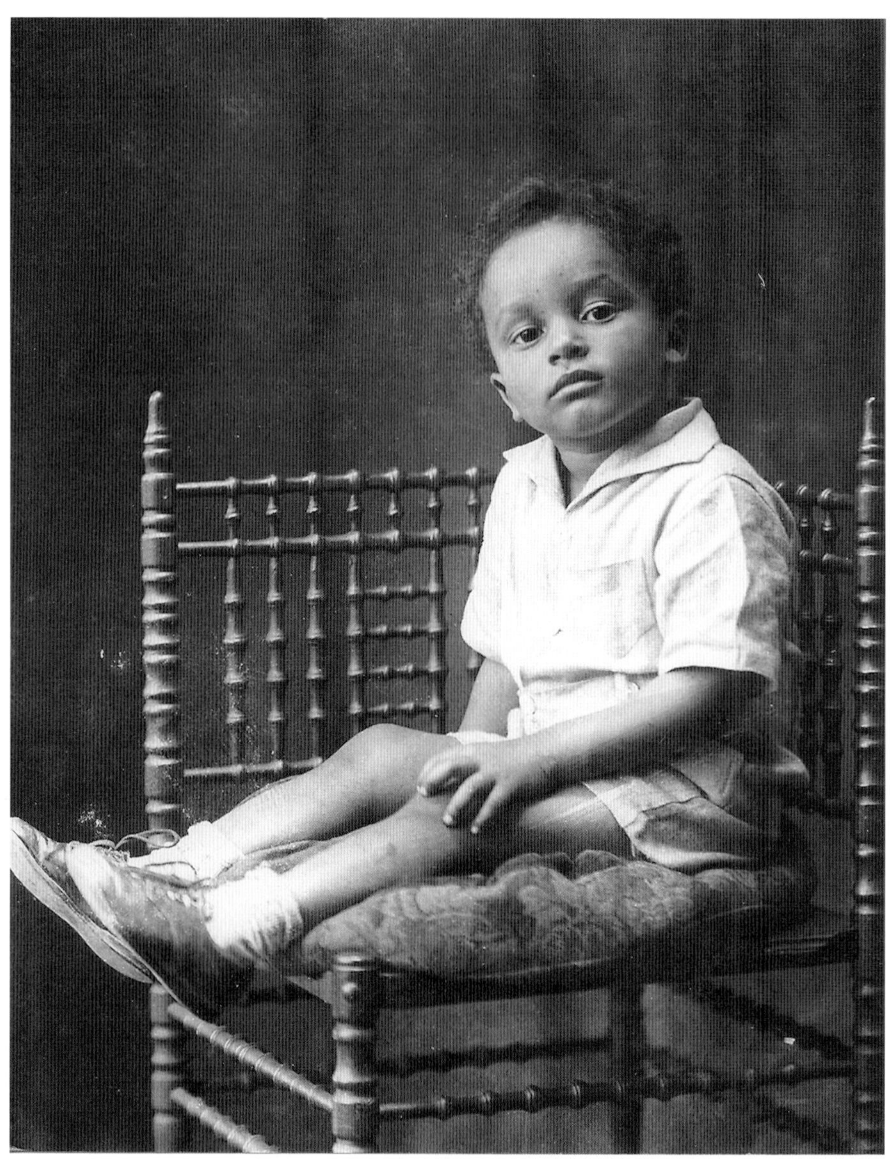

Seated Child, c. 1922–1931

The young child in this beautiful composition sits comfortably and looks at the camera with curiosity and intelligence. Harleston took several studio photographs of children, including her many nieces and nephews.

photographer, sculptor, and filmmaker.) She was one of two African Americans and the only woman student that attended the school. A year after she left for the photography school in New York, she married Edwin Harleston as planned. After she graduated, Edwin Harleston insisted she also enroll at Tuskegee Institute in Alabama where, in 1921, she took graduate courses in photography taught by Cornelius M. Battey who was head of the school's photography division. After her return to Charleston, the couple opened a joint studio and exhibition space in Charleston that lasted for a decade. Visited by poet Langston Hughes and Pulitzer Prize-winning author, Julia Peterkin, the Harleston Studio on 118 Calhoun Street would acquire a national reputation.

Together Edwin and Elise Harleston were business owners, image makers, and community activists. Edwin Harleston co-founded the Charleston branch of the National Association for the Advancement of Colored People (N.A.A.C.P) in 1917 and served as its first president. He also was involved in the Charleston Civic League and the National Negro Business League. Both were active churchgoers and contributed to services. Elise Harleston also was active in the Phyllis Wheatley Literary and Social Club and spent one year as its president.

Edwin Harleston often painted from Elise's photographic portraits of clients and genre scenes. This technique of painting from photographs pleased clients who did not have to pose for a long time. Edwin's studies made him aware of the work of French Impressionist painters influenced by photography such as Edgar Degas and Edouard Manet. He explained that he planned to carry on the legacy of Henry Ossawa Tanner, the first internationally acclaimed African American artist.

Elise Harleston photographed a broad cross section of African American Charleston residents. She took pictures of people she found interesting. Some were well educated and affluent, such as a family member wearing a fur-collared coat, a young boy sitting comfortably on a fine piece of furniture, and a high school

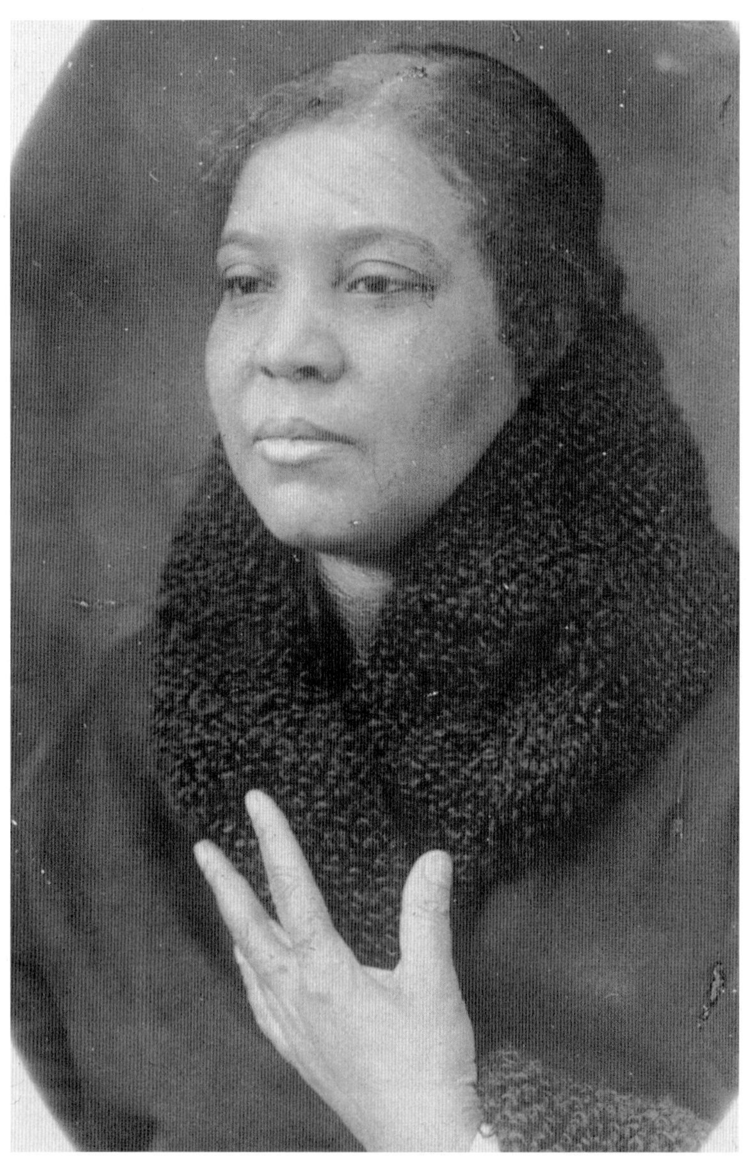

Rosalie Mickey, c. 1922–1931

Rosalie Mickey was Edwin Harleston's first cousin and the daughter of Hannah Harleston and Edward H. Mickey, owners of the Mickey Funeral Home in Charleston. She and Elise Harleston both were members of the Phyllis Wheatley Literary and Social Club. The hand of the family member holding onto the fur collar of her coat balances the composition of this carefully composed portrait.

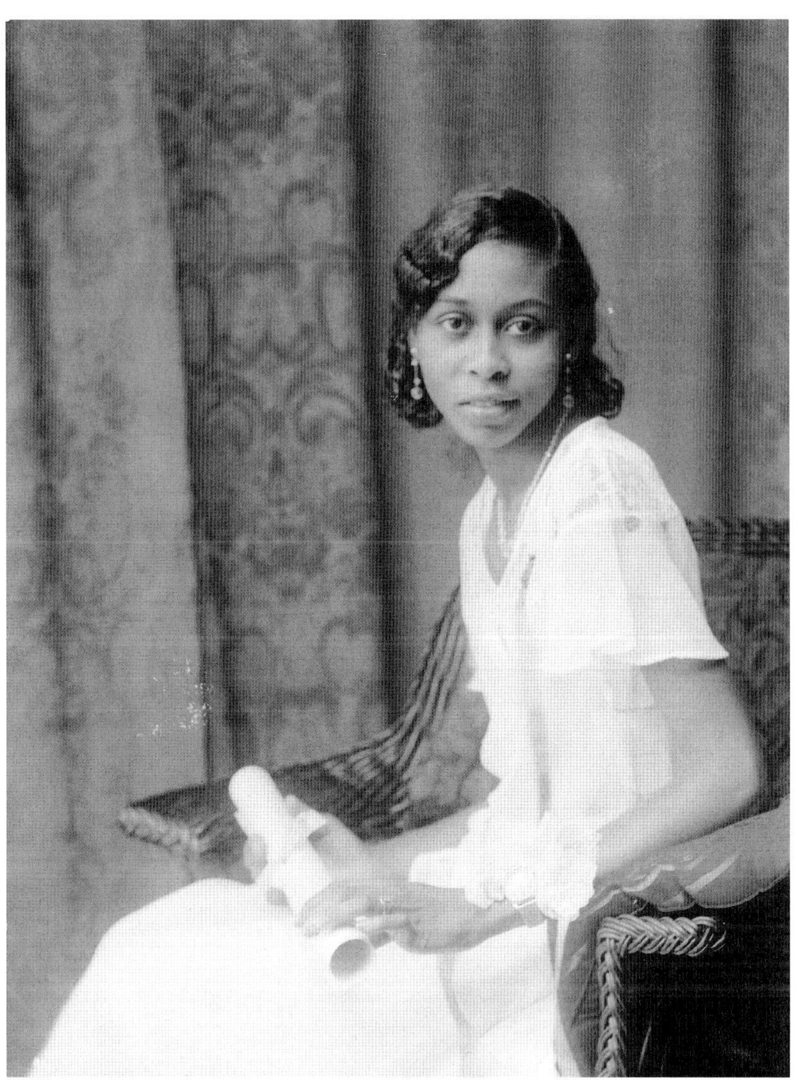

***Girl with Diploma*, c. 1922 1931**

The elegantly dressed high school graduate holds her diploma and wears her class ring. She was likely a graduate of Avery Normal Institute, a college-preparatory school established by the American Missionary Association after the Civil War. Because public schools for African American students in Charleston went only to eighth grade, parents who could afford it sent their children to the private Avery Institute. That the girl posed with her diploma indicates the importance of education to Chareston's African American middle class in the early twentieth century.

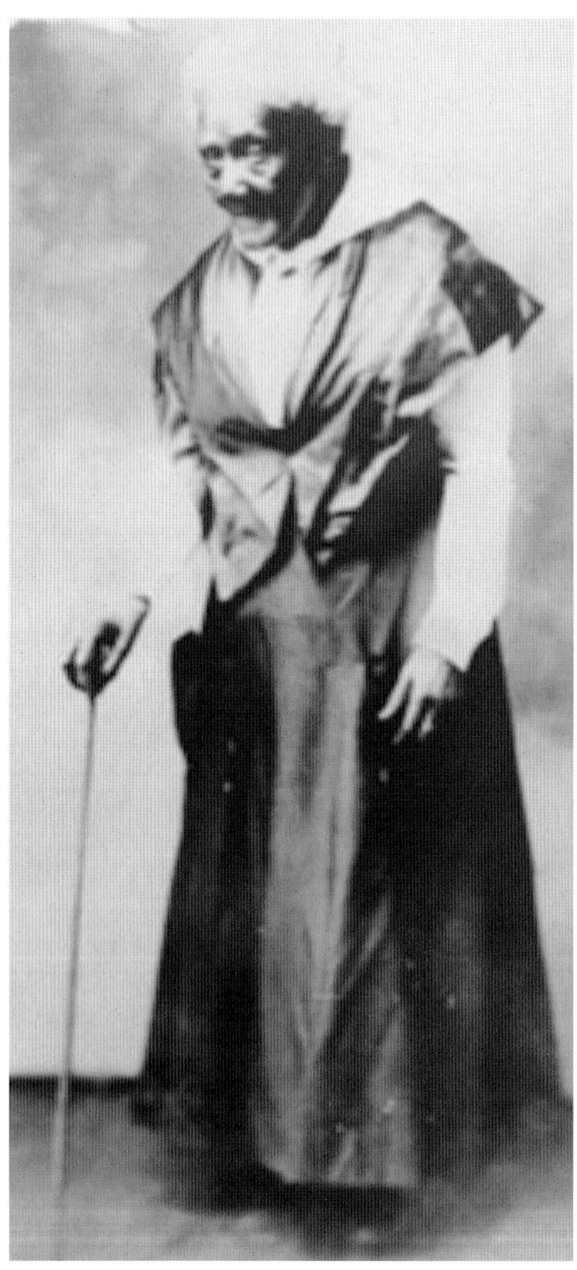

Old Woman from The Borough, c. 1922–1931

This photograph of an unidentified person, most likely a slave, is one of two pictures Elise created, one in which she is standing with a cane and one in which she is seated.

graduate holding her diploma and wearing a class ring. She also photographed Smart Chisholm, a member of the 128th Regiment of the U.S. Colored Infantry during the Civil War and an elderly woman, likely a former slave who lived in Charleston's Ansonborough neighborhood, known at the time as "the Borough."

Edwin Harleston received recognition for his work, but Elise Harleston's role was seldom publicly mentioned. After he died of pneumonia on May 10, 1931, Harleston closed her studio and remarried on August 15, 1932 to schoolteacher John J. Wheeler. She moved to Baltimore, then to Chicago, and then to southern California where she remained until her death from a brain aneurysm in 1970. Much of the couple's papers are now located at the Robert W. Woodruff Library of Emory University. Mae Whitlock Gentry, the great-niece of Edwin and Elise Harleston, is the keeper of her family's archives.

Elise Forrest Harleston is South Carolina's first African American female photographer. Known mostly as a portrait photographer, she was ahead of her time as the only professional African American photographer in the early twentieth century who took photographs outside a studio setting as well.

READING LIST

Horwitz, Margot F. *A Female Focus: Great Women Photographers.* Danbury: Franklin Watts, 1996.

Moutoussamy-Ashe, Jeanne. *Viewfinders: Black Women Photographers.* New York: Dodd Mean & Co., 1986.

Rosenblum, Naomi. *A History of Women Photographers.* New York: Abbeville Press, 1994.

Teal, Harvey S. *Partners with the Sun. South Carolina Photographers 1840–1940.* Columbia: University of South Carolina Press, 2001.

Willis, Deborah. *Reflections in Black: A History of Black Photographers: 1840 to the Present.* New York: W.W. Norton & Co., 2000.

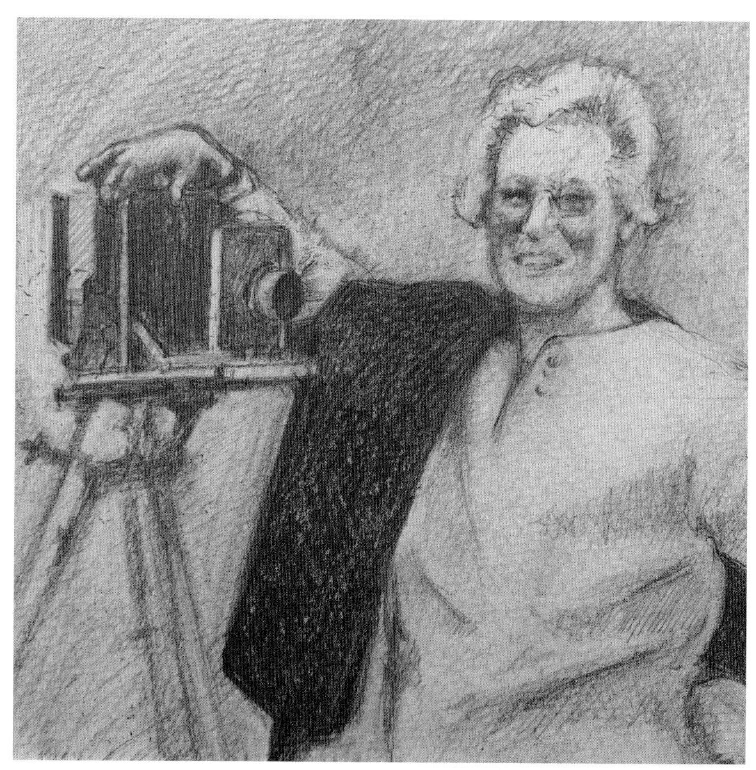

Laura Gilpin

11

Laura Gilpin

(1891–1979)

Landscapes of the Southwest

LAURA GILPIN was born in 1891 in Colorado. For her twelfth birthday, Gilpin received a Brownie camera from her parents. The next year, she visited the Louisiana Purchase Exposition in St. Louis, Missouri, her first world's fair. While there, she took snapshots of its architecture as well as Philippine natives. This is where she first became interested in native cultures.[1]

Going to the world's fair was an experience she would never forget for other reasons. She went to the fair every other day for over a month with her mother's best friend, Laura Perry, for whom she had been named. Since her traveling companion was blind, Gilpin had

1. Also known as the St. Louis World's Fair, the Louisiana Purchase Exposition was an international fair held in 1904. More than 60 countries maintained exhibition spaces at the fair, which was attended by more than 19 million people.

to describe every exhibit to her in detail. As Gilpin explained, "The experience taught me the kind of observation I would have never learned otherwise." Observing for another person made Gilpin even more interested in photography.

Two years later, Gilpin's mother arranged for a family portrait session with Gertrude Käsebier in New York City. Fourteen years old, Gilpin's first meeting with the most well-known woman photographer of her time was the beginning of a long-lasting relationship.

Gilpin became increasingly interested in photography, and as a teenager, experimented with photographic processes. Her first autochrome was made in 1908 when she was 17—the same year the color photographic process became commercially available. (A color photograph made by the autochrome process is an early form of photography using plates coated with red, green, and blue dyes.)

In the fall of 1915, she traveled to California to see the Panama-Pacific International Exposition in San Francisco and the Panama-California Exposition in San Diego. At these world's fairs, she photographed the buildings and sculpture, an experience that she would later call the beginning of her serious interest in art and photography.[2]

When Gilpin decided to study photography, she took the advice of her mentor and fellow Coloradan, Gertrude Käsebier. She moved to New York City to study at the Clarence H. White School, which was the nation's only art photography school during this time. Although she was a self-taught amateur, Gilpin felt confident she was talented and considered herself an artist. Clarence H. White, who

2. The 1915 Panama-Pacific International Exposition was held in San Francisco to celebrate the completion of the Panama Canal and showcase the recovery of San Francisco from the 1906 earthquake and fires. The Panama-California Exposition in San Diego was another world's fair meant to celebrate the completion of the Panama Canal as well as to advertise San Diego as the first port of call for ships traveling north after passing westward through the canal.

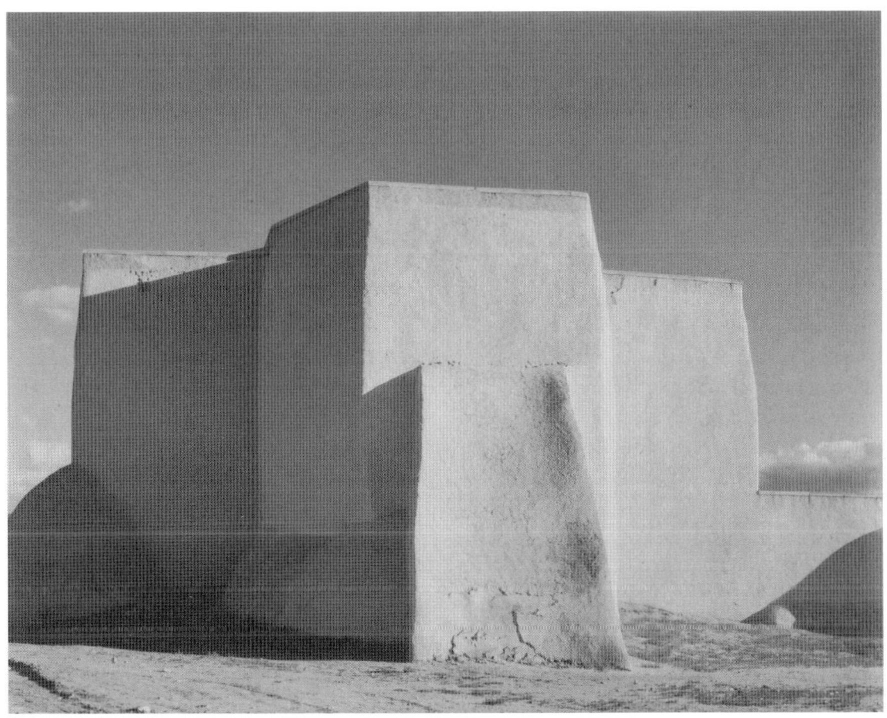

Rancho de Taos Mission, 1930

Made of adobe, a brick composed of straw and mud, the walls of this mission slope outward to buttress the structure and prevent water damage from torrential rains. Although the building was constructed in 1772 by Spanish missionaries and Native Americans, Gilpin's view appears abstract and modern as a series of rectangular surfaces in light and shadow. The Mission Church near Gilpin's home was recorded in photographs and drawings by the Historic American Buildings Survey in the 1930s.

believed photography could be a career as well as an art, was one of Gilpin's greatest teachers.

In 1918, Gilpin returned home to Colorado to photograph the place of bright land and open space she knew and loved best. When she developed the flu, her mother hired Betsy Forster, a nurse, to help Gilpin get well. The two women became best friends and would stay together for more than fifty years.

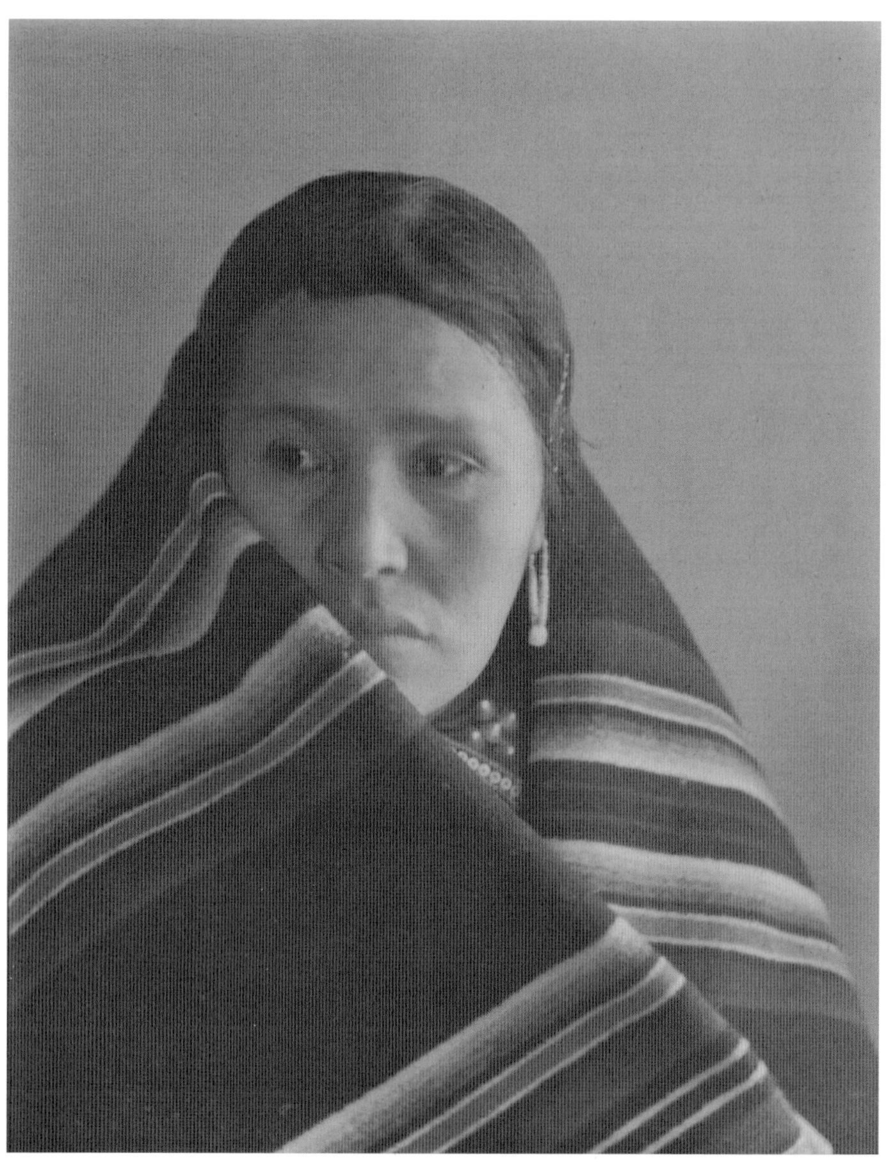

Mrs. Francis Nakai, New Mexico, 1932

Gilpin learned that the longer it took her to set up a photograph, the more important the act of taking a picture seemed to the Navajo people. Her sensitive photograph of Mrs. Francis Nakai, a Navajo neighbor and friend, reflects the quiet rapport Gilpin established with her sitters. She would photograph the Nakai family many times.

While Gilpin submitted still lifes, architectural photos, and portraits to competitive photographic exhibitions, her greatest accomplishments were her western landscapes—a field of work she pursued for over sixty years. Even after studying the art and architecture of England and France in 1922, Gilpin wrote home, "The more I see of the rest of the world, the gladder I am that I am not only American, but a Westerner. I look for the greatest art the world has yet produced to come from the West."

Gilpin also made promotional brochures, and she established a publishing company to produce guide books that she wrote and illustrated. The work of the visionary poet William Blake inspired Gilpin to make her own photographic books.[3]

As Gilpin explained, "What I consider really fine landscapes are very few and far between. I consider this field one of the greatest challenges and it is the principal reason I live in the West. I am willing to drive many miles, expose a lot of film, wait untold hours, camp out to be somewhere at sunrise, make many return trips to get what I am after."

Gilpin documented the Navaho people to show the physical landscape of the community and their way of life in a dignified and empathetic way. She was aware that "it will only be a short time before most traces of the old life are gone." Located in the New Mexico, Utah, and Arizona region, the Navaho people have the largest reservation in the United States. Gilpin's photographs illustrate their strong sense of tradition, family ties, and a love of the land where they live. This project culminated 18 years later in the publication of *The Enduring Navaho* (1968).

In New Mexico, Gilpin also photographed the Pueblo tribe, and published *The Pueblos* in 1941, although production of the book was delayed by the bombing of Pearl Harbor. Proud of the land which contains one of the nation's oldest cultures, Gilpin knew

3. William Blake (1757–1827) is now considered one of the greatest English poets of all time. He also was a painter and printmaker.

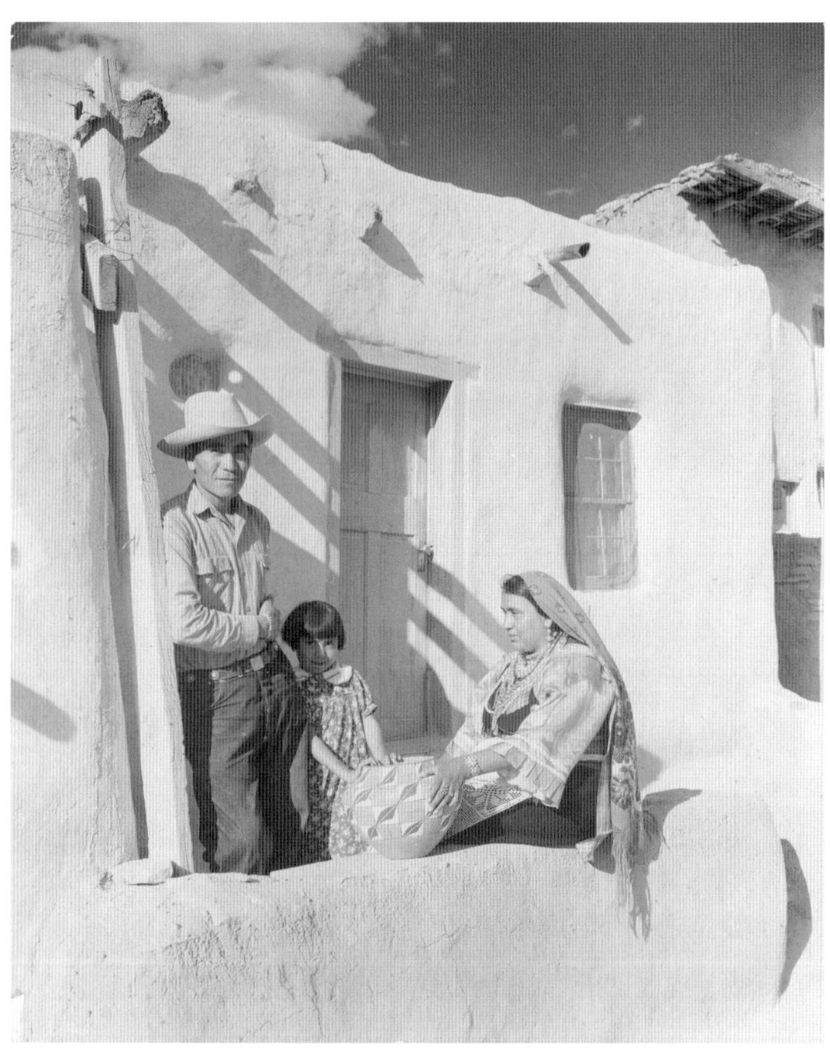

Indian Family, Acoma Pueblo, c. 1939

Gilpin's respectful portrayal of this Native American family in front of their adobe dwelling shows that she understood their desire to retain the best of their traditions while adapting to the modern American world. One of the nation's oldest continuously inhabited communities, the present-day Acoma Pueblo, about 60 miles west of Albuquerque, New Mexico, is a National Historic Landmark. The fact that their architecture, constructed by hand of the earth, has survived for hundreds of years is due to their ongoing preservation efforts. They are also responsible for the revitalization of their culture and language.

that her photographs were not a complete visual record, but her book makes it clear that the Pueblo culture should be preserved. Her other photography books include *Temples in Yucatan* (1948) and *The Rio Grande* (1949).[4]

For her book *The Rio Grande*, Gilpin photographed the entire length of the river from its headwaters in the San Juan mountains of southern Colorado to its effluence in the Gulf of Mexico—showing how people sustained themselves along the river through agriculture and irrigation practices.

Even though she struggled to make a living with her photos, Gilpin took care of her father for 16 years, and for 26 years she devoted herself to the care of her partner, Betsy Forster. Her photographs show that she also cared for Native Americans and nature. Everyone who knew her described her as a loving person.

Gilpin's career spanned 76 years. She received honorary doctorates and many awards. Her work, which has been seen in more than one hundred exhibitions, is now archived at the Amon Carter Museum of American Art in Fort Worth, Texas, where her friend, Mitchell Wilder, created a major collection of American photography.

Weeks before her death of heart failure in 1979, a film crew from the museum was sent to make a documentary about her long career. It was decided that she would make a trip in a small plane over the Rio Grande Valley. In the air, Gilpin leaned out the window to take yet another photograph. She was 88 years old.

Distinguished for her landscape photography of the Southwest and the culture of its native peoples, Laura Gilpin preferred wide, sweeping views of the land to show the impact of the environment on patterns of human settlement. Armed with a keen sense of composition and a kind heart, she devoted much time and energy

4. The Yucatan is one of 31 Mexican states, consisting of 14,827 square miles. The Rio Grande, 1896 miles long, is one of the main rivers of the southwestern United States and northern Mexico.

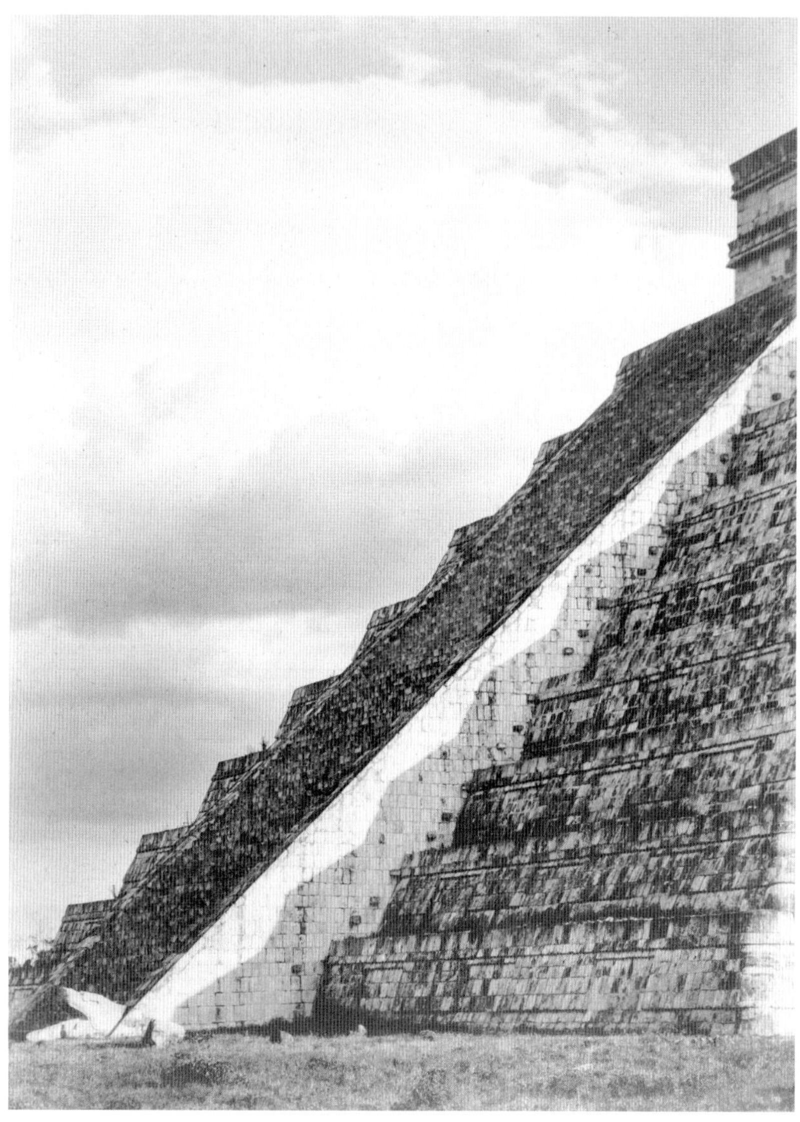

Steps of the Castillo, Chichen Itza, 1932

The ruins of Chichen Itza were a logical choice of subject for Gilpin, since she was interested in architecture, sculptural form, and cultural artifacts. In this photograph, Gilpin focused on the contrasting patterns formed by the dark shadows on the white limestone to emphasize the Mayans' sense of design that she admired so much. Although she admitted that it was difficult for her, Gilpin retained the proportions and decorative features of the ruins in this historically evocative image.

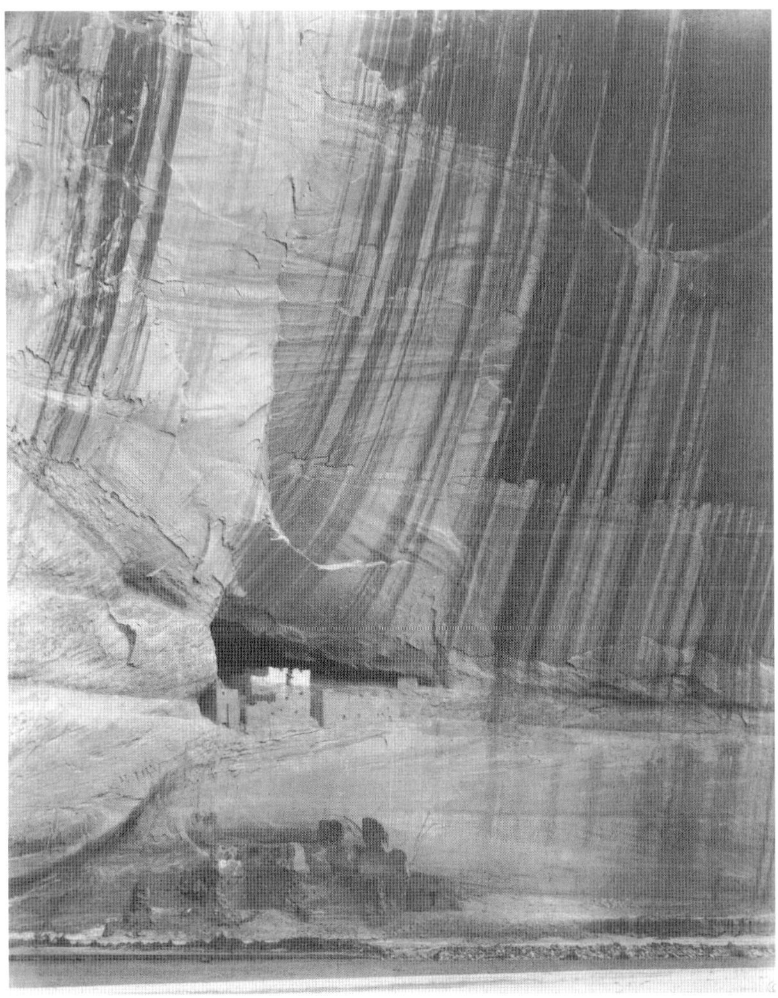

Casa Blanca, Canyon de Chelly, 1930

Canyon de Chelly was familiar to Gilpin since her family had a copy of a 1904 Edward Curtis photograph of Navajo horsemen that hung inside their home. Gilpin, along with her partner, Betsy Forster, went down into the canyon and traveled in a horse-pulled wagon to the White House ruins. Gilpin's first exposure was "the same old shot that everybody has done from [Timothy] O'Sullivan down." Then Gilpin moved to the other side of the ruins and photographed them again with this result.

The upper two thirds of the image show the long vertical striations of the canyon's cliffs. The lower section focuses on the built environment—the longest continuously inhabited landscape of North America.

to explore and document cultural sites of the Navajo and Pueblo tribes. Gilpin's photography led the way for present-day landscape photographers such as Patricia Davidson, Sarah Marino, Jean Day, and Christine Hauber.

READING LIST

Laura Gilpin Retrospective, 1910–1974. Santa Fe: Museum of New Mexico, 1974.

Sandweiss, Martha A. *Laura Gilpin: An Enduring Grace*. Fort Worth: Amon Carter Museum, 1986.

Dorothea Lange
(1895–1965)
Photographer of the Great Depression

DOROTHEA LANGE was born in Hoboken, New Jersey, in 1895. As a child she contracted polio, which left her with a permanent limp. But polio also gave her a strong will and a deep compassion for the less fortunate.

"I think it perhaps was the most important thing that happened to me," she explained. "It formed me, guided me, instructed me; helped me, and humiliated me. All those things at once. I've never gotten over it, and I am aware of the force and the power of it."

Her father abandoned the family when she was only twelve years old. She always remembered how after finding out she loved to read Shakespeare, he hired a carriage to take her to *A Midsummer Night's Dream.* Arriving late for the performance, her father held

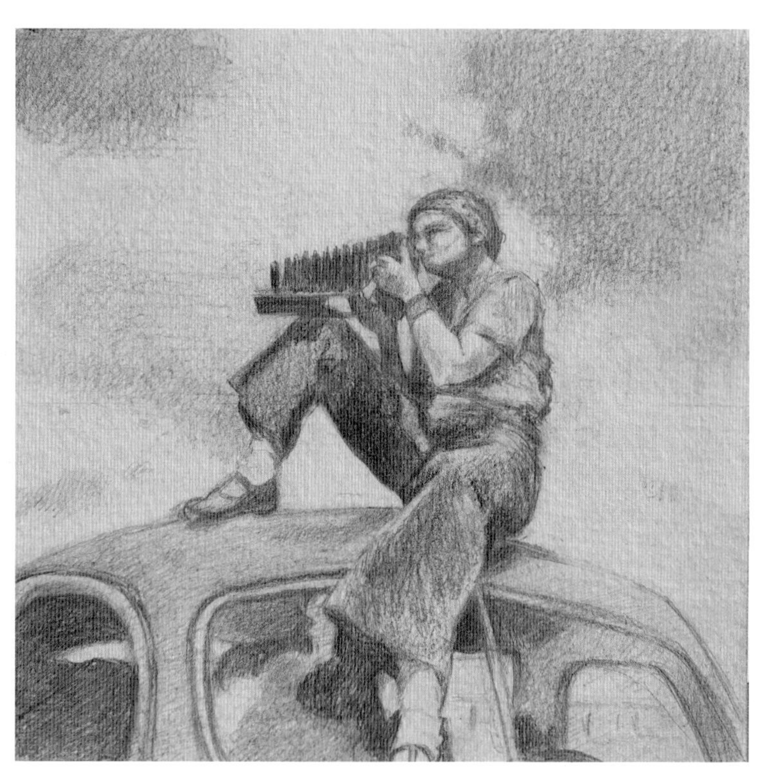

Dorothea Lange

her high on his shoulders in the back of the room so she could see. But although her father had been her greatest inspiration, Lange could not forgive him for walking out on the family and later took her mother's maiden name.

To support the family, Lange's mother got a job at the New York Public Library in the Lower East Side of New York. Lange traveled to the city with her mother and went to school near her mother's workplace. She did not like school because she thought it was boring, and did not get good grades. She spent hours after school in the library where her mother worked, looking at pictures in books. Other times, she would visit museums and take long walks.

By the time she graduated from high school, Lange knew she wanted to be a photographer. She had never taken a picture or owned a camera, but she loved photography because, as she explained, "a camera teaches you how to see without a camera."

To make her mother happy, she enrolled in a teachers' training school. While studying to become an elementary school teacher, she asked photographer Arnold Genthe for a job at his Fifth Avenue studio where wealthy people and celebrities had their portraits taken. Over the next few years, she worked at other studios and learned about photography on the job. She also took a photography course at Columbia University. Clarence H. White, the only teacher in the country who taught photography as an art, inspired Lange to keep her dream of being a full-time photographer alive. She eventually dropped out of school, and bought a large camera so she could take pictures of people she knew.

When Lange was 22, she and a girlfriend set out to travel around the world. Their trip ended in San Francisco, where they were robbed of all their money. Lange soon found work photo-processing at a store, and within a few months, she rented her own photography studio, a beautiful building. The main floor had a large room with a fireplace at one end and a large velvet couch in front of it. Downstairs was the darkroom, where she developed the portraits she had taken upstairs.

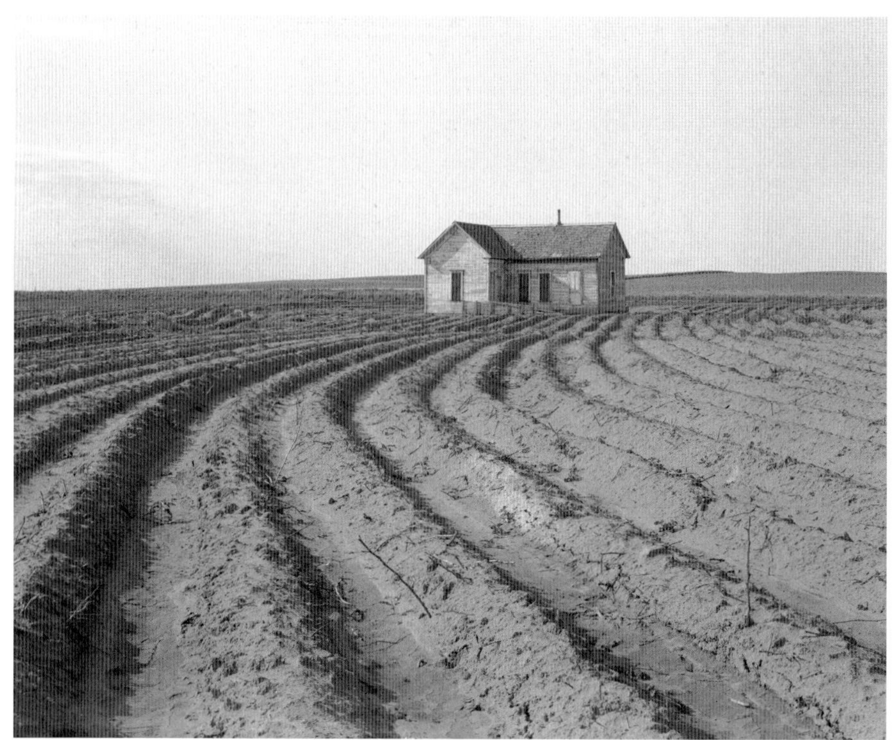

Childress County, Texas 1938

This image of an abandoned farmhouse surrounded by barren furrowed fields is a poignant reminder that the farmers were pushed off their property due to the destruction of the dust storms. This photograph was included in a book published by Lange and her husband, historian Paul S. Taylor, entitled *An American Exodus* (1939). The caption reads: "Tractors replace not only mules but people. They cultivate to the very door of the houses of those whom they replace."

Lange loved San Francisco because she found many good friends there, including the photographer Imogen Cunningham and her husband. She was surrounded by painters, writers, musicians, and playwrights who "lived according to their own standards and did what they wanted to do in the way they wanted to do it."

In 1920, she married Maynard Dixon, a painter of western scenes, and the couple had two sons, but their marriage did not last. For one thing, they had money problems, and Maynard's long trips left

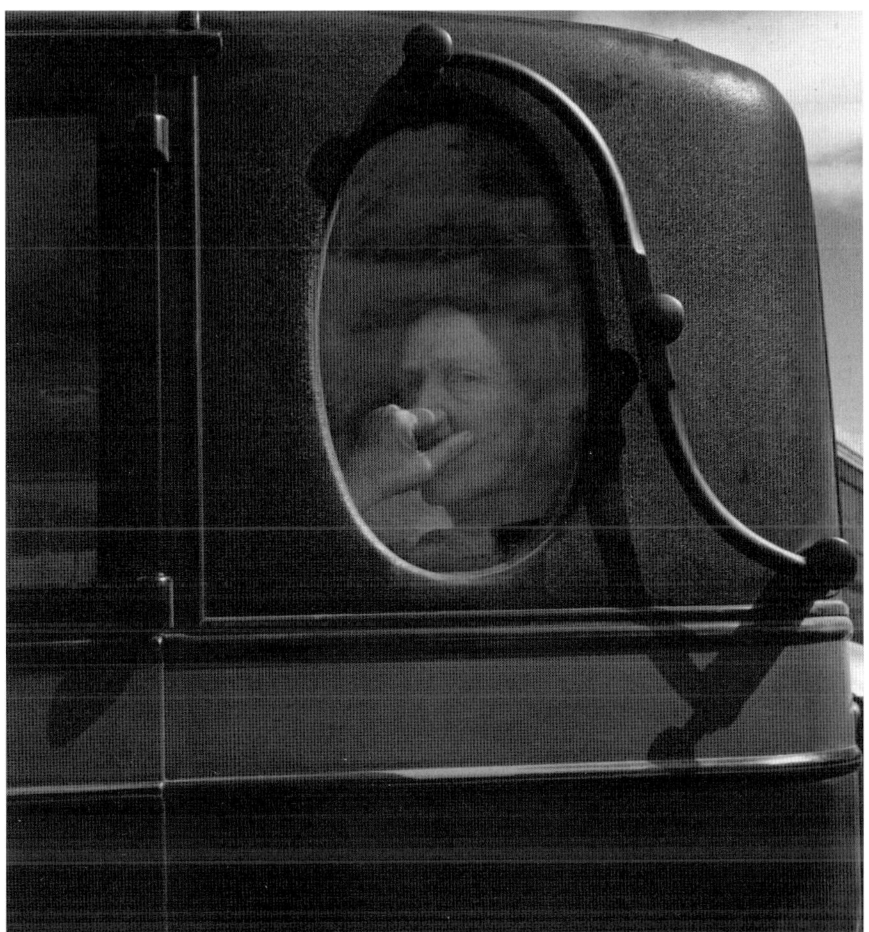

Funeral Cortege, End of an Era in a Small Valley Town, California, 1938

A hard-faced woman sitting in the back seat leans against the inside of a car. She holds her hand to her face as she looks out the oval window in grief. In this haunting funeral scene, Lange brings to mind a sense of displacement resulting from tragedy. The mourner appears deeply uncertain about her future.

Lange alone with the children so that it was difficult for her to do her own work.

Lange continued to spend long hours making portraits for people who could afford them. But she could not help seeing what

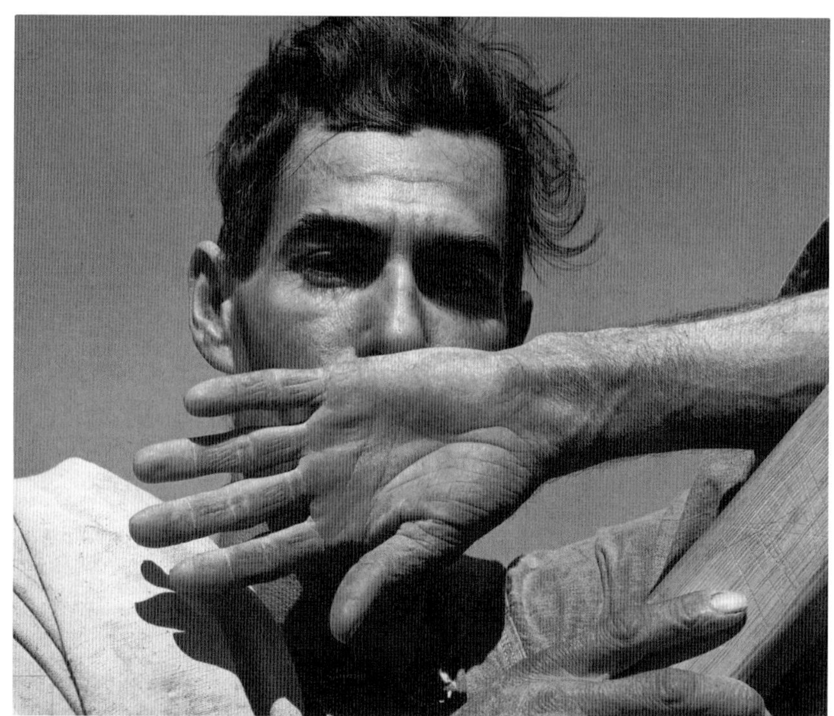

Migratory Cotton Picker, Eloy, Arizona, 1940

Dorothea Lange traveled to Arizona in 1940 to document the working conditions of cotton workers. In this close-up portrait, cropped from a larger image, a migrant worker leans against a fence with his cotton sack thrown over his shoulder. Lange wrote in her notes, "Resting at cotton wagon before returning to work in the field. He has been picking cotton all day. A good picker earns about $2 a day working at this time of year."

Lange took the picture as the gentleman attempted to hide his face in front of the camera. His worn fingertips and the deep lines of his weathered palm reveal the harsh working conditions. The intimate portrait makes us realize how our wellbeing is dependent on someone else's job. It also makes us question how much we owe each other for that relationship.

was going on in the street. Looking down from her second-story window, she saw hungry, homeless people wandering aimlessly along the sidewalks. What she saw was happening to the whole nation, because more than fifteen million people were out of work due to the stock market crash of 1929, the worst economic event in world history. Lange knew she had to take her camera to the streets to document the disastrous human consequences of the Great Depression. After fifteen successful years, Lange ended her portrait studio business.

After her divorce, Lange married Paul Schuster Taylor, an economics professor. He admired her work and together they documented the lives of poor people in America. She took photographs that complemented her husband's research.

The American government soon hired Lange to chronicle the Great Depression. She began to photograph some of the people who were hardest hit by the depression, such as farm workers who moved from the Oklahoma dust storms to find work in the West.[1]

Lange's technique made her photographs memorable. She used close-ups of facial features and gestures to arouse compassion. "I had to get my camera to register the things that were more important than how poor they were—their pride, their strength, their spirit."

Her most recognized photograph, and one of the most reproduced photographs worldwide, is "Migrant Mother," a photograph of Florence Owens Thompson with her children.

Many years after the photograph was taken, Lange explained, "I saw and approached the hungry and desperate mother, as if drawn by a magnet. I do not remember how I explained my presence or my camera to her, but I do remember she asked me no questions. I made five exposures, working closer and closer from the same direction. I did not ask her name or her history. She told me her age, that she was thirty-two. She said that they had been living on frozen vegetables from the surrounding fields, and birds that the children killed. She had just sold the tires from her car to buy food.

1. A severe worldwide economic depression, the Great Depression started in the United States after a major fall in stock prices and was made worse by the 1930s dust storms. President Franklin D. Roosevelt responded to the crisis by implementing programs to relieve poverty.

There she sat in that lean-to tent with her children huddled around her, and seemed to know that my pictures might help her, and so she helped me. There was a sort of equality about it."

When they finished taking pictures of the effects of the Great Depression along the West Coast, Lange and her husband took long trips into the South to document struggling farmworkers.

World War II began in the United States in 1942 when Japanese military planes attacked the American naval base at Pearl Harbor in Hawaii. Innocent Japanese Americans were forced to move from their comfortable homes along the West Coast, leaving behind many possessions to settle into internment camps in the desert. Large families were housed in cramped quarters with only tar paper covering the exterior walls. Without any privacy, life was very hard and depressing. For example, there were no partitions between toilets. Residents had to wait in long lines for meals in communal dining halls. Lange's photographs of these temporary settlements document what is now considered one of the worst violations of American civil rights.

After the war, photographer Ansel Adams invited Lange to teach art photography at what is now called the San Francisco Art Institute.[2]

Her health had already declined over the last two decades of her life, but she never gave up. Lange co-founded *Aperture*, a photography magazine, in 1952. Two years later, she was a staff photographer for *Life* magazine.

Sadly, she died of cancer in 1965 at the age of 70. The year of her death, the Museum of Modern Art mounted a large exhibit of her photographs that she had helped organize. Although she was shy about sharing her most personal pictures for the world to see, she wanted to display her most important work because of its strong

2. The San Francisco Art Institute, formed in 1871, is one of America's oldest art schools.

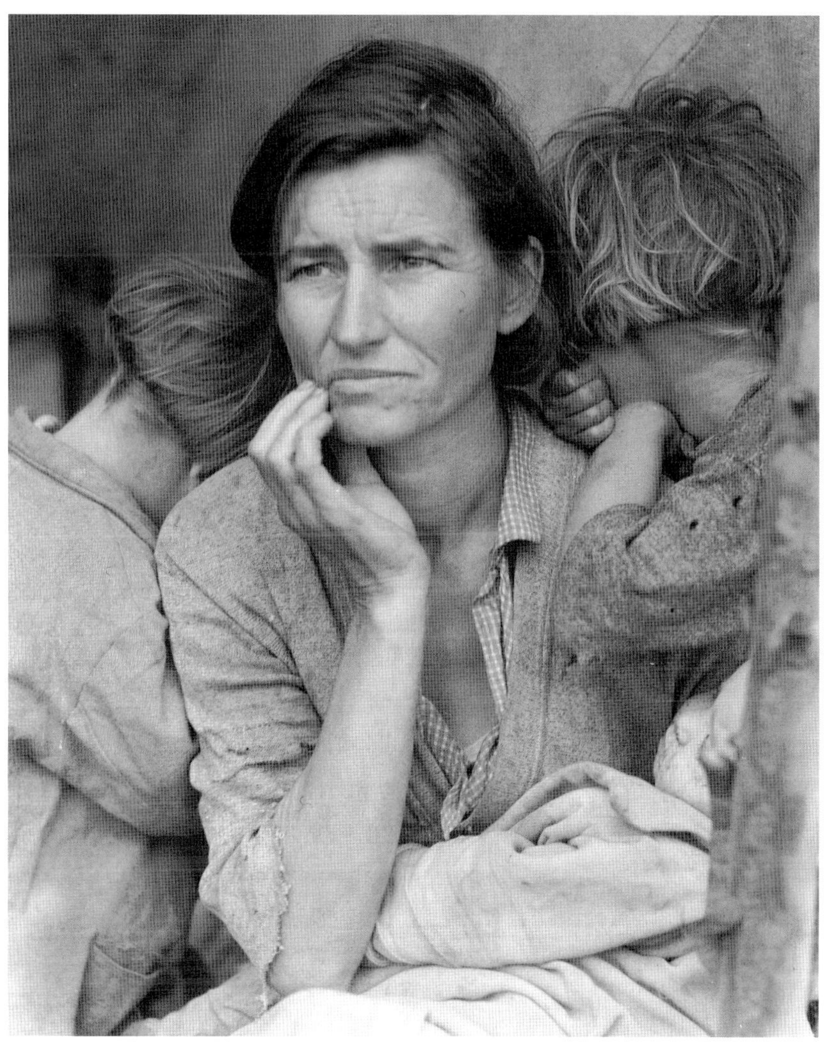

Migrant Mother, Nipomo, California, 1936

Lange took this photograph while employed by the United States Farm Security Administration, formed during the Great Depression to raise awareness and provide aid to impoverished farmers. At the center of this portrait is a mother's worried face. On either side of her are two young children who turn away from the camera and rest their weary heads on her shoulders. The mother looks older than she really is. She touches the side of her mouth with one hand as she is thinking. This picture, more than any other, humanized the cost of the Great Depression by focusing on the suffering mother's face.

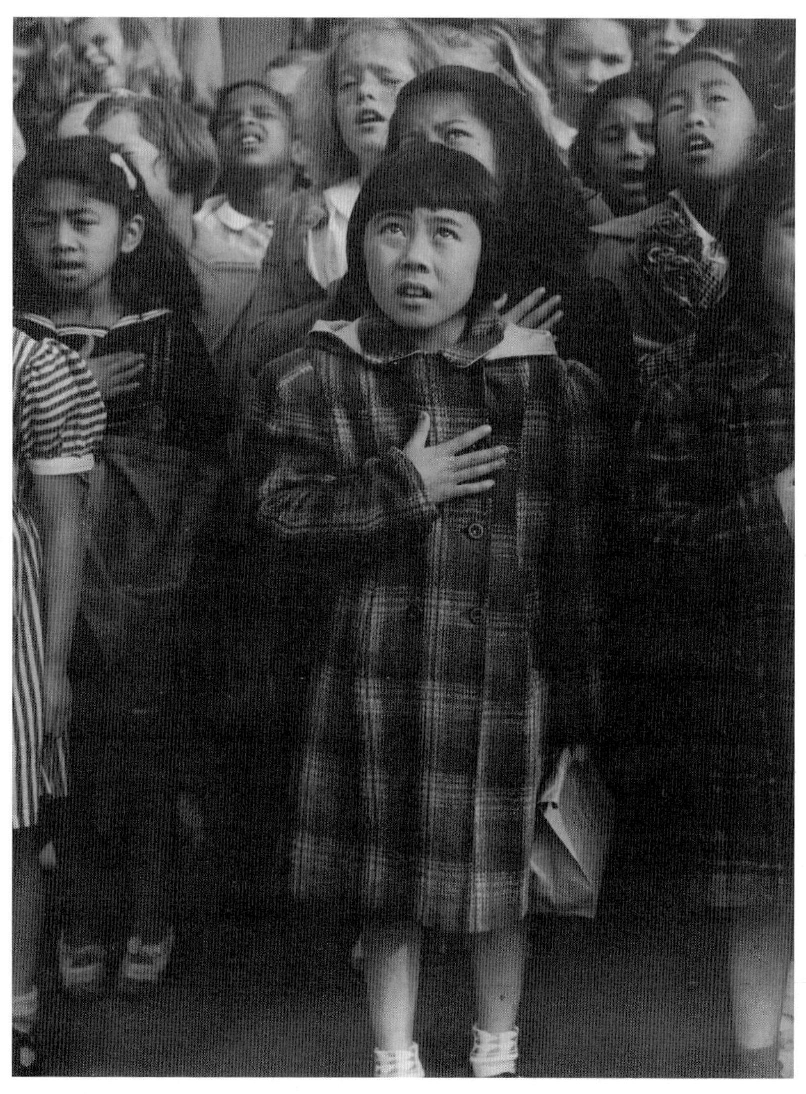

One Nation Indivisible, 1942

Dorothea Lange focuses on one girl who is standing in front of a group of children, all of whom are respectfully pledging allegiance to the American flag at the Rafael Weill Elementary School in San Francisco. The young child holds her right hand over her chest while clutching her paper lunch bag with her left hand. We the viewers, at her eye level, can see that she means what she says. She is sweet and innocent and obviously no threat to anyone, and yet she is about to be taken away and put into an internment camp due to her supposed risk to national security.

emotional impact. Now, Dorothea Lange's photographs are located at the National Archives in Washington, D.C., and at the Bancroft Library of the University of California in Berkeley.

Lange set the standard for engaged, empathetic documentary photography. Her greatest achievements are the photographs she took during the Great Depression. These socially conscious pictures made an enormous impact on how millions of ordinary Americans understood the plight of the poor. Her photographs, relevant to current events, made people realize how anyone could experience the same fate. Lange's images of poverty, forced migration, social disruption, environmental devastation, and racism continue to have impact today, inspiring generations of photographers such as Ken Light, who takes pictures of present-day migrant farmworkers; Janet Delaney, whose images document gentrification; and Jason Jaacks, who photographs Mexican migrants.

READING LIST

Dorothea Lange: Photographs of a Lifetime. Millerton, New York: Aperture, 1982.

Heyman, Therese Thau. *Celebrating a Collection: The Work of Dorothea Lange,* Documentary Photographer. Oakland, California: Oakland Museum, 1978.

Meister, Sarah Hermanson. *Dorothea Lange: Words and Pictures.* New York: Museum of Modern Art, 2019.

Partridge, Elizabeth. *Restless Spirit: The Life and Work of Dorothea Lange.* New York: Puffin Books, 1998.

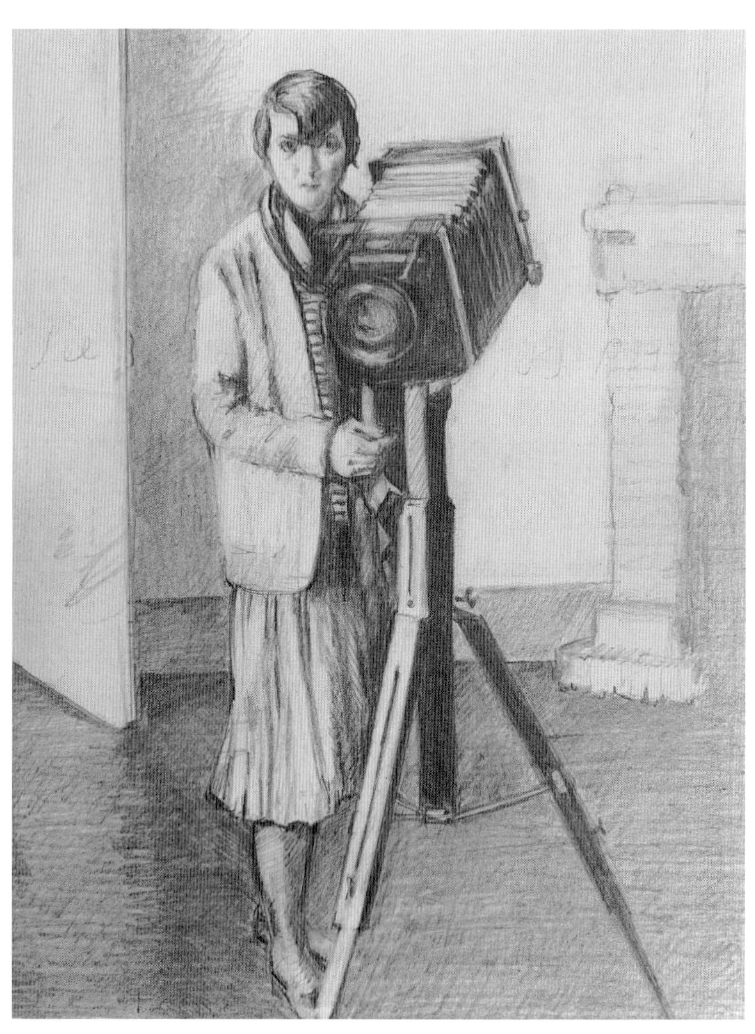

Berenice Abbott

13

Berenice Abbott
(1898–1991)
Changing New York

BERENICE ABBOTT was born in 1898 in Springfield, Ohio. She lived mostly with her mother, separated from her father and siblings, and also at times with members of her extended family.

She briefly attended classes at Ohio State University, and received high grades only in French. She left in 1918 with friends for a more adventurous life in New York City, where she explored sculpture by herself for four years. Settling in Greenwich Village, she played small parts in Eugene O'Neill plays and became good friends with other artists and writers.

There she met Man Ray, a Brooklyn artist who had turned to portrait photography for a larger income. Through him, she also met the artist Marcel Duchamp. She became good friends with both, and they encouraged her to visit Paris.

Abbott spent the next eight years in Paris. First drawn to journalism and later theater and sculpture, Abbott originally planned to attend a high-ranking art school run by a sculptor. However, she could not afford it, so she turned to "pay-as-you-go" drawing sessions, discovering photography only later.

After Man Ray arrived in Paris, Abbott became his darkroom assistant. The two friends worked well together. Abbott admitted that she knew nothing about photography when she started. But with a bit of technical information from Man Ray and a lot of trial and error, Abbott became an expert.

As she explained, "Half the fun of photography is fooling around, mixing solutions, playing with papers ..."

Abbott eventually left Man Ray's studio, and at the age of 28, opened her own. Usually she took only one sitter each day because, "In those days in Paris, no one was rushed." She took photographs of prominent cultural figures including writer James Joyce, filmmaker Jean Cocteau, collector Peggy Guggenheim, and writer Edna St. Vincent Millay.

Critics praised Abbott's studio portraits. They called them "precious and living documents of elegant style and of the most beautiful faces in the world." All this praise made Man Ray jealous!

While in Paris, Abbott met the French photographer Eugène Atget, and they got along well. Berenice realized he was a lot like her: solitary and self-reliant. She admired his style, how he lived entirely for his work, and how all his imagery focused on the city—its streets, buildings, and landscapes. Eugène Atget tried to document all of the historic architecture and street scenes of Paris that existed before the French Revolution before their systematic demolition in the early 1900s. It was clear that Eugène Atget was in love with Paris.

Abbott realized that she wanted to take photographs like he did. "Let us say what photography is not. A photograph is not a painting, a poem, a symphony, a dance. It is not just a pretty picture ... It is or should be a significant document, a penetrating statement, which can be described in a very simple term—selectivity."

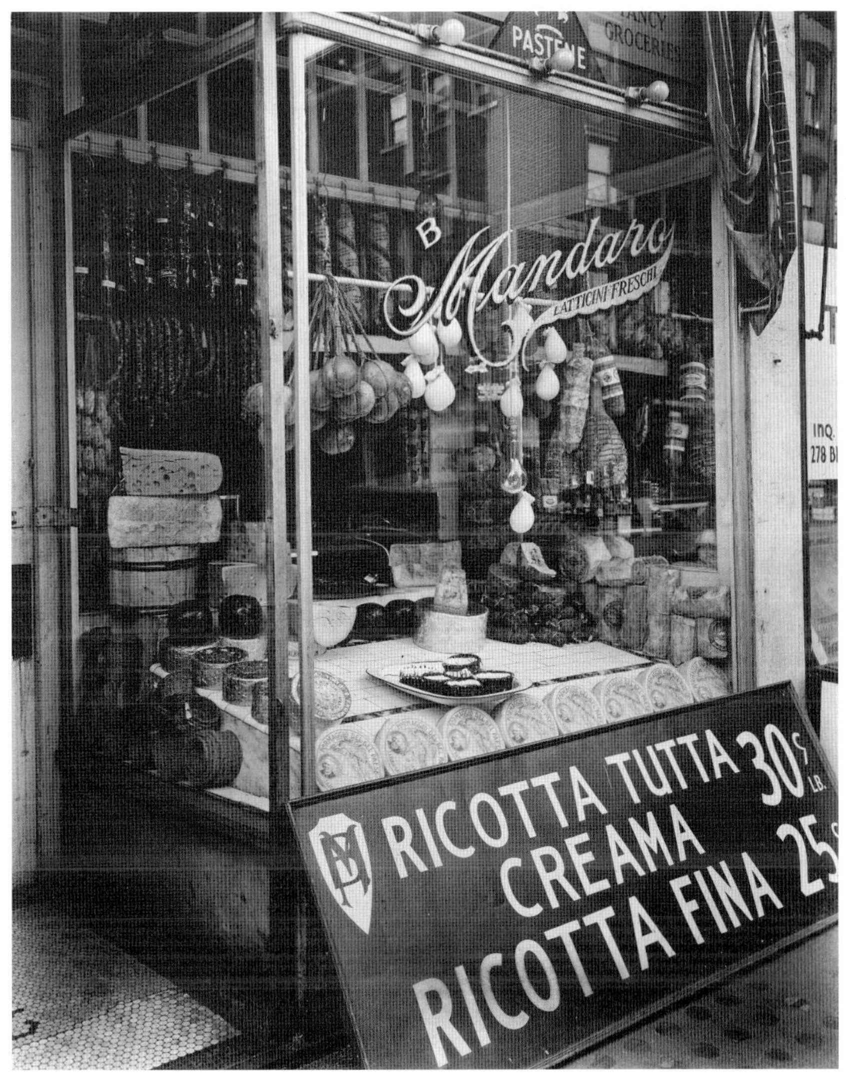

Cheese Store, 1937

The storefront window of this once thriving cheese store at 276 Bleecker Street in the South Village of Manhattan showcases its offerings for all who pass by. The sign on the window reads "Mandaro Latticini Freschi," which translates to "fresh dairy products." Below the window is an advertisement for whole milk ricotta and fine ricotta. A variety of cheese wedges and wheels are displayed along the window ledge. Mandaro's was one of the many businesses that catered to the growing Little Italy neighborhood, which developed between the 1880s and 1930s.

After Atget died in 1927, Abbott acquired his prints and negatives. Since Atget's documentation of Paris was little known, Abbott sailed back to New York in order to preserve and promote all of his work. Her main focus was to find places where she could exhibit his work, along with her own. Berenice Abbott said that Atget "will be remembered as an urbanist historian, a genuine romanticist, a lover of Paris, a Balzac of the camera, from whose work we can weave a large tapestry of French civilization."

She said she loved cities the way other women loved fur coats. "They mean something to me. They have a personality. Not the people in them, but the buildings, the little odd corners." Abbott soon realized her tenderness toward New York City was the same feeling Atget had for Paris.

In 1929, 30-year-old Abbott began to systematically photograph New York, a fast-changing city where historic buildings were being torn down almost quicker than she could preserve them on film—the same problem Atget had in Paris. Abbott hoped to preserve the architectural and social history of New York through her photography. She was especially interested in the relationship between old and new buildings.

During this time, Abbott met art historian and critic Elizabeth McCausland, and they became life partners. While working in New York City, Abbott and McCausland moved to Greenwich Village in Manhattan, and many of Abbott's images are of this neighborhood. Abbott's project would take her a decade to complete. Funded by the Federal Art Project, her work was then published in 1935 with captions provided by Elizabeth McCausland. The photographs from this project are now at the Museum of the City of New York.

Abbott also helped to organize the Photo League, a group of photographers interested in documenting urban life, and she taught classes in photography at the New School. She later became interested in scientific photography and joined a project at the Massachusetts Institute of Technology to illustrate science course materials.

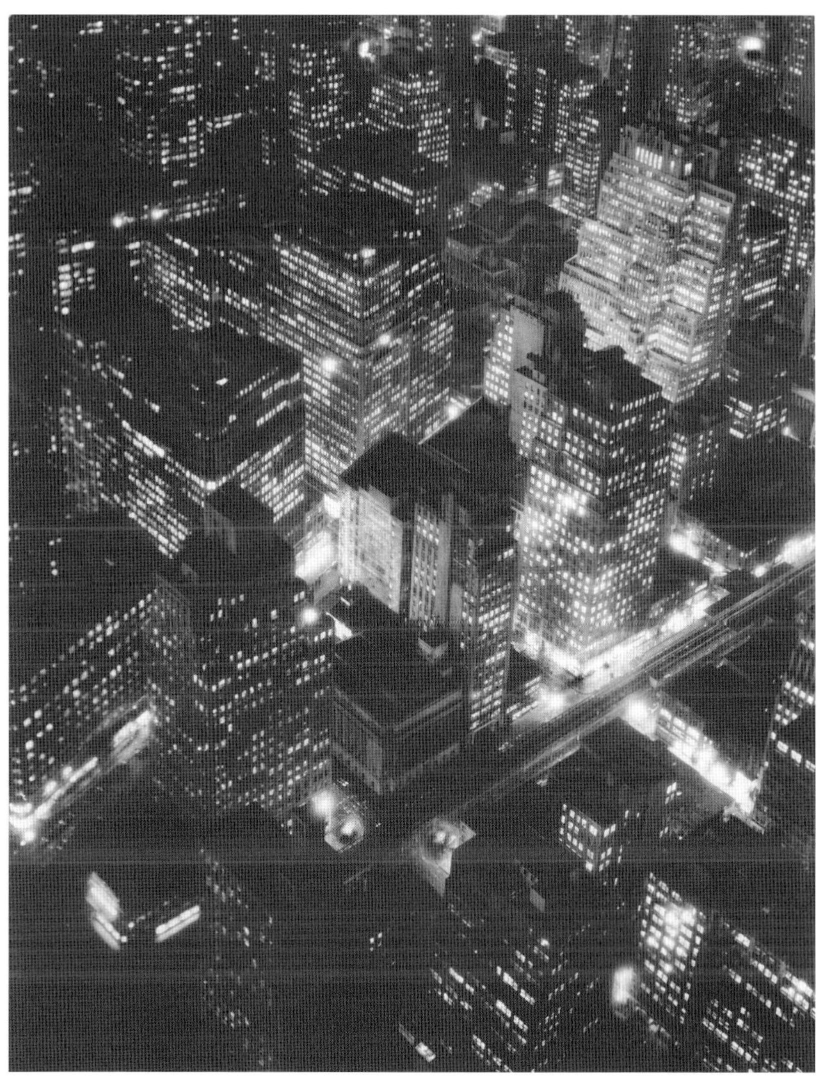

New York at Night, 1932

Berenice Abbott was unique in documenting New York City from either a bird's-eye view or from ground level. This nighttime shot of New York City captures its vibrancy and bustle by documenting the twinkling lights of illuminated skyscrapers and vehicles' headlights. It is as though we are looking into an ant farm to witness activity that appears both frenzied and purposeful, and which we might find amusing and unfathomable at the same time.

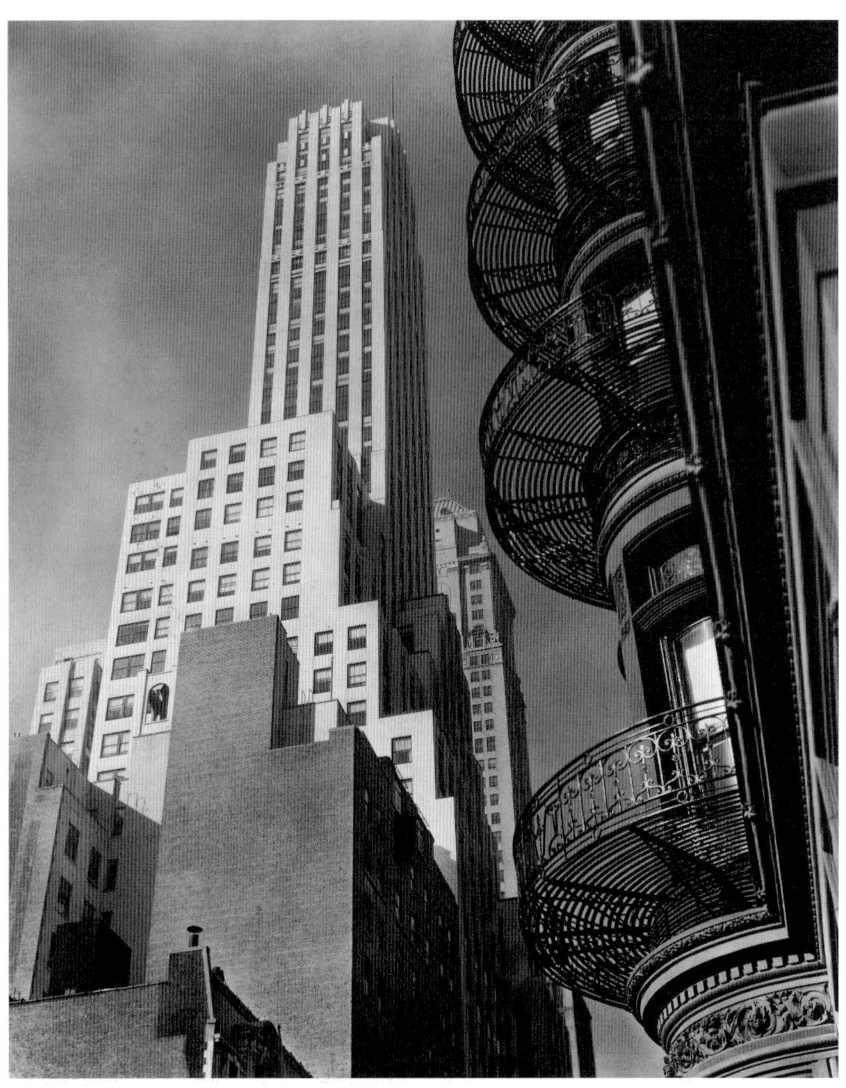

Murray Hill Hotel, Spiral, 112 Park Avenue, 1935

Abbott documents the contrasting geometric shapes created by the contours of New York City buildings. She uses an unusual camera angle, looking upward in such a way that the viewer's eye sweeps up on an exciting journey and then tumbles down the jagged step shapes of what would have been a small skyscraper at that time. These forms are juxtaposed against the curvy wrought-iron balconies of an older building across the street, creating a jazzy interplay of disparate elements and a visual metaphor for the essence of New York City.

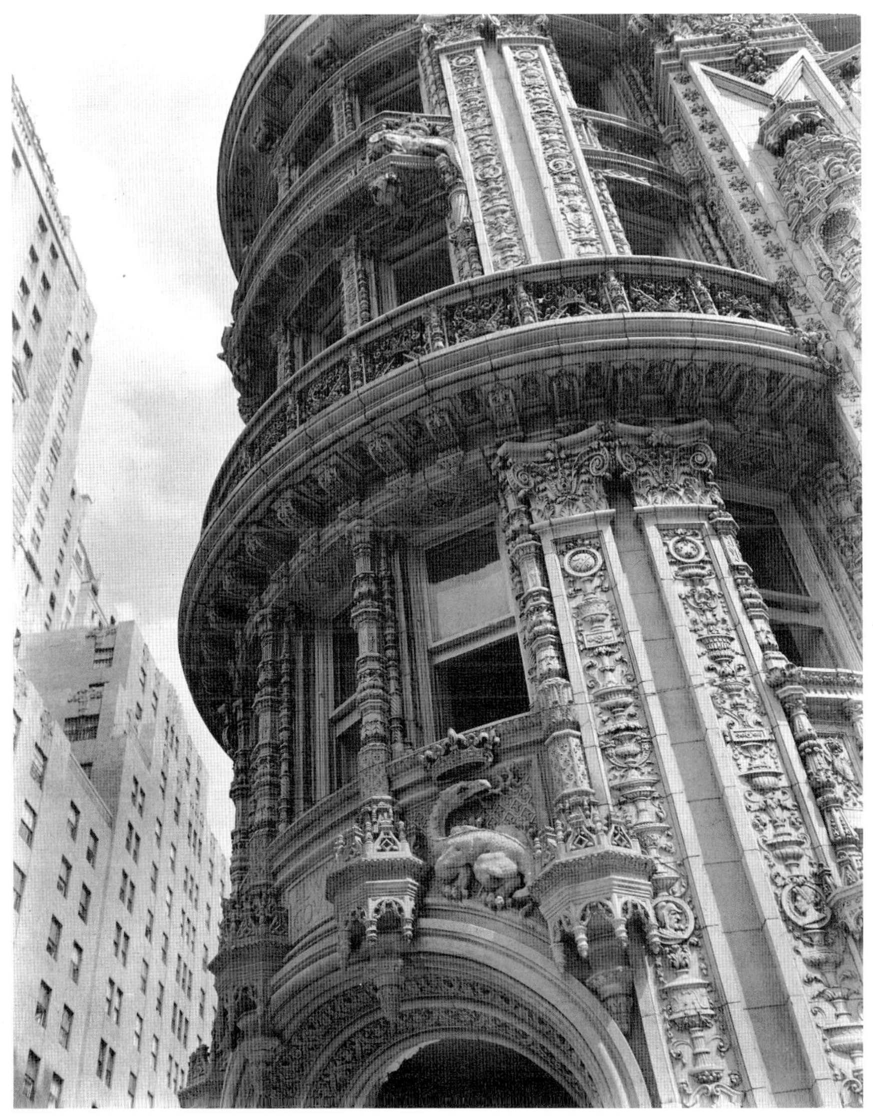

Facade: Alwyn Court, 1938

Abbott focuses on the exquisite sculptural details of the facade of Alwyn Court, a twelve-story 1907 French Renaissance building located on West 58th Street and Seventh Avenue in Midtown Manhattan. This photograph was taken for a federal project to document the changing nature of New York. It's good to know that this building became a New York Landmark in 1966, was added to the National Register of Historic Places in 1979, and restored in 1980.

In 1968, Abbott sold Eugène Atget's archive to the Museum of Modern Art and then settled in Maine. She made prints of her work until her death in 1991 at the age of 93.

Berenice Abbott's legacy lives on today for those photographers who see the city as a valid subject for long-term documentary work. A bridge between the photographic circles of Paris and New York, Abbott is responsible for bringing international recognition to the work of French photographer Eugène Atget. She is also best known for her photographs of a rapidly changing New York during the 1930s. Historians, city planners, historic preservationists, architects, and artists have benefitted from Abbott's images. She successfully documented the architectural and social history of New York while at the same time questioning the relationship of old and new buildings. "To me photography is a means—perhaps the best means of our age—of widening knowledge of our world ..."

READING LIST

Berenice Abbott: Photographs. New York: Horizon, 1970.

McCausland, Elizabeth and Berenice Abbott. *Changing New York.* New York: E.P. Dutton, 1939.

O'Neal, Hank. *Berenice Abbott: American Photographer.* New York: McGraw-Hill, Art Press, 1982.

Van Haaften, Julia, ed. *Berenice Abbott, Photographer: A Modern Vision.* New York: New York Public Library, 1989.

14

Margaret Bourke-White

(1904–1971)

Fearless Foreign Correspondent

MARGARET BOURKE-WHITE was born in New York in 1904. As a young girl, Bourke-White did not take any pictures. Instead, her father asked her to take notes about what he photographed, mostly family, flowers, and birds. Both her father and Margaret shared a love for nature.

The family lived in a small New Jersey town, and near them were woods and a low mountain range. Bourke-White treasured the nature hikes they took together and she appreciated how her father taught her the names of the stars.

Learning to do things fearlessly was important to both of her parents. They wanted her to enjoy being alone. At home, she took care of snakes, turtles, rabbits, and hamsters, and decided she wanted to be a biologist. But when she went to college, she changed her mind.

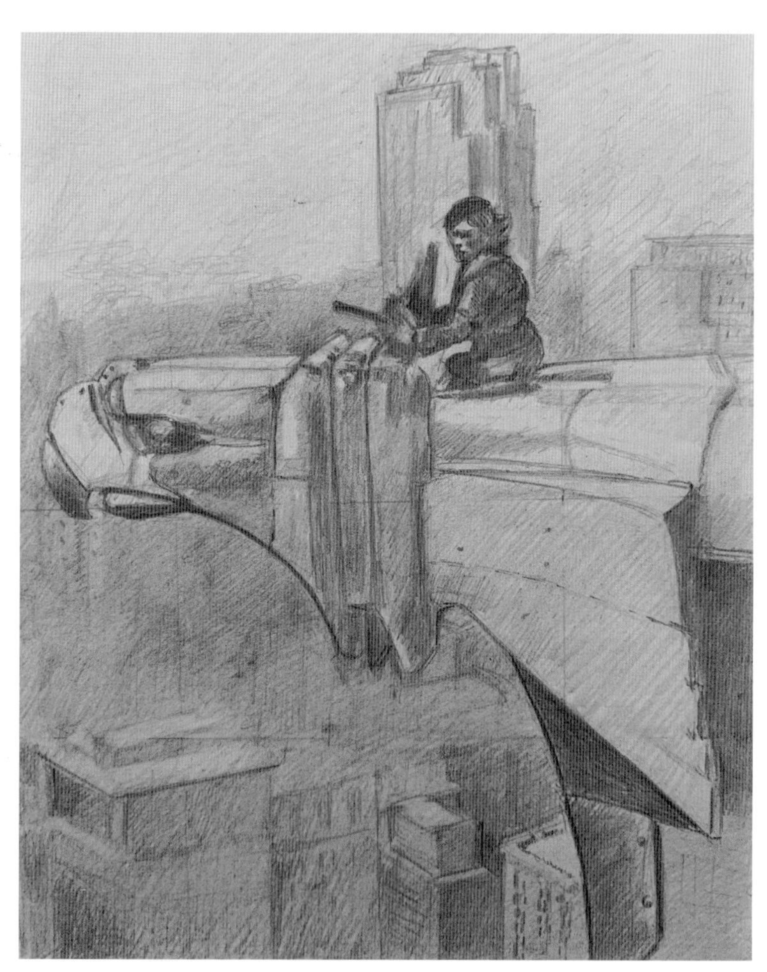

Margaret Bourke-White

Margaret Bourke-White fell in love with photography during her first photography class at Columbia University, where she studied with Clarence White. Then, after transferring during her freshman year to the University of Michigan, she met Everett Chapman (whom she would call "Chappie") in a revolving door. He kept the door turning with her inside until she made a date with him.

They married in 1924 and moved to Cleveland, where she taught children at the Cleveland Museum of Natural History and attended night school at Case Western University. Bourke-White was determined to finish college and get a diploma. She finally completed her bachelor's degree at Cornell University in Ithaca, New York, after which she and Chapman officially divorced.

Bourke-White's professional career began when she returned to Cleveland, Ohio, where her widowed mother and brother had already moved. Bourke-White opened a studio in her apartment. She processed her photographs in the kitchen, and rinsed them in the bathtub. The living room served as a reception room "when the in-a-door bed was pushed out of the way."

Bourke-White walked around the city searching for images to photograph, and discovered a part of town along Lake Erie known as the Flats, an industrial district of factories and foundries. She started taking pictures of trains, bridges, and buildings like the Terminal Tower. By the end of 1927, the owners of Terminal Tower hired her as their official photographer and soon she was renting a studio on the twelfth floor of the building.

Although women were not allowed in the factory for safety reasons, Bourke-White managed to photograph an industrial series on the Otis Steel Mills, where metal products were made for cars and skyscrapers. As she explained, "To me ... industrial forms were all the more beautiful because they were never designed to be beautiful. They had a simplicity of line that came from their direct application of purpose. Industry had evolved an unconscious beauty—often a hidden beauty that was waiting to be discovered." This work inspired Henry Luce, publisher of *Fortune* magazine, to

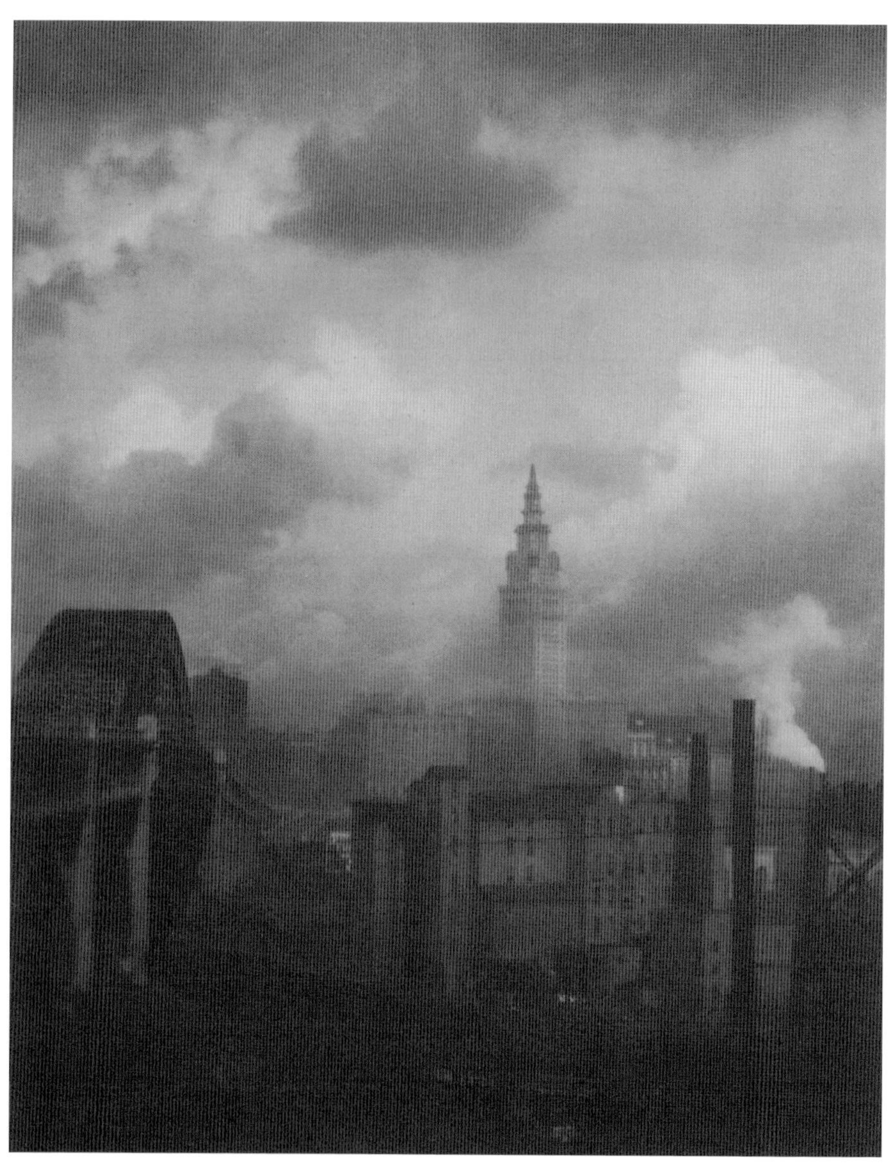

Terminal Tower, Cleveland, 1927

Active in Cleveland in the late 1920s, Bourke-White was attracted to the city's most distinctive landmark. Terminal Tower was at that time the second tallest building in the nation. She documented the building from various vantage points at different times of the day. Atmospheric conditions varied as well in this industrial city. Here, the tower can be seen softly focused due to clouds and steam.

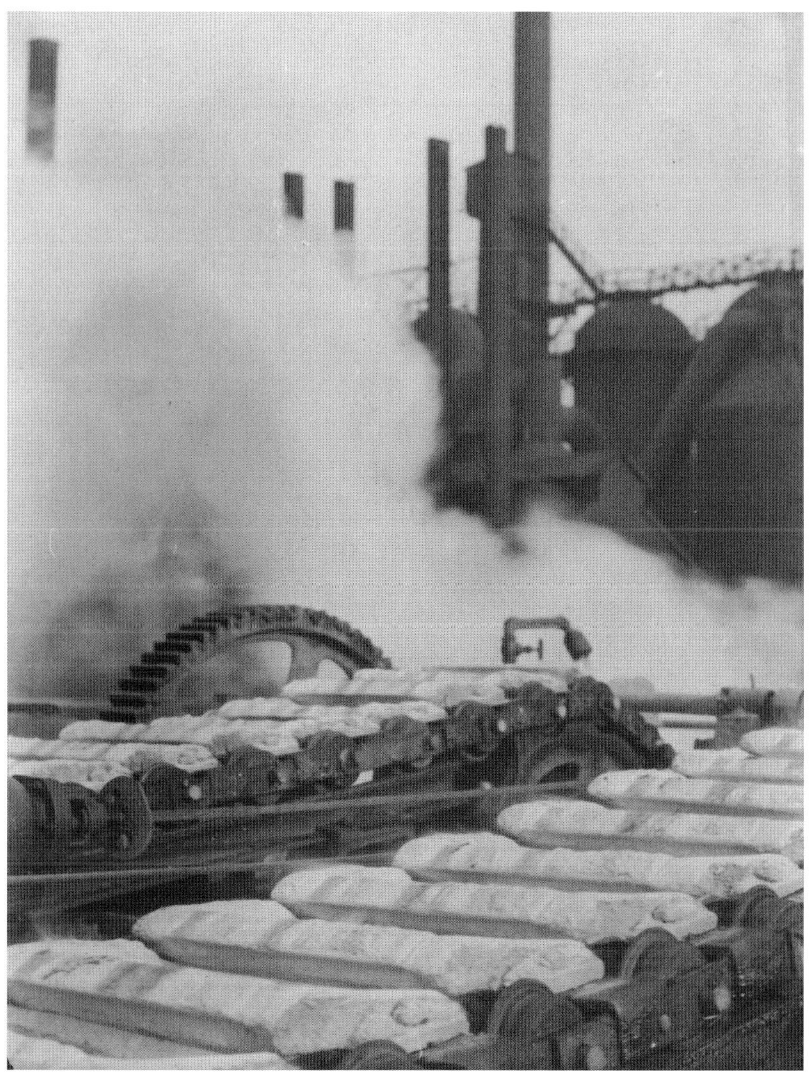

Hot Pigs, Otis Steel Company, 1927–29

Launching her career in Cleveland, Bourke–White received permission to photograph activities at the Otis Steel Company, a major firm with a mill located on the Lake Erie shore, and another on the bank of the Cuyahoga River. Some of her pictures, like this one, have an abstract, patterned quality. Used for making steel, pig iron is crude iron obtained from a smelting furnace in the form of oblong blocks. Magazine founder Henry Luce hired Bourke–White to work as a photojournalist after he saw her images of this steel company.

hire her as a staff photographer in 1929 when she was 25 years old.

Fortune magazine was a success even during the Great Depression of the 1930s. Assignments for Bourke-White ranged from a story on coal mining in Pennsylvania to one about the Campbell Soup Company in New Jersey.

After photographing the construction of the Chrysler Building, Bourke-White moved her office there the same year she was hired by Luce. While photographing the building, she understood that the architects of the Chrysler Building were involved in a battle for the tallest skyscraper, and took pictures 800 feet above the ground. She heeded the advice of the welders and construction workers who told her to pretend she was only eight feet up, "and relax, take it easy."[1]

The next year, Henry Luce sent her to the Soviet Union. Here was a chance to see a country in transition between a medieval past and an industrial future. Bourke-White became the first foreign photographer of Soviet industry. She enjoyed being first. "Nothing attracts me like a closed door. I cannot let my camera rest until I have pried it open ..."

For Bourke-White, this time the people became more important than the machines they used. In a few weeks, she took 800 shots of people working in mills, factories, quarries, and farms. Her book about the country, *Eyes on Russia*, was published in 1931.

Three years later, Bourke-White was sent by *Fortune* magazine to the Midwest to cover the terrible conditions of the Dust Bowl. When she saw people suffering, she promised herself she would try to understand people and tell their stories with her photographs.[2]

---

1. The Chrysler Building, a romantic Art Deco skyscraper in New York City built in the late 1920s, is distinguished by its abundant automotive imagery. The 77-story high building was the world's tallest for 11 months until the construction of the Empire State Building.
2. The Dust Bowl, which occurred right after the 1929 stock market crash, was a time of great economic hardship. Many farmers affected by the dust storms migrated to the West for work.

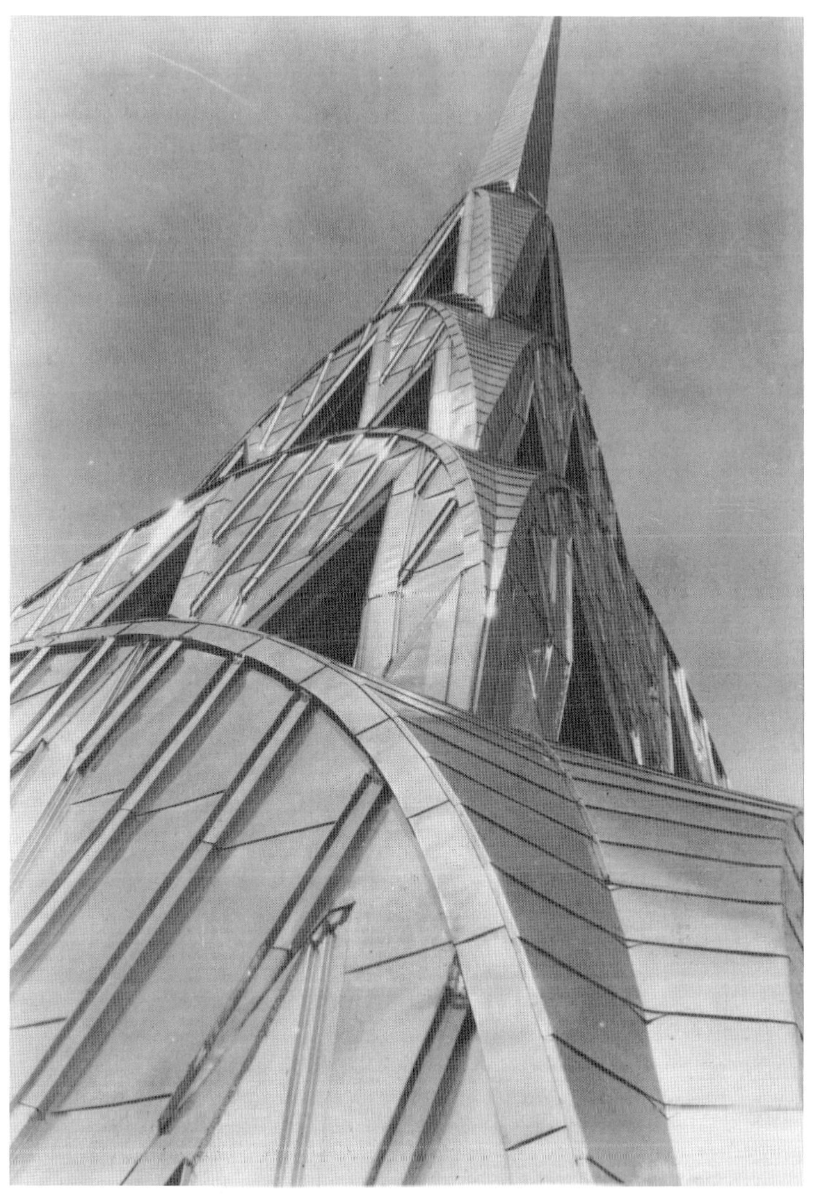

Chrysler Building, New York, 1931

The spire of the famous Art Deco building seen from below juts upward into the sky. After moving from Cleveland, Bourke–White used this majestic image on a card to proudly announce the beginning of her new, rapidly rising career. Her New York City address was located inside the Chrysler Building.

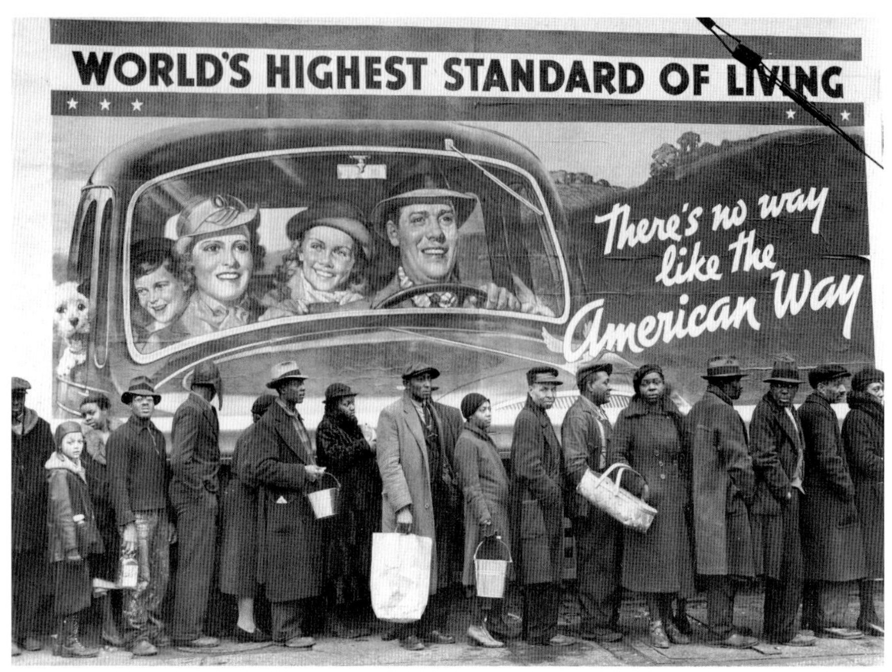

Louisville Flood Victims, 1937

A group of well-dressed adults stands in line under a billboard advertising, "There's no way like the American way." They carry baskets, buckets, and bags to receive food from a disaster relief agency, not because they are poor, but because they are victims of devastating floods. But neither are they enjoying "the world's highest standard of living" like the happy white family in the billboard, because as African Americans, they are subject to prejudice, lower wages, and discrimination.

Bourke-White collaborated with Erskine Caldwell, a Southern novelist, on three illustrated books. Her best-known illustrations of Southern tenant farmers and their families were featured in *You Have Seen Their Faces* (1937). One of her most famous photographs, "Louisville Flood Victims," ironically depicts homeless refugees lining up for emergency supplies in front of a billboard proclaiming the prosperity of the typical American family.

Bourke-White loved Caldwell, and described him as a gifted, difficult man whose gentleness contrasted with the turbulence of

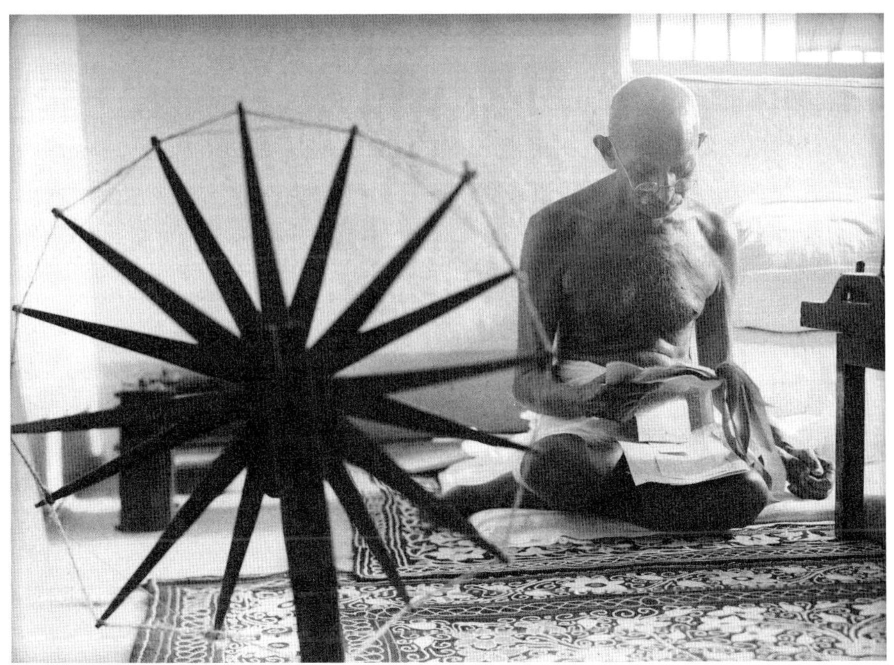

Mohandas Gandhi Reading at Spinning Wheel, 1946

Also known as "Mahatma" (or "great-souled"), Gandhi started out as a lawyer, but later became an anticolonial nationalist and spiritual leader. He believed that if India could take charge of its own needs, for example, by spinning and weaving its own cloth, it would no longer need to depend on England. Here, Gandhi sits at his spinning wheel, or "charkha," a habit he adapted as a comfort during a long stint in prison. The charkha became a symbol of Gandhi and an emblem of solidarity with India's poor. Gandhi employed other forms of nonviolent protest, like long fasts, marches, and organizing workers to protest discrimination. In this regard, he had an enormous influence on leaders like Martin Luther King, Jr., Nelson Mandela, and the Dalai Lama. This image has become an icon of the humility, love of justice, and civil disobedience of Mahatma Gandhi.

his writings. She married him, but their marriage only lasted a short while.

Work for Bourke-White was a top priority, which meant she could spend little time at home. She had been hired by Henry Luce to become one of Life magazine's four original staff photographers. Her photographs became historical documents that shaped the consciousness of millions of people. She traveled throughout the United States and around the world to pursue images that would inform American people of major events.

In 1939, she was sent by *Life* to cover World War II in Europe. The first American female war photojournalist, Bourke-White witnessed the atrocities of war. The Germans bombed Moscow 22 times, and Bourke-White photographed almost every attack to let Americans see what Germany was doing in Europe. In Italy, Great Britain, North Africa, and Germany, she took photographs from ditches, the air, and in hospital tents.

At the end of World War II, Bourke-White arrived with General George Patton, an important military leader, to record the liberation of one of the Nazi concentration camps. Her photograph, "The Living Dead of Buchenwald" (1945), became an unforgettable image of the Holocaust.

In 1946, Bourke-White was sent to India to cover the impending independence of India from Britain, and the splitting of India into two nations: India and Pakistan, based on religious differences. No single picture of Gandhi has become more closely associated with his life than her portrait of him at his spinning wheel. For him, it was a symbol of India's struggle for independence. Gandhi reasoned that if the people of India could make their own cloth, they would not need expensive cloth made by British machinery. In Bourke-White's photograph, Gandhi sits behind his spinning wheel reading. She admired Gandhi for caring more about reshaping the human heart than restructuring society. He tried to reach for the best in every person.

On her last day there, Gandhi was killed. She explained, "Nothing in all my life has affected me more deeply, and the memory will never leave me."

Bourke-White retired from *Life* magazine in 1956 after working there for 30 years, due to Parkinson's disease. Her last photo essay for *Life* was made one year later. During the last seven years of her life, she wrote her autobiography, *Portrait of Myself,* and died at the age of 67 in 1971.

Margaret Bourke-White was responsible for many firsts. She was the first industrial photographer, *Life*'s first female photographer, the first American female war photojournalist, the first woman to take her camera into combat zones, the first Western photographer to be officially allowed into the USSR, one of the first to document the horrors of Nazi concentration camps after they were liberated ... The list goes on and on. Bourke-White's mortally dangerous assignments ranged from riding along on bombing runs over Nazi Germany to getting stranded in the Arctic and surviving a helicopter crash in Chesapeake Bay. A fearless trailblazer, Bourke-White set the stage for countless future generations of professional women photographers, many of them war correspondents, including Lynsey Addario, Mary Ellen Mark, Susan Meiselas, Dickey Chapelle, and Gerda Taro.

READING LIST

Bourke-White, Margaret. *Portrait of Myself.* New York: Simon and Schuster, 1963.

Caldwell, Erskine and Margaret Bourke-White. *You Have Seen Their Faces.* New York: Viking Press, 1937.

Callahan, Sean, ed. *The Photographs of Margaret Bourke-White.* New York: Bonanza, 1972.

Goldberg, Vicki. *Margaret Bourke-White: A Biography.* New York: Harper and Row, 1986.

Silverman, Jonathan. *For the World to See: The Life of Margaret Bourke-White.* New York: Viking Press, 1983.

Rubin, Susan Goldman. *Margaret Bourke-White: Her Pictures Were Her Life.* New York: Harry N. Abrams, 1999.

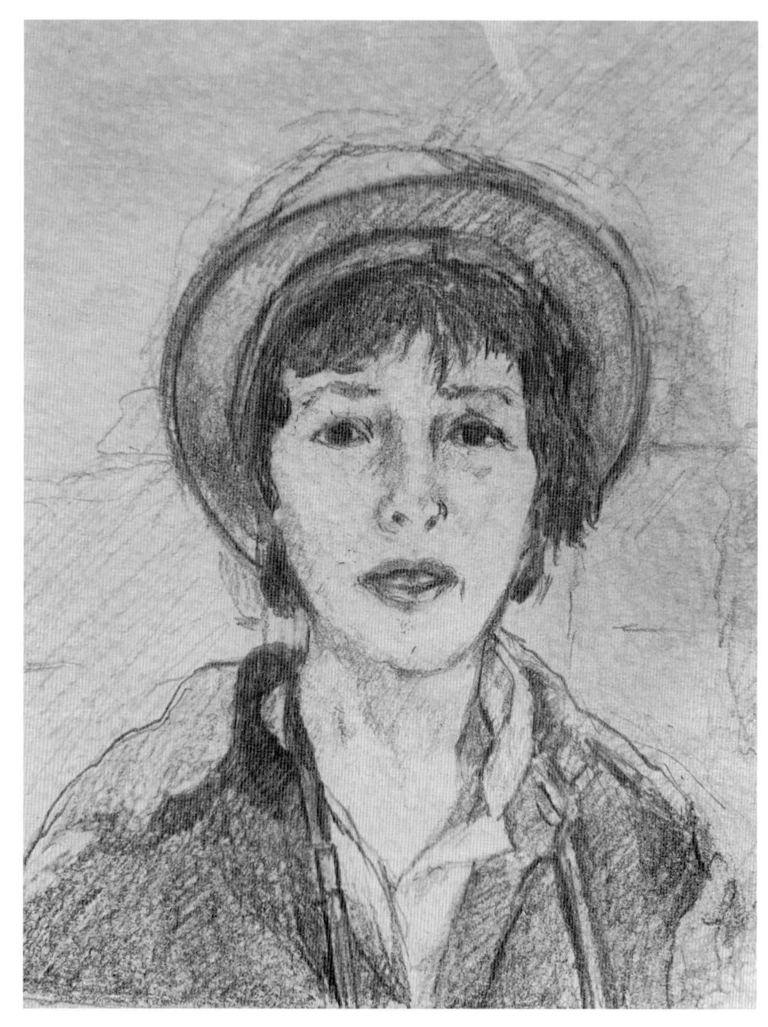

Helen Levitt

15

Helen Levitt

(1913–2009)

Life in the Streets of New York

HELEN LEVITT was born in Brooklyn, New York, in 1913. She was the daughter of May Kane, a bookkeeper, and Sam Levitt, a Russian-Jewish immigrant who ran a wholesale knit-goods business.

Levitt dropped out of high school during her senior year, and at the age of 18, began apprenticing with a commercial photographer in the Bronx. She learned darkroom techniques and continued working there for several years. Through publications and exhibitions, Levitt was influenced by the Photo League. Its leader, Sid Grossman, encouraged members to "photograph with a social conscience."[1]

1. The Photo League (1936–1951) was a cooperative association of photographers co-founded by Berenice Abbott that included many famous photographers of the mid-twentieth century. One third of the members were women. Also active in the League or supportive of their activities was Margaret Bourke–White.

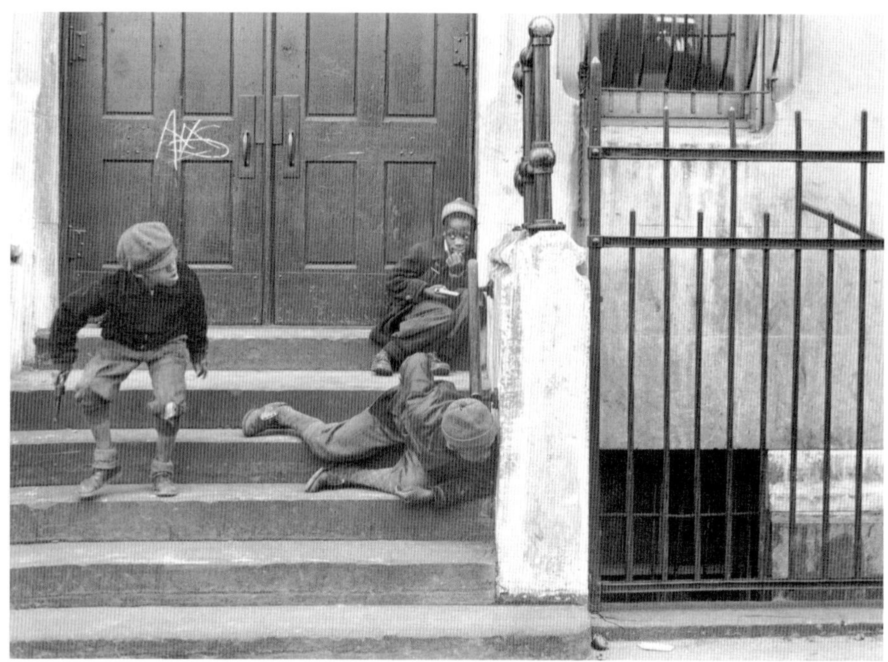

New York, 1938

The boys playing with toy guns on a stoop of an apartment building mirror the world of adults. In this shot, Levitt shows her fascination with the power of children's imagination. Caught in a fleeting moment as they are hiding from a possible attacker, the children display fear, curiosity and thoughtfulness.

During that time, Levitt was introduced to the work of Henri Cartier-Bresson, a French photojournalist whose striking images depicted decisive social moments in well-organized, elegant compositions. Levitt claimed that she originally wanted to be an artist, and that she had turned to photography because she couldn't draw. But seeing Cartier-Bresson's photographs, she knew that photography could be art, too. After meeting him in 1935, she purchased a lightweight Leica camera exactly like his. She also visited museums and art galleries to work on the compositions of her photographs.

Levitt, a lifelong New Yorker, chose the people of New York City as her subjects. Teaching art to children, she delighted in the chalk

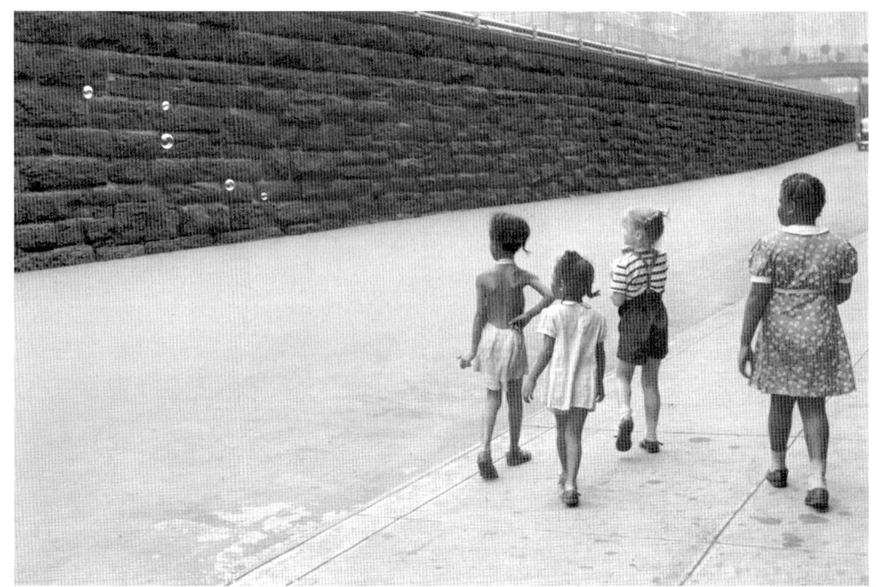

New York, c. 1945

Four young girls watch soap bubbles magically drift across a city street. The bubbles in front of an imposing stone wall dramatically change the forbidden area into a place of wonder. Levitt documents what it means to be human, and focuses on how people interact with their environment.

drawings that they made, and began to photograph them and the children who made them. She also began taking pictures of people, especially children, in the streets of Harlem and the Lower East Side. She wanted to document how people are vitally connected to each other, and took candid shots of children playing games and adults in the midst of conversations or sitting on their stoops.

In spite of the poverty and occasional brutality she sometimes portrayed, Levitt was always interested in capturing the humanity of her subjects. As she developed her own personal vision, she did not feel the need to promote any political or social agenda other than her belief in the dignity of the common man or woman.

In 1938, Levitt met the photographer Walker Evans and showed him her portfolio. He praised her work and became her mentor and friend. He liked the way Levitt captured the bustle, squalor, and

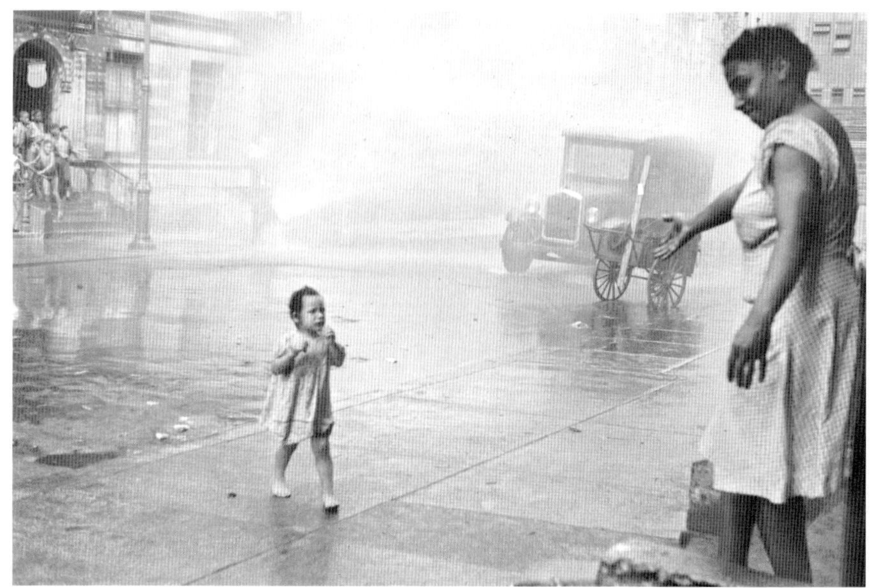

New York, c. 1942

In this photograph, Levitt reveals the paramount love between a mother and child. A mother beckons her young child to come to her, away from double danger—a spraying fire hydrant and an approaching car. On the opposite side of the street, a crowd of children stands on a stoop and watches the unfolding scene. The worried child concentrates on her mother's confident smile as she walks towards her.

beauty of everyday life in New York. Soon she was sharing Walker's kitchen darkroom and helping him print his photographs.[2]

Levitt frequently accompanied Evans on his photoshoots of the city. Together they worked on a series showing people in New York subways. Walker hid his camera inside his coat and avoided using a flash. For several hours at a time, Levitt sat beside him dressed up like a wealthy lady as a cover so he would not be noticed. Levitt also

2. Walker Evans is best known for documenting poverty in the South during the Great Depression. His collaboration with writer James Agee, *Let Us Now Praise Famous Men*, is now considered a classic. The book documents the struggles of poor white sharecroppers in southern Alabama.

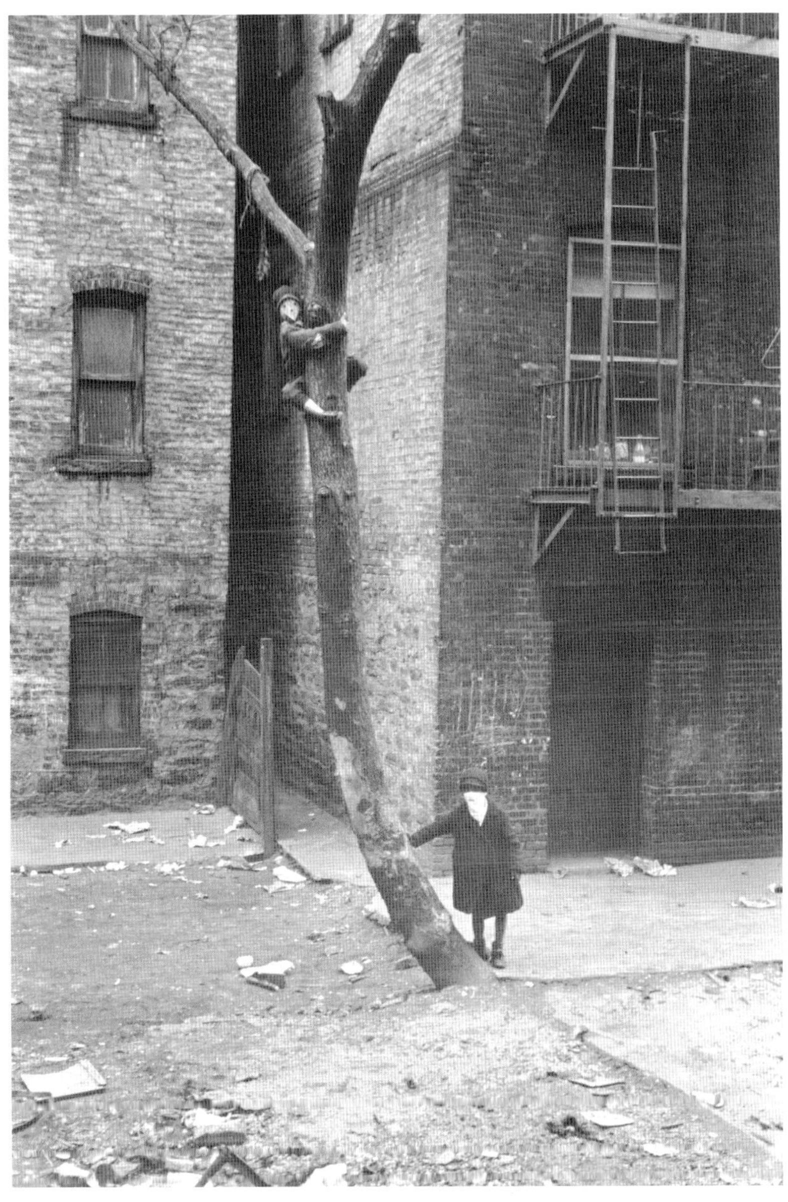

New York, 1938

Levitt shows how children find a way to play and have fun, regardless of their surroundings. Somewhere along 113th Street, two masked boys play behind an apartment building. One climbs the trunk of a young tree as if it were a jungle gym pole, while the other boy stands next to it, posing for the camera.

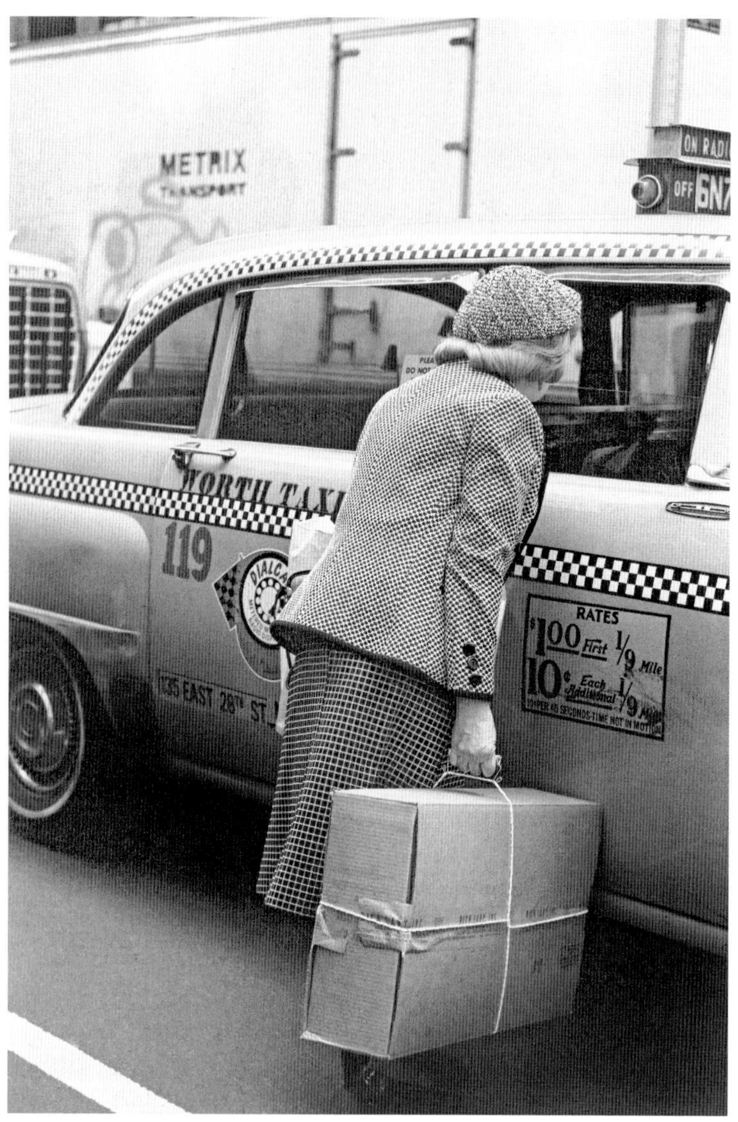

New York, 1982

In this typical city scene, Levitt shows how a street becomes a place of quiet drama when a formally dressed woman holding a large package beside her stands next to the front window of a yellow cab, leaning in to negotiate with the unseen taxi driver. The mysterious photograph makes us curious about where she would like to go and how much it will cost for her to travel there. Also, we wonder about the contents of the package that she carries like a suitcase.

took subway photos of her own. Explaining her technique, she said, "It is a peculiar part of the good photographer's adventure to know where luck is most likely to lie in the stream, to hook it, and to bring it in without unfair play and without too much subduing it."

In 1939, Levitt's photographs were published for the first time in the prestigious journal, *Fortune* magazine. In 1943, when she was only 25 years old, she had her first solo exhibition at the Museum of Modern Art in New York. Since then, her art has been included in museum collections around the world, and her photographs have been published in books dedicated to her unique vision.

For almost a decade, Levitt focused on making films, completing two documentaries, *In the Street* and *The Quiet One*, with the artist Janice Loeb and the writer James Agee.

In the late 1950s, she began to experiment with color film, continuing her fascination with people in the street. She explored the garment district, the East Village, and, as before, the Lower East Side. Later in life, she explained, "I go where there is a lot of activity. Children used to be outside. Now the streets are empty. People are indoors looking at television or something."

Other (male) artists, like William Eggleston, got credit for increasing recognition for color photography, even though Levitt exhibited her color photographs two years before he did. But Levitt was very modest and self-effacing. She admitted, "The mere attempt to examine my own confusion would consume volumes," and that she did not have "a way with words." This is one of the main reasons she liked photography. Although intensely private, she allowed others to describe her work, such as writer James Agee and the journalist Adam Gopnik. Her books include *A Way of Seeing* (1965), *In the Street* (1987), *Mexico City* (1997), *Crosstown* (2001), and *Here and There* (2002).[3]

3. James Agee (1909–1955) was an American novelist, journalist, and screenwriter as well as one of the most influential film critics of his time. Adam Gopnik (1956–), an American writer and essayist, is best known as a staff writer for *The New Yorker* magazine.

Levitt died in 2009, at the age of 95. Her legacy lives on through her influence on younger artists who have chosen to document life in all its tumult: the good, the bad, and what some might consider the ugly. She knew that "you must be in tune with the times and prepared to break with tradition."

READING LIST

Agee, James. *A Way of Seeing: Photographs by Helen Levitt.* Durham, North Carolina: Duke University Press, 1989.

Helen Levitt. Vienna: The Albertina Museum, 2018.

Here and There. Photographs by Helen Levitt. Foreword by Adam Gopnik. New York: Powerhouse Books, 2003.

Rathbone, Belinda. *Walker Evans: A Biography.* New York: Houghton Mifflin, 1995.

Carrie Mae Weems
(b. 1953)
Critical Inquiry through Art

Carrie Mae Weems was born in Portland, Oregon in 1953, the second of seven children. As a teenager, she gravitated towards street theatre and dance and moved to San Francisco to study modern dance. She continued her studies at the California Institute of the Arts (B.A.), and at the University of California in San Diego (M.F.A.). She also studied folklore at Berkeley (M.A.)

Before turning to her art, Weems became politically active in the labor movement. She used her camera, a birthday gift from her boyfriend at the age of 21, to document her work as a union organizer. After reading *The Black Photography Annual* about African American photography, she was inspired to become a photographer. She moved to New York City where she met other artists and photographers, and was invited to teach art at the Studio Museum in Harlem. "I came to New York to be with them, to see them, to

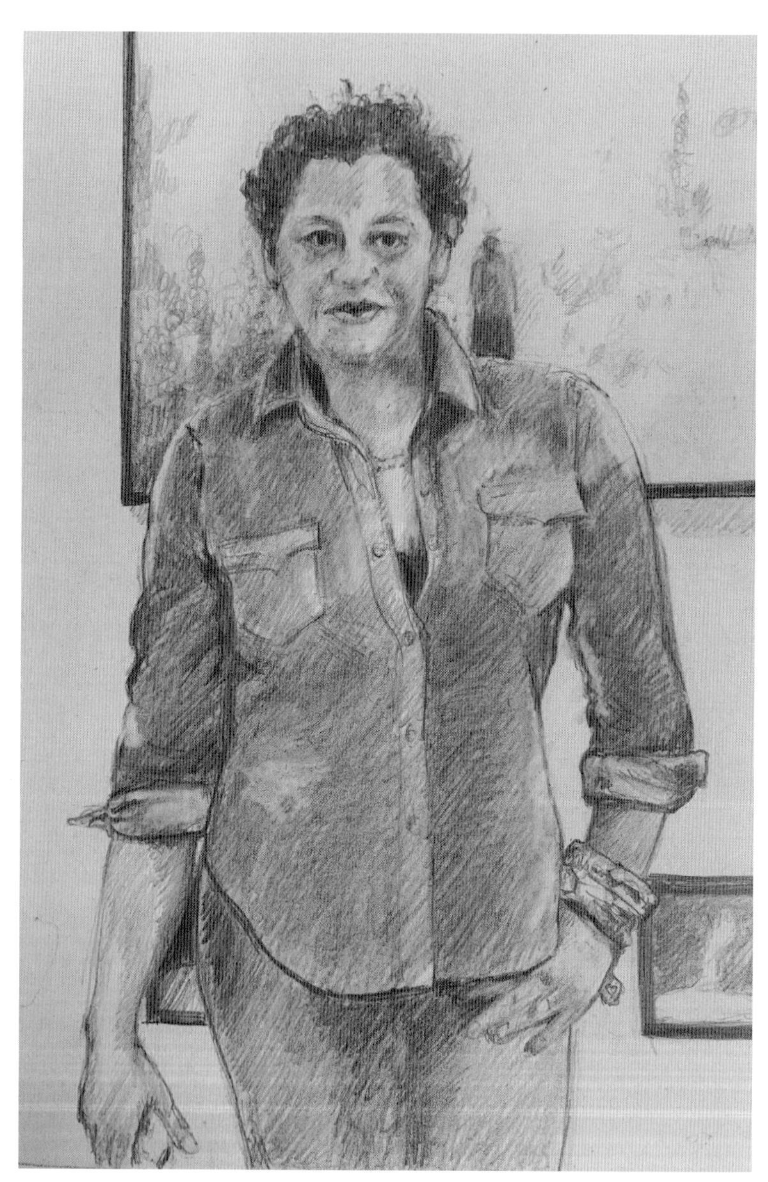

Carrie Mae Weems

talk to them, to interview them, to study with them, to become their friends, to see their exhibitions."

Moving away from documentary photography, Weems began to use staged events accompanied by text to analyze issues of racism, sexism, class inequities, and power. During the 1980s, she completed her first collection of photography, text, and spoken word called *Family Pictures and Stories.* To understand her own history she explored the movement of African American families from the South to the North, using her large, close-knit family as a model.

In her *Kitchen Table Series* (1990), which consists of twenty photographs and took two years to complete, Weems cast herself as the central character near a kitchen table, the place of comfort and discussion in an ordinary home. The skillfully revealing images explore relationships between a woman and a man, a woman and another woman, a woman and a child, and a woman by herself. Involved in the stories presented visually, Weems is a compassionate storyteller that also makes the viewer think about the dynamics behind personal relationships and the African American family experience.

Weems explains that art transforms lives and is about imagining the unimaginable. "I want to make things that are beautiful, seductive, formally challenging, and culturally meaningful. I'm also committed to radical social change ... Any form of human injustice moves me deeply ... the battle against all forms of oppression keeps me going and keeps me focused."

Describing her artistic process, Weems understands that she is responsible for her own construction. Knowing that historians and artists aren't thinking of her own role as an artist, she understands that she alone is responsible for her own actions and her place in history. Weems repeatedly shows how exploring history is a way to better understand the present. While studying the history of art, she asks, "What is left in? What is left out?" Then she tries to think of ways to reposition and insert individuals and groups of people who have not been included in the historical record.

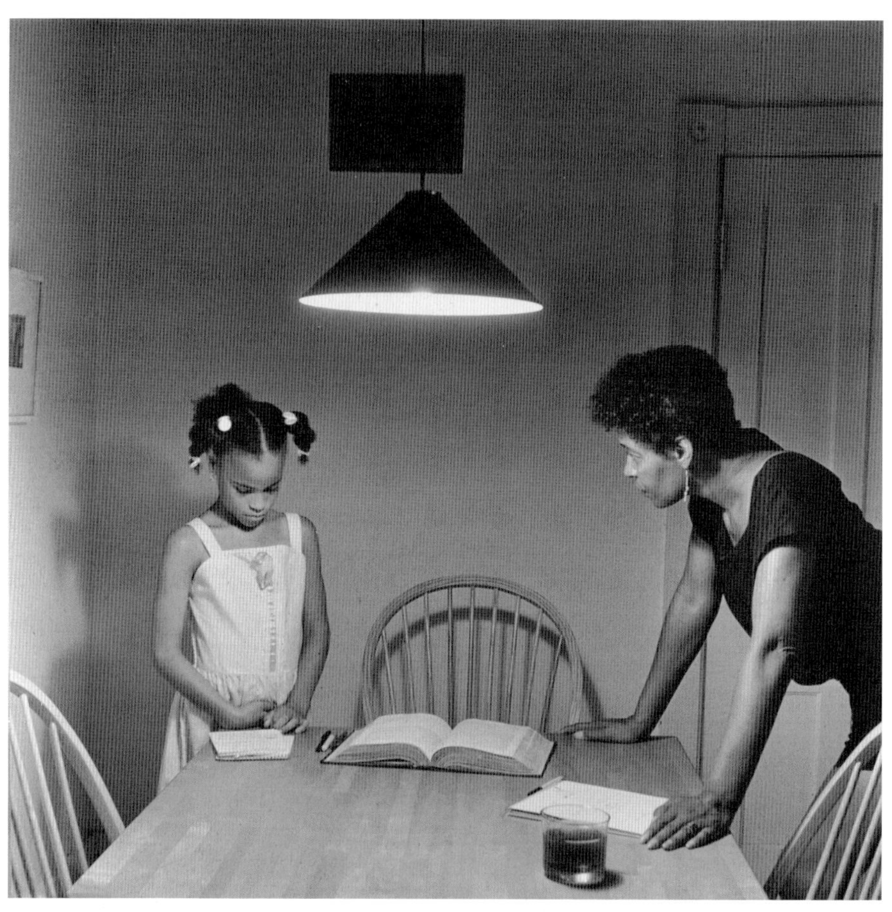

Kitchen Table Series: Untitled (homework, girl looking down), 1990–99

This photograph shows a mother watching her daughter looking down at notes on a pad next to an open book. A single light hangs from the ceiling over the kitchen table, the center of the home and the place where this mother and child work and communicate with each other. The scene is fictional yet documents a realistic, everyday activity, the process of completing homework.

"The lack of representation is stunning. The absence is woven into our social fabric. Disappointed, I realized I work in the shadows, and am waiting for the coming of a new day."

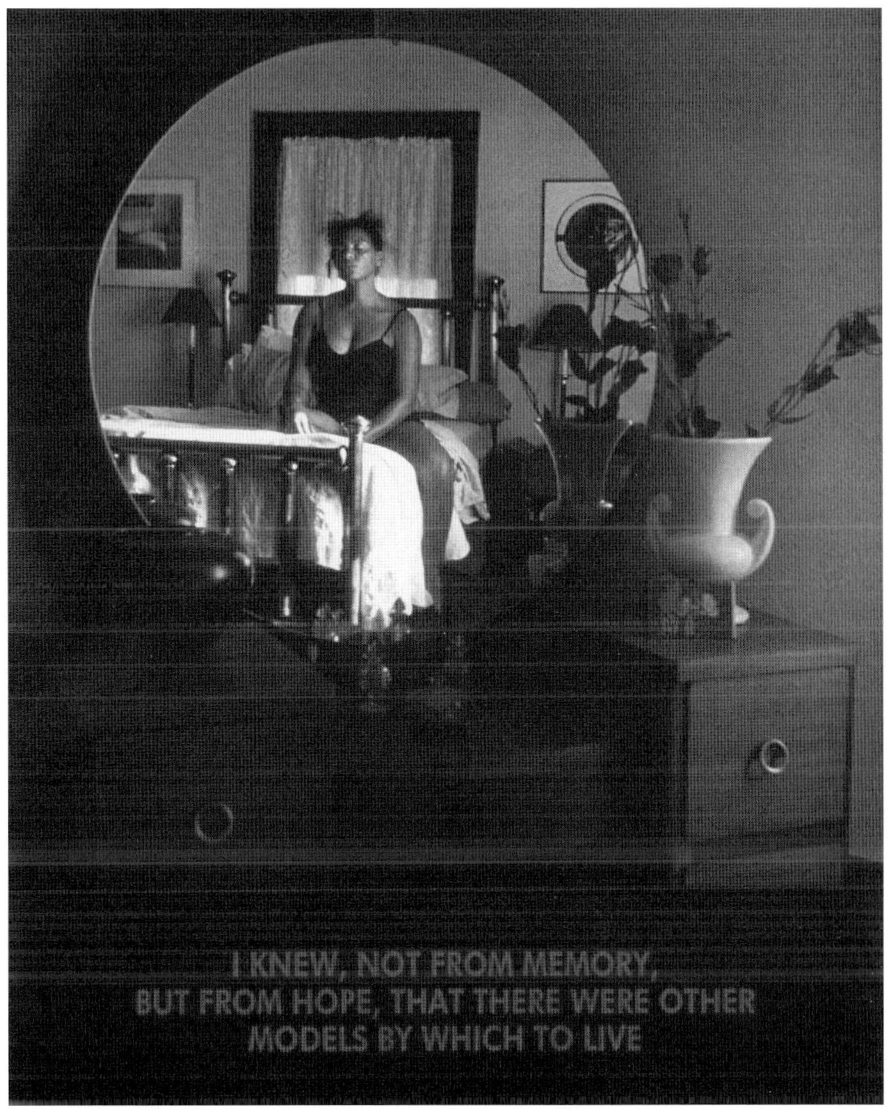

Not Manet's Type 3, 1997

Each of the prints in Weems's five-part series is comprised of a self-portrait. The sardonic statement underneath each photograph relates to how male artists use women's bodies and in particular, the nearly absent role of African American women in art history.

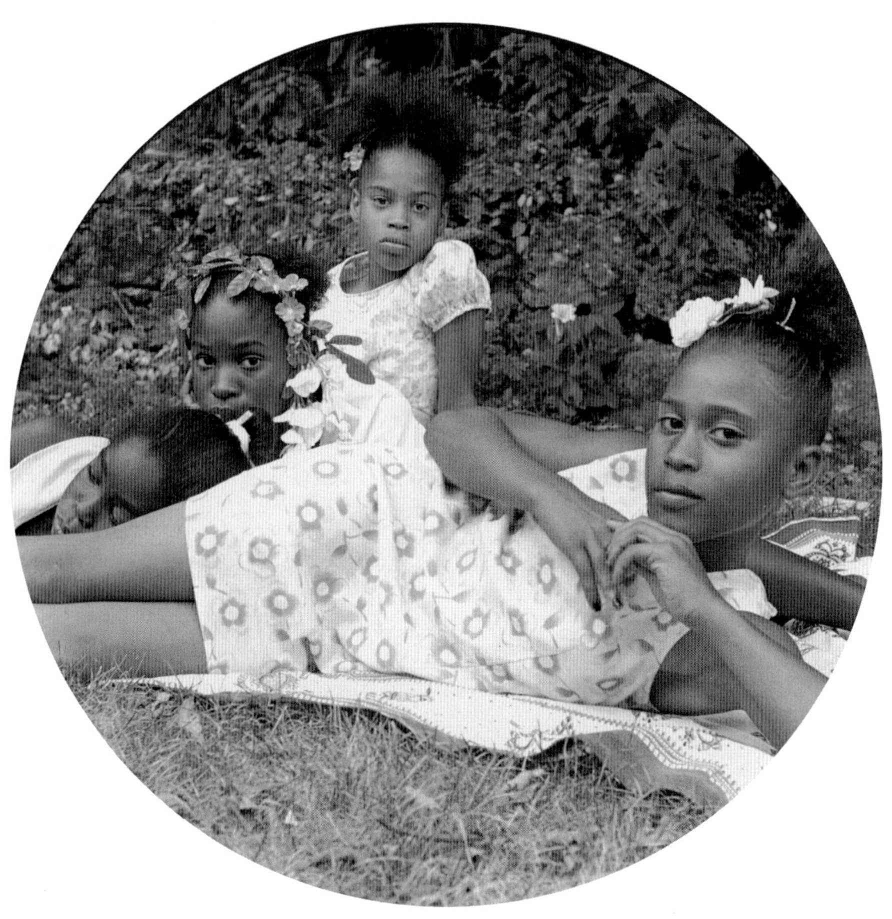

***After Manet: from May Days Long Forgotten*, 2002**

This circular photograph from a nine-part series depicts African American girls in summer dresses with garlands in their hair relaxing on a lawn. Weems first noticed one of the girls, Jessica, on the streets of Syracuse with her mother and approached them to ask if she might model for her.

One of the most influential contemporary American artists, Weems has won many awards and has been recognized by numerous universities. She was awarded the MacArthur Foundation Fellowship in 2013 the year before she became the first African American woman to have a retrospective at the Guggenheim Museum. Her work is included in major museums throughout the United

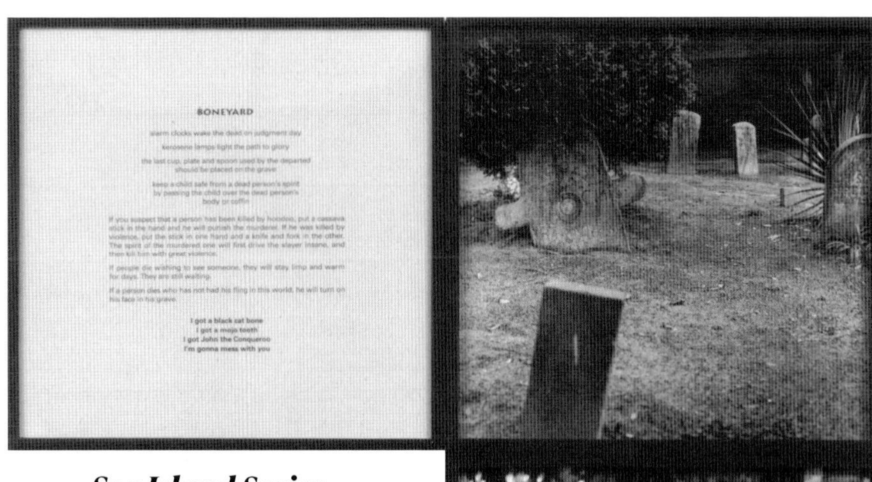

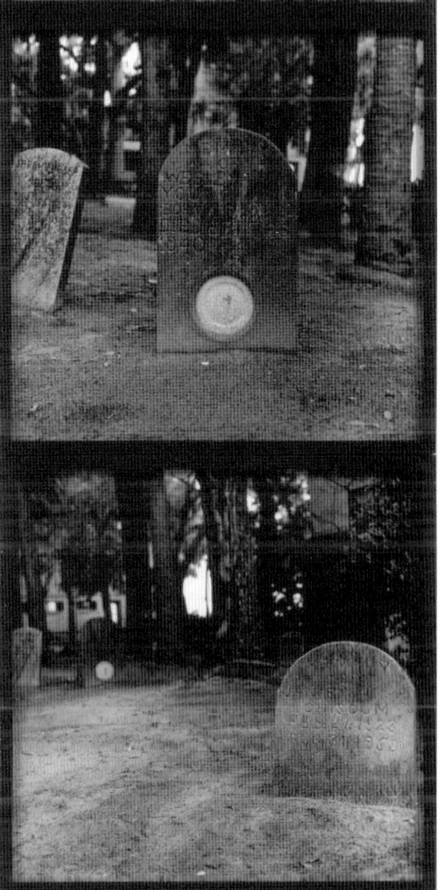

Sea Island Series, Boneyard, 2003

These photographs focus on the Gullah-Geechee culture located on the barrier islands of South Carolina and Georgia. This African American community descended from the slaves that worked on eighteenth- and nineteenth-century rice, indigo, and cotton plantations. Their geographic isolation allowed residents to preserve African traditions that disappeared on the mainland. These photographs show how the landscape helps us remember the past, and how religion and spirituality are part of daily life. In 2006, the Gullah Geechee Cultural Heritage Corridor, a National Heritage Area established by the U.S. Congress, was created to protect sites associated with the culture.

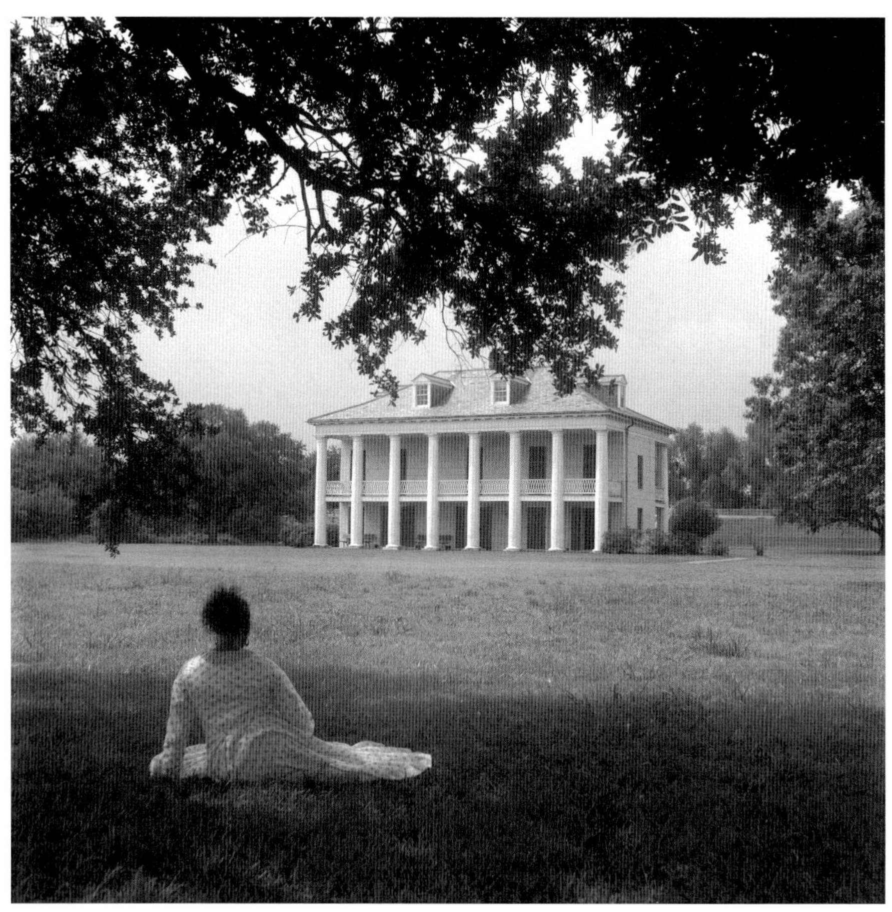

Louisiana Project, A Distant View, 2003

This photograph is one in a series consisting of more than 70 images commemorating the bicentennial of the Louisiana Purchase when the territory of Louisiana was acquired by the United States from France in 1803 doubling its size. Weems places herself in a variety of locations around New Orleans as a witness to the experience of African Americans from the distant past of slavery to the present. In this photograph, she is seen with her back to the camera reclining on the ground looking up at a Greek Revival plantation house in the distance. The scene is reminiscent of Andrew Wyeth's *Christina's World* (1948), often perceived as the embodiment of a strong sense of longing.

States and abroad. She lives in New York where she continues to produce art.

"I cannot lead you to anything, but I hope that [my work] provokes critical inquiry ... If my work encourages you to ask, 'What is that?' and 'What does it mean?' then I think I have done my job."

READING LIST

Borzello, Frances. *Seeing Ourselves: Women's Self-Portraits.* NY: Harry N. Abrams, 1998.

Hirsch, Robert. *Seizing the Light: A History of Photography.* NY: McGraw Hill, 2000.

Weems, Carrie. *Image Maker.* 1995.

----------------------*The Louisiana Project.* 2004.

----------------------*Constructing History.* Savannah College of Art and Design, 2008.

----------------------*Kitchen Table Series.* Damiani/Matsumoto Editions, 2016.

Willis, Deborah. *Reflections in Black: A History of Black Photographers 1840 to the Present.* NY: WW Norton & Co., 2000.

Questions

1. *What is involved in being a pioneer, whether in art or something else? What is the significance of doing something that no one has done before?*
2. *How can a picture of an old building help us learn about the history of a place? What clues can it provide?*
3. *How should old and new buildings coexist in a city?*
4. *In what ways do you express how you see yourself? Which forms of self-expression do you use, and how?*
5. *How can you use photography to show that people are special? Which methods would you use in representing them?*
6. *How can you show empathy in a photograph?*
7. *How should you represent people who are different from you in photography? How do you approach this?*
8. *When do you most feel connected to nature? What is your relationship to nature or the countryside?*

9. *What makes a good landscape photograph?*
10. *Do you have a favorite neighborhood? What do you like about it?*
11. *Do you feel attached to a certain region? What about it draws you in?*
12. *What can others learn from your photographs, either about you or the things, people, and places you are photographing?*
13. *How can photography be used for teaching?*
14. *Is it worth putting yourself in danger to take a photograph? How far should you go to get the photograph you want?*
15. *How do you show street life in a city when there are people that you don't know but want to include in the scene? How do you approach this situation?*

Illustration Credits

1	Kasebier, Gertrude	Flying Hawk	1898	Library of Congress
2	Kasebier, Gertrude	The Manger	1903	Library of Congress
3	Kasebier, Gertrude	Blessed Art Thou Among Women	1899	Library of Congress
4	Kasebier, Gertrude	An Informal Portrait of a Young Woman Surrounded by Laundry	1903	Library of Congress
5	Kasebier, Gertrude	Rose O'Neill, Illustrator and Originator of the "Kewpie" Doll	1907	Library of Congress
6	Johnston, Frances Benjamin	Capital Camera Club	1895	Library of Congress
7	Johnston, Frances Benjamin	The Rebel	1896	Library of Congress

8	Johnston, Frances Benjamin	Booker T. Washington	1906	Library of Congress
9	Johnston, Frances Benjamin	Treasurer's Staircase, Hampton Institute, Virginia	1899	Library of Congress
10	Johnston, Frances Benjamin	Playmakers Theatre, University of North Carolina, Chapel Hill, N.C.	c. 1936	Library of Congress
11	Johnston, Frances Benjamin	Entrance Hall at Fenwick Hall, Johns Island, South Carolina	c. 1938	Library of Congress
12	Austen, Alice	The Darned Club	1891	Collection of Historic Richmond Town
13	Austen, Alice	Quarantine Station	1901	Library of Congress
14	Austen, Alice	S.S. Finland, Steerage at Supper	1909	Collection of Historic Richmond Town
15	Austen, Alice	Peddler with Cart	1896	Library of Congress
16	Austen, Alice	Austen Gray and Wife	1913	Library of Congress
17	Ben-Yusuf, Zaida	Teddy Roosevelt	1899	Library of Congress
18	Ben-Yusuf, Zaida	Mrs. Fiske, "Love Finds the Way"	1896	Library of Congress
19	Ben-Yusuf, Zaida	Self Portrait	1901	Library of Congress
20	Ben-Yusuf, Zaida	Odor of Pomegranates	1901	Library of Congress

21	Ben-Yusuf, Zaida	Elsie de Wolfe	1901	Library of Congress
22	Brigman, Anne	The Bubble	1910	Courtesy of the George Eastman Museum
23	Brigman, Anne	The Dying Cedar	1907	Copyright The Metropolitan Museum of Art, Image source: Art Resource, NY
24	Brigman, Anne	Incantation	1905	Copyright The Metropolitan Museum of Art, Image source: Art Resource, NY
25	Brigman, Anne	The Hamadryads	c. 1910	Courtesy of the Cleveland Museum of Art
26	Brigman, Anne	Invictus	1924	Library of Congress
27	Beals, Jessie Tarbox	Kit Kat Club, New York City	1920	Archives of American Art, Smithsonian Institution
28	Beals, Jessie Tarbox	Diana in the Snow	1915	Library of Congress
29	Beals, Jessie Tarbox	Ink Pot, Greenwich Village, New York	1917	Library of Congress
30	Beals, Jessie Tarbox	Alice Sit by the Fire, The Village Store, Greenwich Village, New York	1917	Library of Congress
31	Beals, Jessie Tarbox	Edna St. Vincent Millay and Edmond Wilson	1923	Library of Congress
32	Beals, Jessie Tarbox	Jessie Tarbox Beals with John Burroughs	1908	Library of Congress

33	Wootten, Bayard	Oak at Middleton Place, Charleston, South Carolina	1930s	Bayard Morgan Wootten Photographic Collection, North Carolina Collection, University of North Carolina at Chapel Hill
34	Wootten, Bayard	Orton Plantation, Winnabow, North Carolina	1930s	Bayard Morgan Wootten Photographic Collection, North Carolina Collection, University of North Carolina at Chapel Hill
35	Wootten, Bayard	A Tobacco Farmer and His Three Sons	1930s	Bayard Morgan Wootten Photographic Collection, North Carolina Collection, University of North Carolina at Chapel Hill
36	Wootten, Bayard	Bain's Store, Near Sevierville, Tennessee	1930s	Bayard Morgan Wootten Photographic Collection, North Carolina Collection, University of North Carolina at Chapel Hill
37	Wootten, Bayard	Reflections from the East, Ocean Drive, South Carolina	1930s	Bayard Morgan Wootten Photographic Collection, North Carolina Collection, University of North Carolina at Chapel Hill
38	Wootten, Bayard	Irons in the Fire	c. 1933	Bayard Morgan Wootten Photographic Collection, North Carolina Collection, University of North Carolina at Chapel Hill
39	Ulmann, Doris	Man with Violin	1930	Library of Congress

40	Ulmann, Doris	Aunt Lou Kitchen, Spinner and Weaver, Shootin' Creek, N.C.	1933	Library of Congress
41	Ulmann, Doris	Katie Jones	1930	Library of Congress
42	Ulmann, Doris	Woman in Sun Bonnet	1930	Library of Congress
43	Ulmann, Doris	Baptism	c. 1929–31	University of Oregon Library
44	Cunningham, Imogen	Magnolia Blossom	1925	Copyright Imogen Cunningham Trust
45	Cunningham, Imogen	Two Cannas	1929	Copyright Imogen Cunningham Trust
46	Cunningham, Imogen	Agave Design I	1920s	Copyright Imogen Cunningham Trust
47	Cunningham, Imogen	Unmade Bed	1957	Copyright Imogen Cunningham Trust
48	Cunningham, Imogen	Frida Kahlo	1931	Copyright Imogen Cunningham Trust
49	Harleston, Elise Forrest	Grand Army Veteran	c. 1922–31	Courtesy of Mae Whitlock Gentry
50	Harleston, Elise Forrest	Seated Child	c. 1922–31	Courtesy of Mae Whitlock Gentry
51	Harleston, Elise Forrest	Rosalie Mickey	c. 1922–31	Courtesy of Mae Whitlock Gentry
52	Harleston, Elise Forrest	Girl with Diploma	c. 1922–31	Courtesy of Mae Whitlock Gentry
53	Harleston, Elise Forrest	Old Woman from the Borough	c. 1922–31	Courtesy of Mae Whitlock Gentry
54	Gilpin, Laura	Rancho de Taos Mission, New Mexico	1930	Library of Congress/ Copyright 1979 Amon Carter Museum of American Art

55	Gilpin, Laura	Mrs. Francis Nakai, New Mexico	1932	Library of Congress/ Copyright 1979 Amon Carter Museum of American Art
56	Gilpin, Laura	Indian Family, Acoma Pueblo	c. 1939	Library of Congress/ Copyright 1979 Amon Carter Museum of American Art
57	Gilpin, Laura	Steps of Castillo, Chichen Itza	1932	Library of Congress/ Copyright 1979 Amon Carter Museum of American Art
58	Gilpin, Laura	Casa Blanca, Canyon de Chelly	1930	Library of Congress/ Copyright 1979 Amon Carter Museum of American Art
59	Lange, Dorothea	Childress County, Texas	1938	Library of Congress
60	Lange, Dorothea	Funeral Cortege, End of an Era in a Small Valley Town, California	1938	Courtesy of the Cleveland Museum of Art
61	Lange, Dorothea	Migratory Cotton Picker, Eloy, Arizona	1940	Copyright The Museum of Modern Art/ Licensed by SCALA/Art Resource, N.Y.
62	Lange, Dorothea	Migrant Mother, Nipomo, California	1936	Library of Congress
63	Lange, Dorothea	One Nation Indivisible, San Francisco	1942	Copyright The Museum of Modern Art/ Licensed by SCALA/Art Resource, N.Y.

64	Abbott, Berenice	Cheese Store: 276 Bleeker Street, Manhattan	1937	Brooklyn Museum/ Getty Images
65	Abbott, Berenice	New York at Night	1932	Library of Congress/ Getty Images
66	Abbott, Berenice	Murray Hill Hotel, Spiral, 112 Park Avenue	1935	Getty Images
67	Abbott, Berenice	Façade Alwyn Court	1938	Brooklyn Museum/ Getty Images
68	Bourke-White, Margaret	Terminal Tower, Cleveland	1927	Courtesy of the Cleveland Museum of Art/Copyright 2020 Estate of Margaret Bourke-White/Licensed by VAGA at Artists Rights Society (ARS), NY
69	Bourke-White, Margaret	Hot Pigs, Otis Steel Company	1927–29	Courtesy of the Cleveland Museum of Art/Copyright 2020 Estate of Margaret Bourke-White/Licensed by VAGA at Artists Rights Society (ARS), NY
70	Bourke-White, Margaret	Chrysler Building	1931	Copyright The Metropolitan Museum of Art/Image Source: Art Resource, N.Y./ Copyright 2020 Estate of Margaret Bourke-White/Licensed by VAGA at Artists Rights Society (ARS), NY
71	Bourke-White, Margaret	Louisville Flood Victims	1937	Getty Images

72	Bourke-White, Margaret	Gandhi Reading at Spinning Wheel	1946	Getty Images
73	Levitt, Helen	New York	1938	Copyright Helen Levitt Film Documents LLC
74	Levitt, Helen	New York	c. 1945	Copyright Helen Levitt Film Documents LLC
75	Levitt, Helen	New York	c. 1942	Copyright Helen Levitt Film Documents LLC
76	Levitt, Helen	New York	1938	Copyright Helen Levitt Film Documents LLC
77	Levitt, Helen	New York	1982	Copyright Helen Levitt Film Documents LLC
78	Weems, Carrie Mae	Kitchen Table Series: Untitled (homework, girl looking down)	1990–99	Copyright Carrie Mae Weems, Courtesy of the Artist and Jack Shainman Gallery, N.Y.
79	Weems, Carrie Mae	Not Manet's Type 3	1997	Copyright Carrie Mae Weems, Courtesy of the Artist and Jack Shainman Gallery, N.Y.
80	Weems, Carrie Mae	After Manet: From May Days Long Forgotten	2002	Copyright Carrie Mae Weems, Courtesy of the Artist and Jack Shainman Gallery, N.Y.
81	Weems, Carrie Mae	Sea Island Series, Boneyard	2003	Copyright Carrie Mae Weems, Courtesy of the Artist and Jack Shainman Gallery, N.Y.
82	Weems, Carrie Mae	Louisiana Project, A Distant View	2003	Copyright Carrie Mae Weems, Courtesy of the Artist and Jack Shainman Gallery, N.Y.

About the Author & Contributors

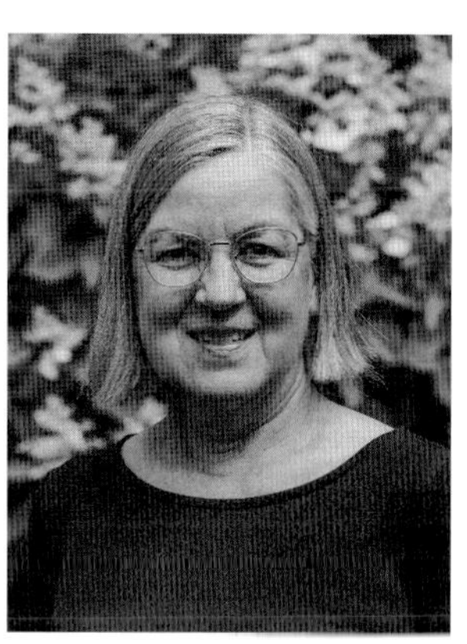

Maria Ausherman is a high school teacher and independent scholar residing in Stuyvesant, New York. She is the author of *The Photographic Legacy of Frances Benjamin Johnston* published by the University Press of Florida in 2009 as well as co-author with Patricia Jennings of *Georgia O'Keeffe's Hawaii* published by Koa Press in 2011. Ms. Ausherman completed her B.A. in Geography from the University of North Carolina at Chapel Hill, received an M.A. in Cinema Studies from the City University of New York and an M.Ed. in Social Science Education from the University of Georgia in Athens, where she also obtained a graduate certificate in historic preservation and completed coursework and a dissertation for a Ph.D. in Art.

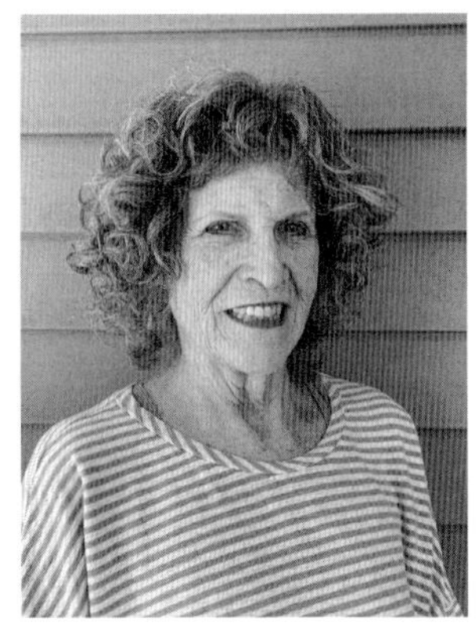

Fontaine Dunn is an artist and writer currently living in upstate New York. She has taught painting and drawing at Sarah Lawrence College, Princeton University, and the Nova Scotia College of Art and Design. In addition, she has been an instructor of English for speakers of other languages. Ms. Dunn received her B.F.A. from Tulane University and her M.F.A. from Carnegie-Mellon University. She is the recipient of grants from the National Endowment for the Arts and the Pollock-Krasner Foundation.

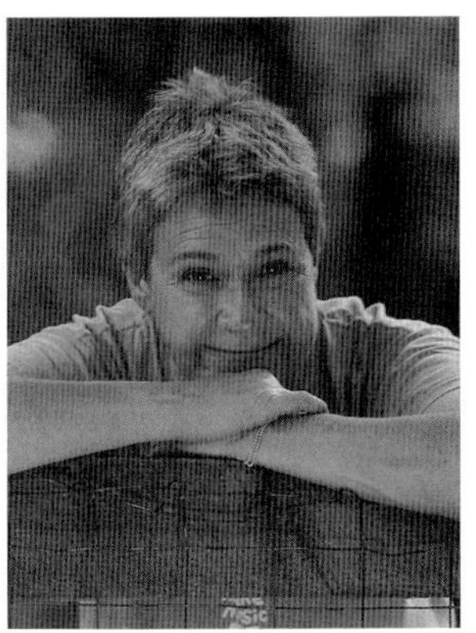

Amy Sancetta covered many of the world's biggest sporting events during her long career with the Associated Press. She photographed numerous Olympics, Super Bowls, World Series, Masters, and the FIFA World Cup, as well as the September 11th terrorist attack in NYC, political conventions, and feature stories across the country. She was the Associated Press's national enterprise photographer, and won the 1993 Pulitzer Prize in feature photography along with a group of her colleagues for coverage of the 1992 presidential campaign.